REALITY

Just a Thought

GREGORY P. LOMB

PAGE PUBLISHING, INC.
New York, NY

First originally published by Page Publishing, Inc. 2017

ISBN 978-1-64082-843-8 (Paperback)
ISBN 978-1-64082-844-5 (Digital)

Printed in the United States of America

This book is dedicated to rational, logical thinkers everywhere,
no matter your sex, race or philosophical beliefs

CONTENTS

INTRODUCTION

What is reality? Is there an "absolute" reality, or is reality merely relative "in nature?" If Isaac Newton were alive today, could Newton make claim to reality as he did gravity, space, and time; or has Einsteinium thought overruled Newtonian thoughts on reality as well as our thoughts on gravity, space, and time? Many make claim reality is nothing more than their personal interpretation of the world, but just about everyone interprets the world differently. Are there really multitudes of realities? Many of us, men and women alike, perceive and then define the world as it best fits their desire of what they wish the world to be. Most people only see and hear what they want to see and hear; they almost never agree as to the objective truth of things as they really are; they almost never agree as to what is reality.

This book is not a scientific study objectively testing reality. The thoughts I put forth herein are merely my attempt at objectively postulating what I believe to be an "absolute" reality pertaining to sometimes-specific and sometimes-general situations in life. Unlike "right and wrong," I believe reality is objective; reality is more absolute than relative. We as a species create right and wrong. We as a myriad of societies spread around this sun-orbiting rock of a terrarium we call home—Earth—decide what is right and what is wrong. And on what is right and what is wrong, no one group agrees. But reality is something entirely different from right and wrong. Some people may believe it right to marry more than one spouse, while others may firmly believe it wrong, but we can all agree the Earth is round—well, anyone of us who thinks rationally.

It is difficult for me to comprehend how anyone can believe other than reality is reality; reality is not something and something else . . . depending upon the observer. Regarding right and wrong, what is right to one group is wrong to another. What is wrong to one group is right to another. Some groups may agree as to a right being a right or a wrong being a wrong, but so few groups and so few individuals agree as to just what is reality even though there can be no rational argument as to what is reality. Can there be? I am herein postulating "reality" is merely and simply reality. I cannot overstate my thought on this matter. In all due respect, I beg to differ with Erwin Schrödinger: the cat is dead or alive, not both. In all due respect, I disagree with George Berkeley. If a tree falls in the woods, it will make a sound. It does not matter if I am present or not; my ego has nothing to do with events exclusive from my cone of influence. Reality is reality is reality.

This book is a compilation of my thoughts, my comments, and my interpretations of events and happenings—realities that have occurred, might occur, or could occur in the world we live in. I do not pronounce my opinions as being anything greater than my personal opinions. Everything I write is just a thought. I end every topic I discuss with the words "just a thought." I have not conducted scientific experiments, nor have I consulted religious texts to derive my conclusions. I do not proclaim my opinions as right and anyone's varying opinions as wrong. I merely state my opinions as to what I personally perceive as "reality." I attempt to be as objective as a rat can be from within the maze. I hear no voices in my head telling me to start a religion. I do not pretend to be smarter than anyone else. You can agree with me, or you can disagree with me. I do not proclaim myself as the final and enlightened "Word" of God, a god, or any fictitious enlightened being. I am not a prophet just as no one else throughout history ever was truly a prophet in the sense most perceive what a prophet to be. I admit what almost everyone else discussing such topics I will cover will not admit, that I am a man born of man and woman; my creators are my parents; that I am one biological being of one species of life on this planet of many species of life on this planet; that I am no one special. I am merely a voice, or more precisely, to those of you reading this book, I am written words. I am merely an opinion. I am merely one being trying to sort out the objective truths—buried or misinterpreted or misrepresented—of various topics, subjects, events, and physics of this world. I hope you too will agree—if not in my examples, but in my belief—that reality is objective, not relative.

I hope you enjoy what you read. I hope you can take away something positive from this book. Most of all, I hope this book makes you think a little more objectively than you think already. I wish for you not to think as you have been taught but think as you were created to think. And that said, I further convey the caveat to not let one's ego grow so separate from reality that one cannot grow. Know that all of us can learn something from everyone else no matter if that something be knowledge to build upon what we already know or knowledge to confirm what we already know or just a different perspective on life. We can, and we should continue to learn until we take our last breath.

Reading this book, I only ask of you the reader to refrain attacks upon this poor author for any message you may rightly or wrongly perceive reading the topics covered herein, and instead if you find you disagree with what you read, formulate and espouse your own opinion(s) in a cogent and courteous manner in your own book, blog, journal, letter, or conversation. Reality is something we should all discuss and we should all agree upon. Knowing reality means knowing life.

I have chosen and divided the topics in this book into chapters titled: science, life, religion and philosophy, political, entertainment, poetry, and questions and answers? And riddles. There are so many other topics I could have added to this book, but I am happy with the choices I made. You can read the chapters in this book in any order you wish. You can pick and choose which topics you wish to read in any given chapter. I suggest you will glean a better understanding of what my thoughts are of any given topic if you read every thought covered in any particular chapter, but again you do not need to read them all. I hope you enjoy the book, and I wish for you a happy life.

Chapter 1

SCIENCE

Gravity and the Strong Force

Could gravity and the strong force be one and the same force? Are there three not four forces in nature? Have you ever thought that maybe, just maybe, Einstein was wrong? Have you ever thought maybe physicists have not got it right yet? I am talking about gravity, and what is gravity? I understand Arthur Eddington (a twentieth-century English astronomer and physicist) was supposed to have proved Einstein's theory of general relativity during a solar eclipse based on the bending of light, but did he prove Einstein's theory? A force bent light and I think most of us will agree that any particle and/or wave can be affected in its directional path by a force exerted upon it. But does that prove Einstein's theory of general relativity? Most, if not all, will say yes . . . but I want to propose something different. Just read and think about it.

What if there are not four forces in our universe but only three forces. What if besides the electromagnetic force and the weak force there is only the STRONG FORCE (aka gravitational force). What if the strong force and gravity are one and the same? Think about it a moment. The strong force is a powerful force, but only in very close approximation to its affected object. Gravity is the weakest of the currently understood four forces of nature in physics. Could not the weakness of gravity be explained by its being redefined as a cumulative effect of the excess strong force from all matter combined on a planetary body? Any number added up enough times has a cumulative effect greater than its singular effect. Well, at least most. Never say *all*—or in this context, *any*. If you add the number 1 a trillion, trillion, trillion times, it becomes a pretty big and powerful number.

Morph that number 1 into $1 dollar bills, and its cumulative value is enough to buy you some pretty expensive toys.

With the small additional excessive force left over from every particle needing the strong force to hold said particle together as a singular unit—with all that excessive force added up—which includes every atom, every stone, every particle of dirt, water, solid, liquid, gas, every tree, mountain, blade of grass, every insect, dog, person, every little and every big thing from the core of this planet Earth to every item—biological or not—sitting in, upon, or above it. ALL this excess strong force could make up the gravitational force that holds our feet to the ground, that makes apples fall down and not up, that makes Michael Jordan's slam dunk tougher rather than easier. Could it be the strong force is gravity?

Just a thought.

A New Theory of Time Travel and Causation Paradoxes

I have expressed and written about this theory of time travel and causation years before now. I even sent tweets to physicists Stephen Hawking, Brian Greene, and Michio Kaku—of course, none of them replied. They are all bigger than life, and I'm not paying them a fee, so why bother responding to a not-famous me. Anyway, this theory of time travel has been rambling around in my head for so long that once again, I feel the need to commit it to paper, electronic media, or any medium someone can read. But before I begin, once again let me lead off with my saying I doubt backward time travel possible. To travel backward in time infers that what was still is—somewhere—in current existence. Now, I suppose if one believes in an infinite universe, then why not believe in infinite planes of time? But do know that time may be relatively related to space, but time is not the same thing as space. I personally tend toward the belief in "something else." By that, I mean the universe ends and something else begins. I personally believe the universe is contained within "something else," which is contained within something else, etc. And this progression of Russian dolls continues ad nauseam. But I suppose that implies an infinite something even if not an infinite universe. So what's the real difference? But I digress—let me focus once again and explain my theory of time travel and causation.

Time paradoxes have been the death knell of theories regarding backward time travel for as long as time itself has been a curiosity. You know the stories. What if you were to travel back in time and kill your father? Would not the death of your father at a time preceding your birth eliminate the you of the present who went back in time to kill your father, thus preventing you from ever having the opportunity of going back in time to kill your father because you killed your father and you were never born . . . what? Where were we? Oh, yes. Another way to look at backward time travel is to reason that anything you changed in the past would already be the present now because you changed past events in time leading up to what was and is now again, now and our present time, right? Exactly, right? Well, what if I told you that either one of the aforementioned paradoxes may not be necessarily true. What if I told you, you can go back in time, change events of the past, and not effect causation—not cause a time paradox. What if.

My paradox-causation-busting theory suggests time exists as unique fragments of space-time coexisting with the present fragments of space-time and the future fragments of space-time. I am not suggesting parallel universes as you might have read about. I am suggesting one universe and one space-time existing in one long timeline. I propose further defining this one-long timeline as similar in nature to a self-contained story or movie with a predefined beginning and end contained on media not unlike a Blu-ray disk. Or better yet think of our universe as an erasable storybook. Each minute fragment of space-time in our universe is equivalent to one page in a storybook or one frame on a Blu-ray disk. We cannot change the events or content of each page in the storybook or the events or content of the video and audio on each frame of the Blu-ray disk, because we are an intricate part of the storybook and/or the Blu-ray disk; a story and a disk cannot rewrite itself. Or can it? A possible way to change a fragment of space-time of said storybook or Blu-ray disk is to either exist outside of the storybook or Blu-ray disk and have the ability to edit the storybook pages or the Blu-ray frames, or to find a way to move oneself outside of the storybook or Blu-ray disk and into some other page of the storybook or some other frame of the Blu-ray disk, thus allowing oneself the ability to interact and possibly change either the storybook pages or the frame content of the Blu-ray disk by at the very least the mere inclusion of oneself where one was not originally. Now then, to say one exists outside of the storybook or to say one exists outside of the Blu-ray disk one must be a being or entity that is not like us—not of this universe. We can call that being a god or merely an author or creator. Not unlike the author who pens and inks the storybook or the digital editor who adds the digital content to Blu-ray disk media. At the very least, we are referring to a being with the ability to edit what was and what will be the content within our storybook universe or within our Blu-ray disk. At the other extreme, if one is not a being existing outside of the storybook or Blu-ray disk, one must have the ability to move oneself about the pages of our storybook (from page to page post-original creation) or amongst the frames of our Blu-ray disk (post original creation). And one might refer to that ability as time travel—backward and forward time travel—as one with said ability is moving amongst the pages of the storybook or the frames of the Blu-ray disk post creation of either or both.

A special note is required here about my referrals to and about time travel. When I refer to time travel in my theory and in my examples within this thought, I do not mean time travel as defined by some modern-day physicists. Based on their definition of time, some modern-day physicists believe—and will have you believe—they have proved the existence of forward time travel. They have, in a sense, but they have not proven forward time travel as many of us laypeople understand and define time travel. All these particular physicists have proved is that it is possible to slow down some objects in their forward progression in time relative to the forward progression in time of other objects. Theoretically, as an object approaches the speed of light, all atoms of that particular object slow down in all aspects of what we define as space-time. The aging of that object slows; the movements of that object slow; the degradation of that object slows—all relative to the speed of the same happening to other nowhere near traveling the speed of light objects. So for example, two twenty-year-old twins . . . one remains on Earth . . . the other twin speeds off in a rocket at near light speed . . . the rocket twin returns to Earth fifty years later according to the Earth twin's time frame . . . the rocket twin appears forty-five years younger than his Earth twin as rocket twin's time frame ran only five years to him. This is very plausible—in fact, it is intellectually simple. But it is not time travel; it is merely the slowing of one's being relative (one's atoms) to other objects. Time travel as we all dream of time travel is actually going back or forward in an interactive way outside of the norm and outside of the universe; it is leaving the storybook on page 25 and entering the storybook on page 10 and rewriting that which was written already. That is not what traveling near the speed of light is doing. Real time, as laypeople and sci-fi fans imagine time travel, is something more. It is actual change of time via interaction.

What my theory suggests is each fragment of time is so unique that each fragment of time can be edited without effecting causation in subsequent fragments of time; hence, no time paradox. Think of it like erasing page 10 of a five-hundred-page storybook and then rewriting page 10 but leaving the rest of the pages of the storybook unchanged. The story may no longer make sense if the storybook is reread from beginning to end, but the changes made on page 10 are unknown to the content and characters on the pages following—that is, pages 11 through 500—so does it really matter anyway? As far as the characters and events existing on pages 11 through 500, nothing has changed. Why? The reason why is because pages 11 through 500 were actually created prior to the editing of page 10. It is also true that pages 1 through 9 still exist as was and also present no problem with the editing of page 10 because to pages 1 through 9, the editing of page 10 is not an editing, but the present happening now and following what always was. Every event that occurs on pages 11 through 500 "remember" the unedited events of page 10, not the edited events of page 10; pages 11 through 500 have no knowledge that page 10 was edited whatsoever. The only way the editing of page 10 can affect the following pages of pages 11 through 500—that is rewrite what we in the present once believed the past to be and kink causation—is if we were to edit all the pages of the storybook following and including page 10 right up to the point in time where one jumped out of his page of the storybook and back in "time" to the beginning of our editing on page 10. In that case, the entire story will have been rewritten. I will let you think of what the analogy using a Blu-ray disk instead of a storybook in this scenario would be.

So my theory suggests that discrete units of space-time coexist with the present unit of space-time. My theory suggests that no time—no events—vanish upon their happening. Space-time survives as discrete units or fragments of space-time on the one and only space-timeline after they happen and into what we call the present. And those space-time fragments, which we refer to as the past, can be edited as discrete units or fragments of space-time—like a page in a storybook—without effecting other units or fragments of space-time and with no paradoxical effects on causation in subsequent fragments of space-time. Hence the theory postulates backward time travel with no paradox in causation—backward and forward time traveling with no son killing his father paradoxes. This is, of course, if you believe in time travel and you believe in coexisting frames of space-time.

Just a thought.

Communicating from the Fourth Dimension

As understood by most of us, we live in a three-dimensional universe. Or do we? We at least perceive three dimensions in our universe. We perceive left/right, forward/backward, up/down. And as beings able to perceive three dimensions, we are also capable of perceiving two- and one-dimensional worlds. This makes sense so far, right? But wait, what if we were a one-dimensional creature and not a three-dimensional creature? Could we as a one-dimensional creature perceive a two-dimensional world? Think about it. What if we were not a one-dimensional creature but instead we were a two-dimensional creature? We could perceive a one-dimensional world, but could we perceive a three-dimensional world? It probably would not be that easy to do as a two-dimensional creature. Edwin Abbott Abbott posed such a scenario—that is, of a two-dimensional creature interacting with a three-dimensional creature and the difficulty his two-dimensional creatures (Flatlanders, as he called them) had perceiving a three-dimensional creature and its three-dimensional world. Oh, by the way, that wasn't a typo. Abbott's middle name is the same as his last name—Edwin Abbott Abbott. Flatlanders is interesting reading; I suggest you read it if you have not already.

String theory and M-theory suggest our universe consists of more than three dimensions. The theory is that these extra dimensions are wrapped up and expressed in such a way that we are unable to perceive them given we only have the physical ability to perceive as three-dimensional creatures. Although both string and M-theories entail double-digit numbers of dimensions, I only want to focus on one extra dimension of space: a fourth spacial dimension. I contend that as three-dimensional beings, we cannot easily, if at all, conceptualize a fourth-dimensional world. So what if there is a fourth dimension of space sharing our universe? And what if there exists within that fourth dimension a creature made up of four dimensions? And what if that fourth-dimensional creature is such that it thinks like us; it can understand us. We cannot communicate with such a creature, because we cannot even perceive its existence; but maybe, just maybe, it can communicate with us.

Just as we can perceive a two-dimensional world and a one-dimensional world, a fourth-dimensional creature should be able to perceive our three-dimensional world. In fact, this fourth-dimensional creature (let's call him 4-D) can see and hear everything we do and think. 4-D can also see what we did, what we are doing now, and what we are going to do, well in advance of our doing it. 4-D experiences our lives much like we experience a film, cell by cell.

So assuming 4-D can communicate with us, at least one way—that is, 4-D can impart information on us but we cannot reciprocate. How would 4-D communicate with us? How would 4-D make itself known to us? Maybe 4-D could communicate via our own media. Maybe 4-D could rewrite our TV shows, our movies, and our newscasts and impart messages in them meant for us to receive. Maybe 4-D could create one of those miracles that religions are always claiming as a way of showing it's here watching us. Maybe the parting of the Red Sea by Moses was made possible by 4-D. Maybe that boxer behind on all the scorecards going into the twelfth round who scores a knockout victory over the overwhelming favorite was helped by 4-D.

What do you think? How would 4-D be able to make its presence known to us? How could you make your presence known to a two-dimensional creature? Think about it.

Just a thought.

Defeating the Time Travel Paradox

Now, I am not a believer in time travel. I have no strong belief that anyone ever will or ever has traveled backward or forward in time, and that goes for objects as well as people. Some physicists will claim that time travel into the future is possible and future time travel has been proven, but as I see it, they are manipulating the meaning of time travel as we laypeople understand the meaning of time travel.

Einstein proved that time is a relative thing. It has been argued that Hermann Minkowski along with Einstein proved that time is a fourth dimension. I do not believe time as a dimension similar in nature to the three dimensions of space (that is, left/right, forward/backward, up/down). I believe time to be no more than a tool of measurement. Time measures the movement of people and objects. That is, time measures objects as large as the universe and as small as one Planck length. If nothing moves, time stands still. But time never runs backward—only forward or not at all.

Time is relative, however. The relative nature of time is where the meaning of time travel, and physicists claim that an object can travel through time into future times makes relative sense. But as I will explain, an object moving near-light speed does not move into the future as you or I think of an object moving through time. Take the twin argument for example. One twin speeds away from the Earth in a rocket traveling near the speed of light. His twin sister remains on Earth with their parents. The rocket twin returns to Earth one year later according to the time on his watch. His sister is there to meet her rocket twin at the landing site. She is alone, however, as their parents passed away ten years after rocket twin left the Earth. Earth twin is now fifteen years older than her rocket twin brother.

This is possible. This I believe. But this is not time travel as most of us laypeople understand time travel. What really happened in the scenario is the smallest particles to the largest particles that make up rocket twin slowed as rocket twin approached the speed of light. Rocket twin's internal clock slowed relative to his Earth twin's internal clock. Neither Earth twin nor rocket twin noticed any difference in time. Both twins perceived time as running normally. What happened to create a different time for each twin is a proven effect due to the movement of objects slowing down as an object approaches the speed of light. The object, the atom, or the person made up of these objects/atoms does not notice this effect. My point being, this is not time travel as most of us laypeople understand the meaning of time travel. This is relative movement of objects at different rates of speed. Rocket twin's atoms, his processes of life/existence, his very being have slowed relative to his Earth twin sister. And as logic dictates, this effect only happens in a forward direction of movement, never backward.

Now this leads me into the title of this thought: "Defeating the Time Travel Paradox." I do not believe backward time travel is possible, but for argument's sake and to legitimize the title of this thought, let us assume backward time travel is possible. And let me make my point as follows. You may have read or you may have been told of the time travel paradoxes that remove credibility for time travel. For example, if you were to travel back in time and kill your mother before you were born, the question then arises, how then could you have existed in your current time to travel back in time to kill your mother? If you killed your mother before you were born, you never would have been born to travel back in time to kill your mother. Well, what if I tell you it is possible to travel back in time and kill your mother and for you to still be alive and to have been born even though you killed your mother before you were born? I am not trying to devise a creative way for you to kill your mother. I love my mother, and I am sure your mother is a loving and caring person with whom you wish no harm to befall. But I do believe you can have your cake and eat it too. Let me explain.

If time travel forward or backward is possible, there must be a place for these—let us call them segments of time—to exist at the same time as our current time. You cannot travel to a place or a time if it does not exist. As I type these words, I am in my current time. As soon as I have finished typing a paragraph, a word, or even an alphabetical letter—the act of typing that paragraph, word, or letter has now become part of the past. It happened; it is not current. What I have yet to type is the potential future. It may happen, but it is yet to be. I am not going to discuss the future here, just the past. If I plan to travel backward in time, to the past, I have to have a past to which to travel. The past has to exist somewhere, or if you prefer, sometime. First we must have an idea of what a time past maybe. One way of looking at time is to compare time to a video clip imported into a nonlinear editing software program. Computer geeks should relate to what I am suggesting. If you video some event you want to save to watch again and again, you may want to save it to some media, such as a DVD disk. You may want to add a menu to the disk and maybe add some special effects to the video clip itself. So you import the video clip into some nonlinear editing software like Adobe Premiere Pro or Final Cut Pro. If you are familiar with nonlinear editing software, you know the imported video clip is laid out cell by cell. Any video cell you may currently view on the editing timeline is comparable to current time. Any video cell to the left of the current video cell (current time) is comparable to the past, and any video cell to the right of the current time is comparable to the future.

Now, if you want to edit one of the video cells using your nonlinear editing software, you bring a particular video cell into focus and begin the editing process—adding video effects or video transitions. By editing a video cell to the left of another video cell, you are changing the past of the video clip you imported relative to the cells to its right. What if backward time travel is similar in nature to nonlinear editing? What if you can change one, two, or one hundred video cells (Planck units of time) to the left of all the video cells to the right without affecting a change in the cells to the right? You would have effectively changed the past, thrown a wrench into causation, and defeated the time travel paradox. As previously suggested, using your poor mother as an example, you could travel backward in time and kill your mother. You could then return to the present to find not only you still exist but your sweet mother has stopped over to your house with your favorite dessert as a surprise. You have defeated the time travel paradox. And no one remembers you visiting the past. To them, and our current time, nothing has changed.

Now, this does screw up causation, but then again, it does not screw up causation. Let me explain. I never promised a perfect world, and you should never expect a perfect world, which means no perfect answers. However, I contend that upon your return to the present, your mother—whom you killed during your trip backward in time—is not only alive, but she has no recollection of your visiting her in the past or you killing her. Your mother's memory of the past is unchanged from what her memory was before you made your trip into the past. Why? How can this be? Well, if we think of time as discrete units of Planck time, what you did in your backward travel in time was change only a specific number of those Planck units of time. You only changed the Planck units of time running from your entry into the past up until your existence from the past and return to your current time. All other Planck units of time (video cells) preceding your entry into the past and following your exit from the past remain as they were before your backward trip in time; they remain unchanged. So you changed the past, but only a specific unit of time in the past. You get to have your cake and eat it too.

A possible theory for time to be a dimension with the possibility of traversing it in a backward direction time must never die. Events in time must reproduce similar to the bodies' cells, continually splitting off and recreating them, but it must be done in a smooth fashion such that we do notice or see time left behind or time out ahead. This is similar to the multi-universe idea but not the same idea. I am not suggesting multiple yous and multiple mes within multiple universes. I am suggesting our universe is a three-dimensional video strip existing within a fourth dimension. I am suggesting our universe sits within the fourth dimension much the same way a two-dimensional comic strip sits within our world. As we can easily traverse and know what is happening in every cell of the two-dimensional comic strip, we are visible and traversable via the fourth dimension. And like a two-dimensional comic strip in our world, we can—via the fourth dimension—travel backward in time and change Planck units of time in the past without changing the present or the potential future. And no time travel paradox need ever surface to trouble us.

Just a thought.

Existence Is an Advanced Entity's Kodak Moment

You have now heard the many comparisons made between time and film. A film can be played forward and backward and over and over again. Movie film, now replaced for the most part by digital imaging, is expressed as a timeline by those of us who have dabbled as a hobby or a profession in movie editing. Science also makes use of the "timeline," and science also makes many comparisons between absolute time, relative time, and time in general as laid out on a "timeline." This comparison, although I believe flimsy and not exactly fair, has led some scientists into believing that time—at least mathematically—fails to find restriction in a backward direction. In other words, physics has not disproved time's ability to rewind; hence, time is assumed the possibility of reversing itself. Personally, I believe the thinking on this is flawed. As I believe all time moves forward, it must move forward, because time is not an "object." Time is not a "thing"; time is a measurement of movement. If an object moves, it can move straight ahead or in a reverse direction—up or down, left or right—but it cannot move in a "reverse" direction as reverse is thought of when one things of time travel. This definition of time encompasses and embraces Einstein's relative time and Newton's absolute time, but not anyone's backward moving time. This definition accepts time stoppage but not backward moving time. Time can move forward, and it can stop. Time moves forward if any object in existence moves—in any direction, even the smallest atom and/or particle of matter. Time stops if nothing moves. But time never goes backward. What has occurred has occurred. It can occur again, but forward in time when it occurs again. It cannot recur in the sense of going back in time and repeating—for example

1920 came and went; it will not occur again. You can never go back in time and shake the hand of Abraham Lincoln.

But all this talk of time and timelines is just to set the background of what this thought is really about. As said, many physicists—and many fiction writers as well—have made the comparison of existence in time to a film, to a film on a timeline. Some have proposed that we—that is, existence—are nothing more than a film on a timeline, a predetermined movie set out by the hand of God in which we are but character actors playing our parts. We are just character actors playing our parts for the amusement of or out of love by and for some godly being. Well, I have another proposal of what is happening. I have a different idea—somewhat similar to us being a film laid out like a timeline, but somewhat different from that idea as well. A movie is an amazing scientific achievement, if you think about it. We take photographs—film, digital imaging—all for granted, but they are really incredible technological achievements. We are able, by such amazing technology, to capture still images of ourselves—moving images of ourselves—and play them back for our enjoyment, time and time again. Watching movies one can become so engrossed in the imaging that it is easy to forget it is a movie and not real life. It appears as if we are watching real people doing real things with sound to boot. That is really amazing if you stop and think about it. It only seems not so amazing because we have grown up with the technology and it is second nature to us now. But think of someone who is so far divorced from such technology. Think about what they would might think while watching a movie for the first time. Amazing, right?

We can think of film as comparable to a two-dimensional world. We live in a three-dimensional world with length, width, and depth. A two-dimensional world lacks that third dimension of depth. If you existed within a two-dimensional world, you would be unable to conceptualize a three-dimensional being as that third dimension is lost to you. A third dimension is not in your vocabulary, so to speak; it would be beyond your comprehension, much as a fourth dimension is beyond our comprehension now. If the two worlds of second and third dimensions intersected, the two-dimensional being would not see the three-dimensional being as the third-dimensional being really appears, but merely as a slice of a two-dimensional portion of said being. The 2-D being could not appreciate or build a 3-D object. But we, as 3-D beings, can and do create 2-D objects all the time, as well as 3-D objects. What if a 4-D being created a 3-D object—that 3-D object, he or she created being us and our universe.

What if the science of said 4-D being was so advanced in relation to ours—as well as having the benefit of an extra dimension to build with and within—that said 4-D being created a "movie" of which we are characters within? What is similar to our 3-D film and digital imaging in its 4-D world and creation and the result of the 4-D beings filmmaking is our existence and our universe. Everything that we are is connected similar to an image and sound on film. The air we breathe, the atoms that make up our bodies, and so much more. The water we drink. The ground we stand on. The space our world situates itself within, and the energy that drives us and the life given us by our stars. All this is connected to each other. All this is self-contained within our universe. Just as all the props for the actors, to the objects, to the backgrounds, to the sounds, to the effects are all self-contained within a film. The only difference is the medium upon which it all plays out. Instead of celluloid and digital media, we are contained within and made up of elements that maybe to a 4-D being are no different than film to us. We may be no more, no less, than a 4-D beings Saturday night entertainment or someone's science experiment. Or possibly, an ornament in the living room of some being's home.

Think about it.

Is Time Travel Possible, or Is It Merely Science Fiction?

There are many science fiction tales about time travel—thousands upon thousands of books, hundreds of movies, and many, many TV series. There are so many tales about time travel that many people take time travel for granted, as if it is a reality. There are even many physicists who have bought into the possibility. But is time travel possible? The answer—yes and no.

Unlike science fiction tales and unlike the many physicists who use complicated language to explain time travel in such a way that makes them appear intelligent but confuses all who listen or read, I will explain it here simply and briefly. Time travel is possible in a forward direction. Time travel is not possible in a backward direction.

So what actually is time travel? First, one must answer the question: what is time? As explained by Albert Einstein and many other great scientists, time is another dimension just as length, width, and depth are dimensions. The latter three dimensions are easily understood as spatial dimensions and need no explanation, but what about time? What is time? Time is the measurement of movement. What does that mean? Let me give some examples. If you brush your teeth, you can recollect all movement you made to do so from the moment you picked up your toothbrush until the moment you put it down. You can recollect the movement of the sun from early morning until it sets late evening (it's actually the Earth doing most of the moving). You can watch the movement of your dog as (s)he chases the stick you threw for him or her. Time is a measurement of movement.

But movement is involved in a deeper way than people, animals, or objects changing positions. Take for example a human being. We are made up of billions of cells, and more than that, we are made up of billions of atoms. All these atoms are in constant motion. Being in constant motion, the movement of these atoms can be measured and, hence, can be said to exhibit time. What if, however, the movement of atoms in all things living or otherwise stopped? It could be argued that time itself had stopped. If nothing is moving from here to there, if not a single atom in anything living or otherwise is moving, time can be understood to have stopped.

Now, how does this relate to time travel forward or backward? Very simply, you can stop atoms from moving, but you cannot make them move backward without doing so in a forward motion, so backward time travel is not possible. You can, however, stop or slow, specific atoms belonging to specific objects while not affecting the movement of atoms in everything else, hence making time travel in a forward direction possible, in a manner of speaking.

Let me explain further with an example. If you can slow every atom of your being relative to every atom not of yourself (the rest of the world), you retard the aging of your body relative to worldly time. By doing so, you could find yourself to have aged slower than everyone around you. This is the time travel example that physicists try to explain with the tale of the rocket speeding away from the Earth at near the speed of light and then returning to Earth only to find the ten years the astronaut believes (s)he was away from the Earth, the ten years his or her body has aged, is not the ten years traveled by those (s)he left on Earth. The astronaut returns to an Earth that has aged, not ten years, but one hundred years. The physics behind this has to do with matter approaching the speed of light. The speed of light is a time barrier. The closer one gets to the speed of light, the slower his or her atoms move, hence slowing time for the speeding astronaut relative to the space surrounding him or her. This is why time travel forward is possible, in a manner of speaking.

But what about backward time travel? Backward time travel is not possible because atoms can be slowed to a stop—which can, in a sense, stop or move someone forward in time relative to everything else—but stopping atoms does only just that. Stop or move someone forward, not backward. And none of this movement is really what science fiction describes as time travel. This forward time travel is a one-way trip. Unlike science fiction, once you move forward in time, you can never go back. Why? Because unlike a science fiction tale, unlike a graph you plot on paper, unlike a timeline in nonlinear editing software—time is not a thing. Time is not an object. Time is a measurement; time is a measurement of movement. And movement can only be in a forward direction as measured by time, or there is no movement at all and, hence, no time.

For a science fiction, tale of backward and forward time travel to bear fruit, every atom that exists in you and everything not in you must replicate and never cease to exist. You would have to exist billions and billions of times over on different planes of existence—in different dimensions, or one long singular timeline of which we find difficulty in comprehending. Some physicists and authors of science fiction explain this possibility with the use of parallel dimensions that sees you and all existence branching off with every thought and movement and every tick of time into multiple dimensions. So that every moment you live is saved like a cell on the timeline of a movie spread across film branching in all directions like an octopus. But that idea is another topic for another time.

Just a thought.

Why I Believe
"Backward Time Travel" Impossible

You can't go back in time, but you can slowly go forward in time, right?

Hey, do you have some time? If I have grabbed your attention on the topic of time, I have another time query I would like to present to you for thought. I am not looking for an answer, merely opinions and thoughts, so read, think, and then rethink. If you have yet to notice, I have been interested in the subject of "time" for some time now (no pun intended . . . or maybe yes, a pun), and I am curious what the professional scientific mind thinks about time traveling in reverse.

Hermann Minkowsky, after analyzing Einstein's theory of special relativity, tied space and time together and banished absolute time in to the Newtonian past. As a result, the dimensions of space and time are now considered to be forever intertwined. Some physicists and scientists in other fields of science, as well as novelists and science-fiction enthusiasts, believe this link between space and time leaves open the possibility of moving through time in a reverse direction. *Star Trek* accomplishes this task by whipping around the Sun at warp speed. It seems the thought being, there is nothing in physics, or science in general, that precludes the possibility of moving in both directions on the timeline, so there is no preclusion to the impossibility of backward time travel. I disagree.

Einsteinium time looks to specific relations of objects in space-time in which to make its measurement of time—for example, a train moving past a railroad platform or the rocket speeding past the other rocket or the ship leaving and returning to port. But what if there is no train, no platform, no rockets, no ship, nor a port to dock a ship? What if all material objects are removed from space-time? What if all elements are removed from space-time? What if the very last atom in existence is removed from space-time? What happens to time? The answer is that time ceases to exist. Why, because time is a measurement of movement. If something exists but does not move, time still exists. The measurement of nonmovement is the equivalent of the Indian (East Indians, not Native American Indians) creation of "0." And if nothing exists—no objects, no elements, no atoms—there is nothing to measure; there are then no objects in relation to other objects to measure. This then is the end of even Einsteinium; time ceases to exist.

So what does this have to do with time travel? Time travel suggests a separation of space from a time. For a man to travel backward in time, he would have to rip a piece of space (himself) apart from a specific point in space-time and paste himself over/into another piece of space in another point in time elsewhere. Does this not violate the first law of thermodynamics? I don't know, I'm just asking. Unless the plural times is considered a true closed unit, what about the hole in space he came from and the space he pasted himself over? Does one supplant the other? Backward time travel has more problems than causation (although that certainly is a major hurdle—but discussed so much by others, I will not discuss it here). To travel backward in time, there must be a backward space-time destination; there must be a place to go. Time travel seems to suggest that matter does not morph itself into a future self but replicates itself similar to a replicating cell; the past never ceases, and so the future always has been because someone's past is always someone's future. This seems very difficult to grasp as reality. This thought leads to the idea of parallel universes, which may exist, but again, that is another topic—which requires much discussion, although not here. It seems logical that objects move in a direction. We label this direction "forward." We define the effects of a movement "forward" by the use of such words as an example, *causation*. But whether an object moves forward or backward, it moves in a direction. When the object moves, we measure that movement by time. The ability to measure said movement does not equate to the ability to "undo" said movement, which is an equivalent of backward movement in time, if time is defined as a measurement of movement. Backward time travel then is tantamount to undoing any measureable movement made forward.

It is very easy with the electronic marvels we have today to confuse film with reality. Movies look extremely realistic these days, especially with HD screens. But because a movie can be rewound does not mean reality can be rewound. Movies are the captured images and sounds of reality on a medium from which they can be shown over and over again. But that is not Clark Gable on the movie being watched. That is the captured reflection of photons that reflected off of Clark Gable and the captured sound waves that emanated from Clark Gable—a Clark Gable who has been dead for some years now. Just as so many of the stars seen in the night sky are reflections of light bounced off celestial bodies—celestial bodies that have long since changed since the light first bounced off of their surface. To further the analogy, backward time travel would imply that that which was still is and always will be—or at least was "captured" and recorded somehow, somewhere, and was still accessible if the means was available.

Wormholes are another interesting subject associated with the possibility of time travel. The bending of space upon itself such that the future cone of one space-time overlaps the past cone of another space-time and a tunnel preexists or is created somehow between the future and the past, creating a shortcut not only through space but time. First I see how the bending of light (photons) or gravity (a force) changes time (movement), relatively speaking. That lucky (or unlucky, depending on how you look at it) man who rockets off into space at near the speed of light then subsequently returns to Earth some twenty years later to find himself (relatively speaking) two hundred years in the future—his family and friends long since deceased. The movement of the rocket man at the speed of light slowed his movement (his timing of growth/aging) relative to his family and friends on Earth. But the rocket man's atomic structural movement was slowed, not reversed. He did not warp into another time; he continued through the same time as everyone else, but slower relatively.

Hopefully, now you see the point I am making. There is a difference between slow movement forward and movement in reverse.

Let's get back to wormholes. Curious, no one mentions how the universe can be so warped, so bent over itself, that a future cone can overlap a past cone and a wormhole can find itself opening a door between the past and the future. That seems quite a bend in the universe. If there was a warranty on the universe (valid past the first five billion years [six-thousand years if you are religious]), something should have called it in for repair before the warranty expired. But even if wormholes do exist, more logically, a connection would be made between two areas of space occupying, relatively, equivalent measurements of movement (time). Causation and the spatial connection(s) would be between close areas of space-time affected by gravitational warping in a specific area, or the connection(s) would be between extremely separated areas of space-time in a curved universe. But the wormhole would be a connection between sections of space, not time.

And what about that well-known *Star Trek* trick of sling-shooting around the sun into the past. It is fact the slingshot effect, using the gravity of celestial bodies such as the moon and Jupiter (to name a couple) has enabled NASA to explore the farthest reaches of our solar system, but it has not propelled space craft into the past, and it still would not do so if we could travel at or beyond the speed of light. And what about that long-sought-after, faster-than-light particle, the tachyon. *Star Trek, the Next Generation* made storyline use of tachyons quite often. Can tachyons send messages to the past defeating causation? Imagine a man made of tachyons (big leap here); let's call him T-Man. T-Man is traveling forward on the timeline at his usual tachyon speed, outracing all other objects/particles that are denied the ability to travel at or near the speed of light. T-Man is even out speeding light itself. So T-Man (when he looks back at us turtles and light also traveling forward on the timeline) sees us moving in reverse. It appears to T-Man he is witnessing time moving backward. But what T-Man is actually witnessing is the late reception of the photons making their way to him. T-Man is so much faster than light that his movement in relation to our movement, and light, does not allow the light to catch up, and so it appears in reverse. But T-Man's movement (timed) and our movement (timed) and the movement of light (timed) are all moving forward. This effect is similar to our reception here on Earth of the light from long-ago stars in the night sky. And similar like playing two movies in a forward direction on a timeline, but at different speeds, from the perspective of the faster-playing movie, the slower-playing movie is moving in reverse. Both movies, however, are moving forward.

The bottom line is this: time travel into the future is possible with the right technology, but only into a future that is yet to exist. It is made possible by slowing a man or woman's movement relative to that of other women and other men. Time travel into the past, however, is not possible. Movement, although it can be in a forward or backward direction, is always measured (timed) in a forward direction. Even the movies we watch over and over again—the movies we rewind to hear the joke the comedian made while our kids were talking—are rewound in a forward (timed) direction. Causation saves us. Even when listening to a garbled audio tape as it is being played in reverse, we are still listening to the reversed audio in forward moving time.

It would be great to travel into the past. Personally, I know I would have been president if I could travel back in time and get an A on that third grade quiz—well, maybe not . . . But it would be a great way to spend my vacation. Think of the fun I could have and the trouble I could get into and then back out of again. And the best part, I could come home before I left; it would not cost a dime in vacation pay.

Just a thought.

What If We Are Traveling Backward in Time Now? Would You Know It?

reverse in running was time if know you Would.

I think I spend too much time obsessing about time. You might think I have too much time on my hands to be so engrossed in such a timeless subject. But then how do you spend your time? Time is a subject that takes hold of the imagination of many of us. I think it is safe to say that most people would love to not only think about time but control time. Dr. Who, where are you? Think of the power one could wield controlling the movement and the speed of time.

Anyway, again I got to thinking about "what if" backward time was possible. And my thoughts went further than time travel, and I thought to muse over the ramifications of backward time travel. I do not believe backward time travel possible, but I believe most physicists will agree that there is nothing mathematically that definitively discounts the possibility of backward time travel. So for the sake of the following discussion, let us say backward time travel is possible. But rather than focusing on scenarios like the time travel exploits of Captain Picard or Doug and Tony through the Time Tunnel, I want to explore a particular idea that has permeated my mind for some time now. What if we are all in a universe where time is traveling backward right now at this moment? Would we know we were running in reverse?

I find nothing to dismiss the possibility of matter moving in more than one direction: up, down, forward, and "backward." Time is tied to space, and just as the clock can be rewound, the space (matter) connected to time can be "undone." But would we know it? As I live my life, and when I take the time to think about how I am living my life and how I am using my time, I have the ever-present feeling that I am doing so in a forward direction. But would I know otherwise? If time were running backward, would I be aware it was running backward? Every event that happened would unwind. Every event that happened would cease to be as if it never were. How would I know this? I do not believe I would.

Too often the motion of time is compared to a filmstrip—a timeline. But when I look at a filmstrip, when I look at each cell on that film strip—forward and/or backward—I am doing so from the outside. I am an outside observer. I am not an object on one of those cells on the filmstrip. Just as we observe the many sci-fi TV shows and movies about time travel, we do so from the advantage point of an outside observer. We are not on the TV show. We are not a character in the sci-fi movie. We are outside. But if our time is traveling backward as I write, it is our time, and we are within that space and time; we are inseparable from our film, our space and time.

I think a better comparison pertaining to this thought than film is that of paper and an eraser. If I total my life from birth to death and set it upon paper, and I then start erasing my life from death to birth, the paper will only evidence as much of my life as still remains on the paper at any given time. What is erased is gone and for all purposes; it never was. Or maybe a better object of comparison is a tape recorder and my voice recorded thereon. As an outside observer, I can listen to my recorded voice in a forward or backward direction, but as the voice on the tape itself—that is to say, if I examine the rewinding of the tape from the vantage point of my recorded voice on the tape and not as an outside observer listening to the recording—I am only aware of what is playing as it is playing, and what has played vanishes from my reality as quickly as played. Our minds are predisposed to think of time as having direction—forward and backward—but maybe direction is our way of labeling time and forward is backward or forward, all dependent on one's relative perspective.

If our time is running backward, all evidence of our movement in that direction is being erased as time moves backward. No different than if time is running forward. We live in the present. Once an event occurs, it is done and gone—erased, but still in our memories. So one might believe that if time is running backward, we would remember the future, and the past would be the new unknown future. But what if that is not how it works? What if causation is fixed relatively and what if relativity exposes another t. What if time moving backward is relative to time moving forward? And what if time affects our memories in only one direction? Then our moving backward in time would leave us oblivious to what just occurred in our past, which is the future for someone living in forward moving time. We would only remember the moment—the present. And we would remember the past, which in reality is our future. But we would perceive time as moving forward and past as having occurred, when in reality our past has yet to happen—"déjà vu."

We grow accustomed to our environment, and we accept that which makes life manageable—physically and psychologically. We perceive time as moving forward, causation intact and moving one direction, and maybe causation is intact. But if our time was such that our time was moving backward, we would perceive that as "the norm" and adjust our thinking and rationalizations accordingly.

For time to exist in the sense of being traversable, I think it necessary to believe that events that are destined to happen have happened—in other words, destiny and/or fate. And if that is so, causation is preserved. But I also believe it possible to have no perception that we are moving in reverse. No perception that our futures have occurred and our futures are unraveling into our pasts, which, for us, have yet to occur.

I leave this topic with this request. Record your voice, and play it back in reverse. And as you listen to your soliloquy unravel, imagine being that voice on the recording. Separate from the you who recorded it. Imagine your world, your memories, unraveling, and think about the possibility of living your life in reverse.

Just a thought.

Schrodinger's Cat

No matter what Erwin Schrodinger proposed and no matter what physicists choose to believe—the cat is dead and alive until observed—the cat still has to shit on the pot.

The truth of the matter is that mathematics does not solve all equations. And some mathematical equations do not represent the real world—much to the consternation of many physicists and mathematicians. Some things are possible mathematically that just are not possible in reality. I'm sorry, but the cat is dead or alive—not both, nor neither—and consciousness has nothing to do with the resultant reality upon observation of the opened box. Chance and chaos and randomness are things that exist in our world of physics, but as Einstein said, "god does not play dice." John Wheeler was correct in surmising that we cannot objectively observe and critique the universe; we are participants. We are the mice in the maze. We are the rice in the pudding. We can only observe with the senses and abilities at our disposal, and the universe is so much more than what we can perceive. But being participants does not mean we can also be the experiment itself. We are but a part of the experiment, an ingredient in the meal, but not the baker of the pie.

To suggest as renowned author Michael Talbot seems to suggest that consciousness makes matter and effects causation is a little on the egocentric side regarding the human feelings of worth and importance. But then, is not ego what drives so many human beings, scientists, and nonscientists alike? When a scientist can defeat permanent death (we are all dying and being reborn every second of our lives until our very end), then and only then can science make a claim to have some conscious effect on the universe. I believe it possible that all life and nonlife—all matter and energy—can be merely waves vibrating at varying speeds: the slower the vibration, the more solid the particle. And if all existence be nothing more than a hologram and/or wave pool inside a box entitled our "universe"—being examined, observed, and reworked by entities existing in a fourth, fifth, etc., spatial dimension—unperceived by us, we still are no more than a series of waves programmed to function and act as a life form as we know within a universe not of our making, design, or control. At least not of our control that is not already programmed into the universal box as a possibility.

To be able to consciously control the life or death of Schrodinger's cat would mean ALL who come in contact with said boxed cat must collectively and consciously agree the said cat is dead or alive upon opening said box. OR those whose conscious decision is for the cat to live must move on a path into a different universe than those whose conscious decision is for the cat not to live. Multiple universes must then exist, and for such a possibility, the number of multiple universes must be an uncountable number near or at infinity. Where is all the real estate for these universes? LOL. This is not to say it is not a possibility, merely that it may be a possibility.

Einstein and many others throughout history were correct in concluding the human equation must be removed from the experiment as best as can possibly be done for objectivity to have any merit. WE are not the masters of our universe. We are part and parcel. We are threads in the fabric. We are cherries in the pie (or pits, depending on your outlook). Ego must be put aside so that truth and reality can be found. And remember, the greatest minds of our world once believed our planet to be the center of our universe, laughing and destroying careers or taking the lives of the few enlightened minds who for thousands of years—even prior to the birth of Copernicus—believed otherwise. Remember, we must refrain from rushing to accept everything told us, and we must always be open-minded to the world around us.

Just a thought.

WE ARE WAVES . . . Electromagnetic Waves to be Precise

We are but a child's science project—a display on a shelf, an experiment, an entertainment sitcom. But we are waves.

Follow along with me on this theoretical ride into supposition. We all must agree that our world is inundated with electromagnetic waves. It is the light we see. It is the light we do not see. It is the sound we hear. It is the sound we do not hear. It is the heat that warms our bodies and warms our Earth. It is the air that we breathe. It is the water that sustains us. It is the energy that allows us to move and thus gives us the "miracle" of life.

Electromagnetic waves (hereinafter merely "waves") are long and short. The length of each wave defines the colors we see. The length of each wave defines whether we perceive a wave with our eyes/mind or our ears/mind. The length of each wave defines the properties of said wave and what said wave can do and what it can be and how we can interact with said wave. Size (length) does matter.

So a fast-moving wave becomes light and magnetic/electrical fields—photons and electrons. On the other extreme, a slow-moving wave becomes a sound, a solid, a rock, a mountain, a human being. Of course, not merely one wave, but many waves held together by fields are the building blocks of what we exist within and what we exist as. All such waves are necessary for the existence and maintenance of the physics of our universe.

How different are we from a two-dimensional drawing? Maybe we are not as different as one might think. Look to Abbott Abbott, a name given a man with an idea so good he had to be named twice, for some amazing possibilities. As Flatland is so much more complicated in its makeup than a one-dimensional world, so too is our three-dimensional world that much more complicated than a two-dimensional world like Flatland. So is it that much of a stretch to think a theoretical four-dimensional world would be based on physics exponentially more complicated than our three-dimensional world? I think not. Given that thought, is it possible a four-dimensional spatial world exists and envelopes our perceivable three-dimensional world? I think it's possible. String theory may not be in vogue these days as its backward experimental proofs of existence have not borne much fruit, but it has yet to be ruled out completely. Other dimensions may exist that we cannot perceive as we are physically equipped to perceive only three-dimensional space-time. Other dimensions wrapped up within or possibly outward and encompassing are beyond our abilities of perception. We are creations of a three-dimensional world, and as such, we are not equipped to perceive more spatial dimensions than length, width, and depth—with time thrown in as a possible dimension but not a dimension of space. So a fourth and a fifth and who knows how many more spatial dimensions may exist, which we are unequipped to perceive and/or conceive the existence thereof?

So I contend it's possible our world, our universe, consisting of our terrarium the planet Earth and all else that we are capable of perceiving given our known physics can possibly be on display on a four-dimensional being's idea of a coffee table or fireplace mantle. That we and all we exist upon and within can be no different than a book of two-dimensional drawings with a storyline told in characters and no different than an old Kodak film where we exist as a story being told frame by frame with a beginning and an ending and available sound—where we and our lives are predetermined and readily accessed at beginning and at end. Think about it.

The afore-written supposition is merely food for thought and nothing more. What do you think?

Just a thought.

The Following Is a Letter I Sent as an Email to UConn Physicist Dr. Ronald Mallett Regarding the Subject Matter of a Book of His I Just Read:

Hi, Dr. Mallett,

I just read your book *Time Traveler*, and I was touched by your personal story and the inspiration of your father to drive you to the success you attained in life, personal and career alike. I too have been driven all my life by family, especially my close family members—they being my wife, who is also my closest friend, and my three children who all excel in academic studies. I am first and foremost proud of my family.

I hope you do not mind my following comments regarding the search for an answer to time travel. I am not a physicist, nor am I a scientist. I am a lawyer by profession. I am fifty-eight years old and an old married man who still has young children of ages nineteen, sixteen, and twelve. I am a late starter at everything in life. But being inquisitive as I am, I read a lot, and physics along with history are the two main topics I read about. I have amassed my own library of mostly nonfictional works as I enjoy reading—and learning— about life as it really is and not about life as it is not. Time and gravity have always fascinated me, and I have purchased and read many books on these topics. I have collected the works of many physicists, as I believe they will have a more accurate tale to tell about the workings of life and the universe than those merely reporting on their works. I am not a mathematician. I love to read about theory, but I am afraid of math—although I did just order a book on tensor calculus, which I am going to try to comprehend.

I have come to my own opinions and theories on time and time travel, as I am sure so many others have before me and will after me. If you do not mind, let me briefly share some thoughts that came to mind after reading your book.

First, I do not believe time travel is possible, nor do I believe anyone has proven it possible. Despite my fascination in time and my hope, others will prove differently. I know some may argue that time travel to the future has been proven, but I disagree, and I believe their claims beg the question as to what exactly is "time." I believe time to be nothing more than a measurement of movement. That is why some may correctly argue that time travel to the future is possible. But it also explains why time travel to the past is not possible. If every single quark, if every single particle—no matter how many, no matter how small—were to stop moving, then time would stop. At that point in space, one could argue that time has stopped. That time has ceased to exist. But you cannot move particles backward. You cannot move beyond zero. Even backward movement (for example, playing a film in reverse) is still measured by time in a forward direction as time is a tool of measurement, not a thing apart and of itself tangible. Interestingly, if one was able to move backward—in time direction, that is—would one even know they were doing so? Could we be in the middle of a universal crunch, moving back in time and not even aware of such? Think of a movie being played backward. Do the characters in the movie realize they are going backward? I don't think so. The movie is rewinding, undoing. There would be no knowledge or feeling of going backward.

Regarding moving forward in time brings to mind the often told twin scenario. The old twins and the rocket tale told by Einstein and by many others does not prove time travel. The twins, one remaining home on Earth and one rocketing off into space near the speed of light, merely prove relativity. Everything is relative to everything else. I know time is glued to the theory, but not time travel as we dream. As goes the twin story, the twin rocketing off into space, along with his or her rocket, experiences a slowing of every particle in his or her being/body as well as the rocket and everything else material traveling due to his or her moving near the speed of light. This is Einstein's theory—a valid logical theory even to me a simple layman. But this is not time travel as understood by us laypeople. This is a slowing of matter relative to what we perceive as the normal speed of matter and our everyday lives, the Earth, and our day-to-day experiences. It is not time travel. The closet analogy I can make in other words is, it is near freezing of oneself and the containing rocket, oxygen, and all else traveling near the speed of light; but it is not time travel as most of us are willing to define and dream of time traveling. Slowing one's very being—and hence, age—is not time travel per se. It is not jumping from one time frame to another. It is still the process of moving along within the same universe as all else, but at a decelerated frame of time relative to others.

I believe that to be able to travel through time as most of us understand time travel, one must take into consideration a different belief or theory of time and the universe itself. One has to believe the universe is more like a "movie" with set frames for every event that occurs. This means that each moment of time that passes for each of us is preserved in space, but where? And on what plane is each moment preserved? How? If and only then does time takes on a different form then that of mere measurement. Then time becomes that dimension of travel possible backward and forward. Because then each frame continually exists and never dies—although the possibility of each frame being malleable then exists. I think this is the mistake many make when considering the possibilities of time travel—especially backward time travel. One can freeze oneself and exist in the future, although they are not really traversing time, but one cannot freeze oneself and backup to traverse time—unless that space that we refer to as yesteryear never went away and still exists somewhere, somehow, on some plane.

Interestingly, if the universe were proven to be an existing timeline where every fraction of time continued to exist and never die—like a movie that can be played over and over again—one could also explain and defeat the time paradoxes that are so often brought up such as how could one accidently kill one's parent and still exist in the present. If time exists as a never-ending series of time frames of space, theoretically, one could go back in time and change a series of frames without creating a paradox. For example, we exist at time frame 58, our current time. I go back in time to time frame 15 when I was fifteen years old. I accidently kill my father (even for an example, I cannot say I could intentionally do such a thing). I continue existing in my backward time from time frame 15 until time frame 20. I then return to our current time frame 58. Now looking back at my personal history and the world history, I come to find my father was not killed by me, but he lived the life I remember him living prior to my backward time travel and the only one who has knowledge of any change whatsoever in history is me. History has not changed for anyone, nor has it changed for me except the memories of my backward travels left in my own mind pursuant to my travels through time. Why, because I changed only time frames 15–20. Time frames 21–58 remained unchanged and any one's historical recollections will only be of those subsequent to frame 20, frames 15–21 noninclusive. I avoided a paradox because I only changed specific time frames and the time frames prior to and subsequent to the ones I changed remain untouched just as if I wrote on frames 15–20 of a movie film but left the remaining parts of the film untouched.

And if the universe does exists as a never-ending timeline of space, new questions need to be asked and different directions need to be explored—for example, how long is each frame of space/time? How is or can each frame be measured? In this type of universe, backward and forward time travel is probable, but how? A two-dimensional being cannot rip him or herself out of its universe and move itself to another frame in its universe without leaving a hole in its universe and potentially destroying itself. Or can it? It seems that for us as three-dimensional beings to be able to traverse time, we would have to rip ourselves out of our three-dimensional terrarium and traverse a fourth spatial dimension to leave frame 58 and enter frame 15, but how to do so? And if possible, one would have to take—most likely—quite a bit of the terrarium with one into the fourth dimension, or one would never survive the trip.

These are just a few thoughts I had after reading your book. Thank you for reading through them. And I agree with Bryce DeWitt, your father would have been proud of you.

I made a few grammatical corrections to the letter before reprinting it, but those are the only change made thereto. And like all my other writings in this book . . .

Just a thought.

Try to Stand Still. You Cannot!

It is impossible to stand still and be able to say you exist at the same time. Kind of like the Uncertainty Principle, I suppose. We are all moving. We are all always and constantly moving. The Earth never stands still. The solar system never stands still. The galaxy never stands still. The universe never stands still. Everything moves. Nothing stands still. You even continue to move when you die. You will never remain in the same spot during your entire life. The planet orbits the sun and seems to return once a year from whence it started, but the solar system and the Milky Way move on, and so are not in the spot from whence they started. Everything moves. So try your best to stand still . . . but you will fail. But that is a good thing, because if you could remain rooted in one spot, you would not exist. Existence is movement. Life is dependent on movement. Time is movement. Life is movement. Existence never stands still.

Just a thought.

Is There a Fourth Spatial Dimension?

If there is a fourth dimension (of space, not time), can life as we understand life exist there? This is just a short thought and commentary, not a paper on extra spatial dimensions. This is merely a whisper in the ear to all who follow the latest in physics and its discussions of possible higher dimensions. String theory suggests at least the possibly of ten-spatial dimensions and one of time. Here I am only discussing the possibility of one more spatial dimension: the fourth dimension. Many well-publicized physicists bandy about conversations of two-, three-, and four-dimensional worlds. In short, the two-dimensional Flatland world of living squares, triangles, and circles; our three-dimensional world of length, width, and depth; and the four-dimensional world that encompasses the three dimensions plus carries the possibilities of seeing our inner workings and thoughts and more in its unique and impossible to picture by us three-dimensional creatures space. Here I am speaking of a fourth dimension existing outside our third dimension, not a dimension wrapped up within our third dimension.

But I have to wonder about the reality of life existing in the former and the latter dimensions. I live in a three-dimensional world, so it is impossible for me to discount its reality. And life obviously abounds in the three-dimensional space we live within. But I have yet to see living entities in a two-dimensional or four-dimensional world. Not bearing witness to fourth-dimensional beings is understandable. I am a three-dimensional being. My senses are made up of three-dimensional and two-dimensional materials and can only perceive three-dimensional, two-dimensional, and one-dimensional objects and beings if they so exist. I am unable to verify the existence of a four-dimensional being, and if it exists, I am also unable to verify its makeup. By being a three-dimensional creature, I can only perceive three-dimensional creatures and two-dimensional creatures if they were to exist. But if I can perceive a two-dimensional creature as I should be able to do as my senses are equipped to do so, why have I not seen such an Abbott Abbott creature?

Odds are that a two-dimensional creature is an impossibility outside Abbott's Flatland. It seems unlikely a two-dimensional creature could exist—let alone survive, if it did exist. Such a creature would cut itself in two whenever it tried to process organic material; it would have to be a totally self-sufficient entity, not needing to process any outside materials to survive. A land of two-dimensional beings, however, is a nice way to make a relative comparison of the differences between spatial dimensions and how it may be impossible for a lower level–dimensional creature to perceive a higher dimension outside of one's lesser-dimensional realm. But the reality of life existing in the lesser dimension is something else altogether. The same can be said for the possibility of life existing in higher-dimensional realms—although the proof is much more difficult to obtain for the existence of a higher-dimensional realm than that of the lower dimensions as one and two exist within three; but four would exist outside, not within three.

So given life seems impossible to exist on a two-dimensional realm and has not been witnessed as far as I know, I question the ability of life to exist on a four-dimensional realm. BUT that does not mean I doubt the existence of a fourth spatial dimension. There may well be four, five, six all the way up to ten or more additional spatial dimensions that exist—dimensions we three-dimensional creatures are unable to perceive. But can life as we know it, or even as we do not know it, exist outside of three dimensions? That is, can a living entity be one made up of four, not merely the known three, dimensions? And if so, what form—if any—would such an entity take? Try to imagine. It boggles the mind in a delightful way.

Just a thought.

Are the Brain and the Mind ONE, or Are They TWO?

Many of the greatest minds in the world differ on the answer to the question of whether the brain and the mind are one and the same or two separate entities. Personally, that many differ on the answer does not surprise me, but it does amaze me. It seems so obvious of an answer. The mind is nothing more than the thoughts and emotions and voices of the brain. That is to say, the brain and the mind are one and the same.

To suggest the mind is some intangible, floating entity that lives within one's head is tantamount to suggesting angels sit on golden chairs on clouds. It just is ridiculous. If the mind is separate from the brain, then why do the emotions and memories and thoughts and attitude and personality change upon brain damage? The mind changes upon damage to the brain because the mind is the brain. There is only the thinking you, and it is the brain.

We hear many voices in our head, and these voices are not the mind speaking to the brain. These voices are the many sections of the brain speaking to the many other sections of the brain. There is no singularity in the brain. There is no central processing unit in the brain like exists within a computer. There is no "mind" controlling and speaking to the brain. There is only the brain. But the brain not having a central processing unit must communicate within itself as well as it must communicate to the rest of the body. That is the voices one hears in one's head—the brain communicating with itself to its various component selves. The voices "from god" religious people hear are nothing more than one section of the brain speaking to another section of the brain. The multiple personalities of mentally ill people are one or more sections of the brain attempting to dominate and refusing to assimilate as "one" as do the average voices of the average brain. We are multiple thoughts and emotions and memories and contradictions of what we want to be should and can be and fear to be and dare to be and must be, and all these contradictions and the greater number of common wants and needs that we are speak together and work together to be one—and believe themselves to be one—and the one is what is us. But all of that is our brain. All of that is physical. Not spiritual. Not intangible.

The brain and the mind are the same thing, or better said, the mind is the totality of the workings of the amazing brain that allows us to think, to breath, to survive, to enjoy life, and to write and to read. The brain is part of us, and we are a physical entity. We are not supernatural, not a single part of us. We are tethered to this planet Earth by the air we must breathe, the organic material we must consume for energy, and the pressures and the strong force that holds are bodies together. We are one with the world as our brain and our mind are one with each other.

Just a thought.

Time, Space, Life . . . It's All a Reality Show

It is. It is not. It births. It dies. It always is, so can never end, but cannot always be, so can never die. Time, space, life . . . are but a dalliance . . . an entertainment . . . a distraction . . . for something beyond what we know and understand. We are beneath recognition to be seen and heard . . . Search too much, and we will be a nuisance and dismissed. Time, space, and life are but relative to that which perceives. Time is movement . . . Space is where time moves about . . . Life is but a collection of programs birthed from inorganic materials. Time, space, life . . . It's all a reality show.

Just a thought.

Chapter 2

LIFE

Secrets to a Successful and Happy Marriage

What are the secrets to a successful and happy marriage? I should think that many people are very curious to know. Well, unlike so many others that claim to know the answers for everyone else, I can only speak for myself. So I am going to tell you what I believe has made my marriage such an amazing success story.

I am now sixty years old, and I will be married twenty-four years this July 4, 2017. And I am more in love with my wife now then I was when I married my love twenty-four years ago. Twenty-four years ago, my wife and I looked a lot different. I have always looked young for my age, and my wife is six years younger than me, so even twenty-four years ago, we both looked pretty good to each other. But that is not why we came together. That is not why I asked her to marry me. When I first met my wife and until three dates thereafter, I had no idea what my wife looked like physically from the neck down. She could have weighed three hundred pounds (ever see the movie *Shallow Hal*), and/or she could have been missing limbs, and/ or she could have been handicapped and missing a body altogether. In fact, I really saw nothing more of my future wife those first three days than her eyes and her smile. She could have been white, black, red, yellow, brown, or an extraterrestrial. It was not what I "saw" of or in my wife. It was what she said and how she said it. What I did see of my love was everything she was inside.

Too many people focus on the physical attributes of their mate. More times than I can recount, I have heard men AND women pronounce they must be physically attracted to someone before they can enter into a relationship with that someone. So as I interpret this pronouncement, it means they must be sexually attracted to someone before they will even consider getting to KNOW that person. And what I see happening more often than not is that these men and women find someone they are physically attracted to who will consider dating them and then convince themselves they are compatible as friends, mates, lovers, and husband and wife. WRONG!

That is the reason most marriages end in divorce. And the sad fact is that very few learn this fact after their first failed marriage, and they then repeat this flawed mating ritual, remarry, and divorce again. My current marriage is my second marriage. I made the same mistake as so many others my first marriage. But I did not my second marriage. And that is why I love my wife more today than I did when I asked her to marry me. Both my wife and I have changed physically these past near twenty-four years. My hair has thinned and grayed, and I have gained some weight. My wife has grayed and gained some weight. We both have wrinkles we never had before. And we both no longer have that youthful glow. But we both love each other so much. We both are each other's best friend. We both count on each other to surmount any obstacle that may present itself. We both trust and have faith in each other. Neither of us doubts the other. We are more in love today than twenty-four years ago, and we were in love then.

Why? Because we never had to convince ourselves we were compatible. We never had to rationalize away differences. We never feel any different about each other as our body's age. We never fooled ourselves about our love. Our love was never based on a physical attraction. Our love was and is based on what we see inside each other.

So the secret to a successful and happy marriage is simple. Before you even decide to date someone, make sure that someone is someone you like—someone you like because of who she or he is, not someone you like because he or she has nice hair, nice boobs, a nice butt, or a pretty face. I am not suggesting that you discount someone who is physically attractive in your eyes. A perfect mate is perfect neither because said mate is attractive or unattractive. What I am suggesting is a perfect mate is someone whose inside attributes click with your inside attributes. Close your eyes, and meet someone. Love should be blind.

Just a thought.

For All Dog Lovers

I've lost my shadow. I moved right; he moved right. I got up; he got up. When I ate, he ate. Whenever I ran on the treadmill, he lay right by the treadmill until I was done. No matter how many times I would go upstairs then downstairs in no matter how short a time, he would follow me. Whenever I left the house and then returned again, no matter how many of us walked back into the house, he made his way through the crowd to greet me first. He always made sure I was there. He never wanted to lose sight of me. He brought me his toys to play. He licked me and wanted me to hug him many times each day. He always wanted to know where I was and that I was there. All four paws left the ground whenever I let him know he and I would go for a ride in the car, and he sat beside me with a smile and now and then a kiss to say how happy he was I brought him with me. He never went upstairs to sleep until I did, and then he would lie near my bed at my side until I went to sleep. He was always again there at my bedside in the morning until I woke and got up out of bed. When he knew I was waking up, he licked my face to say good morning. He never tired of any of this. He never gave me any doubt he loved me. He was my shadow. Now when I look to the sun, my shadow will be gone. The sun has yet to rise, but I already fear it will not be as bright and it will not be the same. My shadow is gone. My shadow is gone.

Just a thought.

Life Is a Gift

Some are born with more tools to open more doors than most of us, but all of us have the possibilities of achieving goals we set for ourselves. Time is always the enemy. We only have so many years to work at and achieve our goals, but then youth, while here, affords one a much greater possibility of success. Know that you have within you a spirit that sometimes you fail to see. Know that you have within you potential to achieve goals you have yet to set for yourself. Time, that great enemy, is not such an enemy when you are young as it becomes when you are much older. Make use of every second . . . every minute . . . every hour, and every day of your youth to explore and find what makes you happy. You have many tools at your disposal that many others of your financial status do not have. Use them. Get to know yourself. Get to know your strengths. Understand your weaknesses. Build on your strengths. Strengthen your weaknesses, but realize ALL have weaknesses, and in that no one is alone.

Now, while time is with you, now is the moment to search . . . to explore . . . to seek the path that will bring you happiness. Your path may shower you with money; it may shower you with fame; it may be bereft of the aforementioned, but it may shower you with happiness and/or contentment. There is more to this world than material possessions, riches, and fame. So EXPLORE. Look for something that you want to do and do it—no matter if it is by way of education, trade, or just plain sweat. Look within yourself and search, and once you know yourself, look for resemblances of yourself in the world that surrounds you, and SEARCH and explore and you will FIND HAPPINESS.

Just a thought.

Too Many People Are Like a Flock of Sheep

Too many people are like a flock of sheep being easily corralled by the day's sheep dog. You don't think so? Or maybe you do, but you believe that describes you? Have you ever seen sheep? They appear oblivious to the world. Human sheep (from here on merely, *sheep*) believe themselves to be very aware of the world and believe they know themselves well, but like their four-legged friends, they are more oblivious than aware of reality and the world around them. Like sheep, they eat and digest all the crap fed them by those in charge. They are oblivious to the reality that the world is controlled by only a few people; they are oblivious to the truth that small groups of people control most of the wealth in this world. Governments rule with an iron hand. Dictatorships thrive in so many countries. Corruption rules in every country; even democracies are corrupt. Sometimes a democracy is no better than a dictatorship; the only difference being control of the populous in a democratic society is usually corporate control—an oligarchy. Is control by ownership of the purse strings that much different than control by military might? Do we not still serve the rich and the privileged? Truth be told, I believe most people want to be controlled; most people are merely sheep. People can be easily manipulated into believing what they are told and then incorporate those beliefs into their minds as if they were their own original thoughts. Why? Because it is so much easier to be told what to do and do it than have an original thought and do it oneself—sheep.

Have you ever wondered why so many countries are ruled by one man? Have you ever wondered why millions upon millions of people allow themselves to be subjugated and controlled, why so many people allow themselves to be kept in poverty and servitude by a small handful of men and sometimes even by just one man while that handful of men or that one man lives a life of privilege and luxury? The answer is that so many people are sheep. There are only a small number of individuals who realize that so few are willing to fight for fairness in life, and these few individuals take advantage of this sheep mentality to control the world. Too many sheep make for a scary world for all of us but a few. There are not enough sheep dogs in this world and too many sheep. What the sheep fail to realize is that there are more of them than the sheep dogs. The sheep should be in control, but then if that were the case, they wouldn't be sheep, would they?

There are too many sheep flocking together spewing propaganda about changes needed in the world, yet as soon as the master speaks, they stop, they listen, and they do nothing to change their life for the better. Too many sheep are why dictatorships thrive and never go away. Too many sheep are why democracies are ripe with corruption. Sheep by nature accept their fate. Sheep will proclaim, "Politicians are corrupt and always will be. There is nothing I can do to change government for the better, and there is nothing I can do to end corruption therein." So the sheep allow our "leaders" to empty our pockets; so the sheep allow our "leaders" to live lavish lifestyles while the flock continues to struggle paying bills for luxuries like food, clothing, and shelter. We are good sheep; we are good followers. We are the armies of sheep following the few who deserve all riches WE make for them. The sheep worship our "leaders" and title them kings, queens, presidents, first families, Congress, and CEOs. The sheep see their "leaders" as their betters; the sheep see their "leaders" as deserving of our praise and homage. Our "leaders" can only praise the sheep for the sheep keep them living in luxury; long live the sheep. I'm sorry, but we have too many sheep living in this world.

Just a thought.

Love Is Love . . . Sex Is Sex

I first acknowledge that many of you will disagree with what I am about to write. And some of you will disagree merely because on an unconscious level some people feel the need to find disagreement because I wrote what many will disagree with; in other words, I am taking the unpopular stance on a popular issue.

The human species is not as far advanced of other species on this planet Earth as its inflated ego tends to believe it to be. Human beings are far beyond many other species in their ability to mold their environment to their wants and needs. Human beings are far beyond many other species in their ability to record and reproduce past discoveries. We are a species of collective intelligence far beyond the others on this life-teeming planet. We are a species with many of the pluses of other individual species combined into our one: physical, mental, social, retentive abilities, reasoning abilities, and more. But still, we are animals with animalistic urges.

Love is that one word that many try to define but always seems to have many different definitions for; many times those definitions are in conflict with each other as much as they may be in harmony with each other. Love is difficult to define. Sex, however, is easy to define. Although more people than not confuse sex with the word *love*, sex is not love. Sex is a biological, animalistic urge that builds within us and then dissipates upon sexual release. We are all attracted to our own definitions of beauty. And we tend to differ on our definitions of just what beauty is. Many people claim they cannot love another person unless they are physically attracted to that other person first. I have to disagree with this wholeheartedly and from years of experience with love and sex. If one bases their pursuit for love on first satisfying a physical attraction to another, they may become one of the more than 50 percent that find themselves with a new partner—or alone—sometime later in their life. Sexual urges are extremely strong in the young but tend to wane as the young become older and wiser. Beauty fades. But the human mind is something so much more than a mere tool to guide the body to sexual satisfaction. Life is so much more than a release of sexual tension. Love is indefinable and confusing because love is so much more than sex. Sex has nothing to do with love at all. Love is caring and being cared for. Love is comfort and comforting. Love is sharing dreams, fears, happiness, and sorrow. Love is thinking alike, dreaming alike. Love is doing things together longer than an hour or two. Love is planning a future together and treasuring the past lived together. Love is children of your own, little ones that are a combination of both of you—raising them, loving them, no matter what—even if they do not feel the same about you. Sex is about hormones and the release of sexual tension and fleeting moments of physical pleasure. Love is an orgasm that lasts a lifetime. It is not fleeting; it grows and grows and survives good times, bad times, aging, and sorrow. Sex is not love. Love is so much more!

We all want to be happy in our brief existences in life. And I think, if possible, we should all do what will make us the happiest as long as doing so does not hurt others. I find nothing wrong with sex—sex of any kind—as long as it hurts no one else. Our sexual bodies were made for a purpose: to procreate. Heterosexual sex is inarguably the natural course of our creation. Man's penis was created for a woman's vagina to procreate and continue the species. Sexual urges and sexual tension was created to coerce man and woman to copulate. If the sexual urge and tension—and pleasure—were not connected to sex, our species might have died out years ago. Many other species risk death just to satisfy their sexual urges—poor spider and praying mantis. But that is not to say that sex between a man and a man is wrong or unnatural. That is not to say, sex between a woman and a woman is wrong or unnatural. It just says that sex is sex and love is love. We should not confuse the two as being the same or what our sexual differences were created for. We need only admit the truth as to what we are and why what is, is.

We were not born with a manual. But we have a brain that helps us sort out what we need and what we want. If sex is more important than love in making one happy, then so be it. If love is more important than sex in making one happy, then so be it. But know the truth. Love is love. Sex is sex. They are not the same thing. Social convention may make them seem the same. Social convention may force one to make a choice between one's sexual preferences over love or love over one's sexual preferences. But never forget that love is love and sex is sex.

Personally, I find love far greater in importance than sex. I fought strong sexual urges as a youth to find love. I copulated with many beautiful women when I was young. I married the first time based on sexual attraction more so than love. But I thought. I learned. I grew. I grew to understand. Love is not sex. I then closed my eyes, and I listened more with my ears. I am not much of a musical fan, but I heard a siren's call. I understood words spoken at me that sounded like me. I heard and felt an understanding of me, a compassion for me, and I felt the same for she who spoke the words. Love is truly blind. Sex is not. I fell in love with my "soul mate," and I am still in love with her today. My body may wither. My sexual desires may wane. But my love continues to grow and grow. I am so happy for meeting my love. I am happier than any sexual encounter ever made me or I believe ever could make me. I have someone I can lean on, not just lie upon. I have someone who will listen to me, not just grunt with me. I have someone to share our children and their lives with. I have a good feeling that stays with me all day, all week, all year, and beyond, not just a few hours. I have love.

I know. Sex is sex, but love is not. Love is love!

Just a thought.

Is There Really an Absolute Definition of Right and Wrong?

I do not believe in an absolute right and wrong. As one incident of proof, I give you an observation I made just tonight watching an episode of a televised show called *Locked Up*. The camera crew was discussing their interview with a female couple incarcerated in an Oklahoma jail who was alleging to be married to one another. The pronouncement by the two women that they were married to each other is not what caught my attention. What caught my attention was the casual response and descriptions by the *Locked Up* crew about the married wife and wife. The camera crew's casual laissez-faire attitude about two women being married is an example of how quickly and easily a society can change its views, opinions, morals, and overall definitions of what is proper, acceptable, and/or right and wrong. THERE IS NO ABSOLUTE RIGHT OR WRONG! I believe Albert Einstein got the idea of relativity right for more things than merely space and time: morals, crimes, marriage, sex, good, evil, right, and wrong—they are all relative. No more than a few years ago, most people would have laughed at the idea of a woman marrying a woman and/or a man marrying a man. Now it is being accepted and being accepted to a greater degree by the day! And most people will probably proclaim they ALWAYS felt that way—LIES, but then people live on lies. Most people want to convince not only the world, but themselves, that they are progressive thinkers and they are BETTER than someone else. Is this the TRUTH? The truth is that most people lie or merely deluded themselves. Most people are sheep, sheep led to whatever is considered popular. Most people do not strive to be different. They CLAIM to do such. They proclaim to be

James Dean, a rebel without a cause. But most people are sheep who just do whatever allows them to be accepted within the herd. Is this a problem? It can be. Sheep live in groups. Groups become mobs. Mobs force their beliefs on everyone else, all the while proclaiming anyone who disagrees with their way of thinking as ignorant, stupid, and someone who must be shown the light—shown the RIGHT WAY to think.

No, Isaac Newton, there is no ABSOLUTE. Albert Einstein was right. Everything is relative, including what is right and what is wrong.

Just a thought.

Our Purpose in Life

Many people think . . . asking themselves and others . . . what is our purpose in life? Why are human beings here, alive, on this planet Earth? Many religious organizations will say, god made us to worship him. And all other life on this Earth was made by god to serve us and god. Mankind is special. Mankind is made in god's image. Secularists will say life is chance. We are born of fortunate circumstances. We exist because of many factors of chance that came together resulting in the Goldilocks effect that is this planet Earth and all life upon this special rock. And secularists will go on to say, we may be smarter, but we are no more special than any other organism that walks, swims, or flies this planet. But what if both the religious make-it-up-as-you-go-as-long-as-it-favors-our-species dreamers AND the secularists who search-for-the-truth-by-examining-facts-but-discount-all-religious-beliefs realists are right AND wrong? What if we do have a purpose, and there is a plan, but not a plan devised by any god of the popular religious organizations of this Earth?

Think for a moment. What if there is a creator or creators of this planet Earth and all that inhabit this rock. What if that creator or those creators are beings existing within a different dimensional plane from that which we know as the third dimension. What if this creator or these creators are four-dimensional beings that we cannot perceive with our physical senses—we cannot see, hear, smell, taste, or touch them? What if this creator or these creators are scientists of the fourth spatial dimension—scientists who are immortal, scientists of great intellect, scientists who are extremely bored with their immortality, so bored with their longevity of existence that they set about to create their own entertainment, the planet Earth. And on this planet, they placed millions upon millions of varied life forms of varying sizes, shapes, forms, intelligence, talents, and strengths. And they programmed the DNA of all these life forms to be curious, to question, to want to survive. And this creator or these creators—who never die and who cannot be seen or perceived by us—sit back and watch. And laugh. And cry. And the only purpose we the created have is to entertain our creators, please our masters with our habitual chaotic, selfish behavior. Entertain with our desire to survive, to best our brothers and sisters, to conquer and dominate other species, to kill and to worship, to beg and to plead, to build and to destroy, to love and help the needy—TO EXIST MERELY TO ENTERTAIN.

This would answer much. But would this satisfy anyone? The religious could claim, "Yea, we have a lord and master." The secularists could shout, "We told you we are no more special than other species and the world is ruled by chaos." But would anyone be happy with this? It would explain much. It would explain the absence of a creator in our everyday lives. It would explain our origin. It would show we have a purpose—finally, a purpose! Finally, everyone gets to be an actor to play out their lives on a stage.

Think about it.

Just a thought.

Is Humankind Really THE Superior Species?

I just finished reading English astronomer's David Darling's book, *Life Everywhere: The New Science of Astrobiology*, and it got me thinking about the possibilities of finding extraterrestrial life. And what that would mean to people here on Earth? It also got me thinking about religious claims that humankind is the center of existence and the special species of some manlike creator many call God, Yahweh, Allah . . .

Many of the world's most popular religions claim man is made in god's image. If true, I have to wonder why a god who has always existed—why a god who was never born; why a god who can and never will die; why such a god needs a mouth, a stomach, a heart, an anus, a penis, hair, arms, legs, lungs . . . well, you get the idea. Can some religious expert explain this to me? And if man is made in god's image, what is woman, an accessory? And what are all other species on this planet, afterthoughts or possibly the result of a bored god?

Many of the world's most popular religions claim humankind is the superior species on this planet. Heck, many of the most popular religions claim there is no life anywhere in the universe other than on this planet, and so humankind is the universally superior species. I wonder if we were to find extraterrestrial life if it might threaten religion's claim that man is their god's chosen superior species— maybe not, but maybe yes? Maybe if extraterrestrial life is found, religion can make the claim extraterrestrial life is just a product of god's practicing his craft of creation off the chosen world of Earth until HE got it right with humankind here on Earth. But what if not only extraterrestrial life is discovered but it is discovered to be of greater intelligence than humankind? Might that threaten religious claims of humankind being God's chosen ones—maybe, maybe not? Maybe religion will just continue moving heaven further and further into the realm of the unexplainable. Historically, heaven began in the clouds and heaven has continued on a pathway further into the unknown as science has grown in knowledge of the universe about us. I guess God doesn't want us visiting his home as he appears to move the smarter we become. Given religious explanations of the heavens can move heaven so easily, I am sure religion can also come up with an explanation as to why god created extraterrestrial life and how to maintain humankind's claim as God's chosen ones.

But I digress. Let us stir back to the religious claim of human superiority. This planet has an incredible number of species living and sharing this world. This planet in its history had even more species in existence in its past than it does today; many species have gone extinct. According to science, humankind was not the first species here, and humankind did not appear on this rock for an extended period of time subsequent to the planet's birth. On the other end of the historical account of mankind, and according to many religions, humankind was here within a week of the birth of the planet. Whatever history you believe and however long humans have truly been on this planet, a question worth posing is, "What makes humankind a superior species?" One answer might be how about the fact that no other species has created the many mechanical wonders created by humankind. No other species has sent probes to other planets, moons, asteroids, and the many celestial bodies in our solar system. Arguably, no other species has amassed as much recorded knowledge about life, physics, and how and why everything is what it is. So what makes humankind superior? What makes humans God's chosen? What makes humans stand out from other species? What I just stated? Or is it something else. There are many similarities as well as differences between humankind and the other species with whom we share this planet. What makes us special?

Humans have an uncontrollable obsession with sex. Does that set us apart from animals? Animals have sex too. Beyond reproducing, some humans seem to obsess about and plan their lives about sex. I have to wonder if humans don't obsess over sex and its importance

78

more so than most animals. Some humans go as far as identifying themselves—not as thinking, intelligent, curious human beings, but as heterosexuals, lesbians, or gay. For some individuals, their sexual identity becomes more important than other reasons for living. For some individuals, their desire for sexual pleasure seems more important than the welfare of others. Does an obsession with sex set humans apart from animals in a good, godly way?

Humankind captures and enslaves other species—for example, chickens and cattle and swine. Humans cage these animals in deplorable conditions then eventually cut their heads off, skin them, cut them up, dress them up for display like birthday presents in supermarkets to then be bought and eaten. And the children and babies of these animals are not spared. What if our children were packaged and sold for food? These species don't count, of course. They don't feel pain. They don't matter. Because humankind is god's chosen species and all other species are merely food for humans to eat. I find it odd, however, that said god made these creatures able to feel pain and fear. I find it odd that the said god made many of these creatures of a caring nature for their offspring. Wouldn't a caring, loving god have made our table food brainless, fearless, and painless? Odd, isn't it? A very odd god design, I think. And why are humans made of the same elements as the animals we eat? Doesn't that make humans food too? Odd, isn't it? I have heard people cry out in disbelief and disgust when they are told of a human being haven been mauled, killed, and eaten by an animal. "We must kill that animal," all will shout. "That animal is wild, crazed, dangerous," all will proclaim. "That animal is not allowed to do what humans do to its species," all will think. However, what humans do to animals is a God-given right many believe; animals doing the same to humans is an abomination most will yell. Why, because humankind is superior. Humankind is god's chosen. So if I understand correctly, what an animal may do for its protection and/or survival is considered evil, but the same done by humans is a good and necessary deed sanctioned by God. We're so special!

Humans love violence. Many will get angry reading my commentary relegating sexual desire to animal instincts. Many will get angry reading my commentary suggesting every species has as much right and as much claim to life or at least equality in their creator's eye as humankind. Why, because humans love to hate. Why, because humans have to feel superior and justified in every act they commit no matter how horrible it may be. If you're a history buff, you must admit, the most popular religions are based on hate and grew on hate. The Jews wandered the desert invading towns and killing men, women, and children—not Jews. That was okay, though, because their God proclaimed them the chosen ones. The Prophet Muhammad had no problem with killing infidels. That was okay, though, because his God proclaimed Islam the true faith. The Christians fought wars killing American Indians and heretics all in the name of their god. Apparently, gods love to hate as long as the hate is directed against a "nonbeliever."

Humans love guns. They demand the right to own guns, but honestly ask yourself, what is the purpose of a gun? The answer is its purpose is to kill. Oh, but I need a gun to protect myself from the other guy or gal who might shoot me with his or her gun, you say. Isn't that just a circular argument, and not a very good argument at that? The truth is people want to own guns with the hope of being able to use said the gun. And what do guns do? Guns kill. Humans love violence.

So what is it that makes humankind superior to all other species? First, ask yourself what it means to be superior. If by *superior*, one means technical skills and the ability to manipulate the environment to one's advantage, then I have to agree that humankind is superior to all other species we know of in this universe. But if by *superior*, one means being a loving, caring, nonviolent, not sexually obsessed, respectful of other species not as technically endowed as our own, then I don't see humankind as superior to any other species on this planet. Most species as we understand them are endowed with a will to survive, reproduce, and prosper. There are many violent species on this planet, but humankind is arguably the most controlling and violent and disrespectful species of the bunch. There are many species that live their lives in nonviolent ways, not caging and/ or eating other species—or at least no more so than necessary for their survival. Humankind is not one of those species. If you believe in a solitary god that created all there is to see, touch, smell, hear, and taste, then you have to admit that god created all species, humankind included, with the need to devour and destroy other species in order to survive. What a cruel and terrible thing to force on any creation is the NEED to kill other species to survive. Does this god so many people worship so much have a cruel streak within him? Making all species have to eat each other to survive is very much like human-run dogfights or cockfights, species forced to fight each other to survive for the entertainment of others.

So ask yourself, does winning those fights against other species, enslaving them, caging them, killing their children, and eating them make humankind the superior species? Does it make humankind special? Does it make humankind godlike? Or does it just make humankind one more of many species, no more special than any other species, except in that we're winning the dogfight? We're winning the cockfight. Think about it.

Just a thought.

People Are So Cold and Scripted in How They Interact throughout Their Lives

As I was shopping at my local grocery store for the fourth time in the same week, I noticed what I usually take for granted whenever I shop—the cold, indifferent "other" shoppers. Oh, sometimes they are nice, friendly shoppers, and believe me, I noticed and I appreciate them when they are nice and friendly and I show them so with a wink and/or a smile. But the vast majority of the others are cold and isolated. Why? Why must they be the norm? We may not know each other, but do we have to act as if we cannot see, hear, or acknowledge each other? What's wrong with being nice to and acknowledging strangers?

Experiment for yourself. Walk through your local grocery store or mall, and watch the "others." Walk real close when you pass by someone, and watch their eyes; try to make eye contact. Most people will look straight through you with the blank, button-eyed stare of a seagull. They won't make eye contact. Notice how many others will rush through the doorway in and out of the store when you enter and leave the store so as not to feel obligated to hold the door for you. Watch how people run their shopping carts through the aisles as if no one else is in the store; be careful they don't run you over.

Even in the parking lot, you must be so careful of being run over. We do not have to be like this. Just this day, I was helping a cart boy pull the parking lot carts together. He thanked me. He appreciated my unsolicited help. Shouldn't we try to help others more often, not just when asked or obligated to do so? After helping the young man, I turned and crossed the parking lot aisle to return to my vehicle, and a driver—whose vehicle was not yet near me, a driver who most definitely saw me crossing the parking lot aisle—I watched her stare right at and through me. This driver never stopped her vehicle for me to cross safely. Oh, she slowed her vehicle a little bit, but she continued to drive right at me until she was nearly within two yards of me, all the while she never acknowledged my being in front of her, and she then sped on by me when I cleared her vehicle by one yard. I guess I inconvenienced her by cutting two seconds out of her time driving through the parking lot.

Meanwhile, back in the store, while I was shopping, I smiled at people, which I usually do. I know that is a cardinal sin these days. Smiling at strangers now means you are dimwitted or gay or flirting. There was a time when such friendly behavior used to be acceptable and meant to others you were a nice, friendly person. I excused myself when crossing in front of someone checking out a grocery item on the shelf. I stopped for two different shoppers, smiling and waving them on, when our paths intersected at aisle intersections. One "other" said nothing; she ignored my presence and continued on her way. One nice older man smiled and acknowledged me and my polite gesture and made brief conversation. The former "other" reminds me of a seagull. A bird that looks stuffed, indifferent, lacking personality, and concerns for all but itself. The latter made me smile and feel a glow inside—a kind man, a kind, personable gentleman. Why can't there be more people like the kind man and less like the "others?" It really isn't that difficult to be pleasant and kind to others. It really isn't that difficult to acknowledge everyone one encounters—not always with words, but with a smile or a less-birdlike stare.

The next time you are shopping. Be that kind gentleman/gentlewoman.

Just a thought.

Stop Being a Watcher. Be a Doer.

Stop watching football, basketball, soccer, baseball, golf, poker, bowling, and any other overpriced spectator pay-to-watch sport of the "best" athletes in the world. Do you really care who is better than you? Does it increase your personal fun to know? Why don't you enjoy **PLAYING** football, basketball, soccer, baseball, golf, poker, bowling, and any other sport that looks like fun? Be part of the game, not a spectator. Don't waste your money watching OTHERS PLAY the game for you. PLAY the game.

Stop watching TV, movies, internet video, and any other over-priced "entertainment" device that cost you more than it ever gives back to you. Buy a video camera and make your own movies. Star in your own movies. ENTERTAIN YOURSELF. Don't waste your money funding the creation of overrated "actors" that your money makes into millionaires by way of your hard-earned money. Spend your money on you and entertain you.

Stop paying exorbitant ticket prices to listen to someone else play a guitar, wind instrument, drums, and sing. They are not worth the ticket prices they are charging. YOU ARE WORTH MORE. Buy an instrument and learn to play. Take singing lessons and learn to sing. Or be like me, even though I am told I cannot sing—and recordings bear that out—SING ANYWAY. Why do any of us sing? I sing because I like to sing. If no one wants to listen, so what! Who cares? Sing because it feels good. Sing because you want to sing. STOP paying others to sing for you. It's much more fun to sing and play than to listen and sit.

DO IT! Doing is more meaningful and more fun and more entertaining. Be a part of the game. Be a part of the entertainment.

Be a part of the song. Don't pay for overpriced tickets to watch others do what you can do yourself. Don't fight crowds just to watch and listen to someone else do what you can and should be doing yourself. Don't waste your time watching others have fun. **YOU HAVE FUN BY DOING, NOT WATCHING.**

Just a thought.

Life Is a Movie

We are programmed biological media, just another variation of digital media. We are a creation of a bored entity or group of entities whose existence has been so timeless and become so dull they have nothing left to learn, and now they amuse themselves with us; they forget reality and try to cure their boredom by amusing themselves with us. Their lives are no different than yours or mine, just watching a movie for lack of something else to do. If the movie is good enough, we can lose ourselves within the movie and forget about our everyday realities, forget about the real world, and live out a fantasy. Maybe that is what we are to them. Maybe we are just something's or someone's fantasy. Like toy soldiers in the hands of a child, we are toys existing within the minds of greater beings—good, evil, happiness, sadness, good lives lived, and bad lives lived. Our existence is nothing godly, merely a scheduled program. We won't die and go to heaven when the show is over. We will merely cease to be and others will take our place. The plot is set. The storyline is sold. Our parts may be scripted or our parts may be ad-libbed. Whatever the reality, our parts are not in our control. We may think we control our destinies, but how many times has that belief seemed more a fantasy than reality. No matter how hard we try to be different than what we believe ourselves to be, we end up being what we believe ourselves to be. Truthfully, we are merely characters in a movie, characters in a play. We are good and bad theater. We are nothing more. We are nothing less. Reality exists for that that created and controls our lives and our existence. Is that good? Is that bad? Good and bad are subjective creations of our minds. It is neither. It just is what it is.

Just a thought.

Please No Heaven for Me

With all the selfish, crazy, violent, self-centered egotists living on this planet, if I find I am wrong and there is a man-god watching over us and there is an afterlife where people are sent upon death and we can go to this heaven—I pray to that man-god that I not be made to suffer eternally by being subjected to and imprisoned within said everlasting eternity living with the same selfish, crazy, violent, self-centered egotists who inhabit and makeup 99.999999999 percent of all men and women who have and do live on this planet. Heaven would be hell for me. To spend eternity living with hypocritical crazies would be hell, not heaven, for me. Human beings are an egotistical species that believe they are better than all other species, and all the while they are butchering other species in what they would describe as "inhumane" if the same butchering was brought upon them. Human beings justify all evil they perpetrate by claiming to be "the chosen ones" merely performing "god's work on Earth" while having convinced themselves that all other species on this planet were created for humankind's pleasure, sport, food, and just overall "do what you want with them." Human beings are collectively an intelligent species, but not any closer to our creator than any other species. Human beings play with guns and shoot each other. The few rule the many. The few eat, sleep, and live well, while the many rarely eat, sleep poorly, and live like they have already been sent to hell. Give me the quiet everlasting silence of the grave rather than an eternity of heaven living with god-fearing human beings.

Just a thought.

My Wife Says I Never Say Anything Nice about Anyone, So Here I Prove Her Wrong:

I love old women living on a fixed income who give a few dollars to charitable causes. I hear these stories a lot. These are women who can barely take care of their own financial needs, and yet they care so much about the needs of others that they give what little they have to give. And the few dollars these kind women folk give is worth more in heart and true concern for others than the millions of dollars given by a woman like Oprah Winfrey or a man like Bill Gates who can both still afford to drive expensive cars, live in mansions, and live like royalty after they give millions. These kind, poor women who give such a larger share of their life savings are so special in my heart.

I love the neighbor who shovels the snow off his elderly neighbor's driveway without being asked. Or who rakes her leaves for only a smile as payment.

I love the parents who treat their children like children while themselves acting like parents. These are parents who love their children and care for their children's future and welfare. Unlike the parents who want to be their child's best friend and spoil the child rotten.

I love my dog Sugar Ray—who recently died at the young age of eight and a half years. He never left my side. He waited for me to fall asleep before he would go to his bed at night. He waited for me to wake in the morning and then kissed me to say hello. He followed me everywhere. All four of his paws left the ground whenever I would tell him we were going for a ride in the car. He loved me unconditionally. I loved him just as much.

I love my wife—who has been my best friend for more than a quarter century now. She listens to me, and I listen to her. She discusses with me. She loves doing things with me, and I love doing things with her. I love her more today and more than a year ago and more than a decade ago. I love her more all the time, and I think she loves me the same—as she shows me over and over again. I hope to be with her to my last breath.

I love and commend anyone who does something nice for someone else selflessly. Many people do nice things for reward or public acknowledgment. But some people do nice things for others merely because they know it will help that other person somehow and/or make that other person happier and/or better off than they might have been beforehand. My hat is off to those selfless people.

I love people who will stand their ground for a worthwhile cause, people who will proclaim their views no matter how unpopular to the mob that rules our world and stand tall. There are so few people who will risk being ostracized by society, by religion, by government, by friends, by potential employers standing up for values and truth they strongly believe to be right and worthwhile but possible unacceptable to the mobs that rule our world. These are a select group of people. Many people delude themselves into believing they are in such groups, but sadly, they delude themselves. They are part of the mob, and that is why THEY shout their views with impudence, knowing the mob will have their backs and knowing very few will come forth to contradict and/or confront them. I love those others who boldly stand up to the mob, those brave souls who are so few in number.

I applaud the actress, the celebrity, and the newswomen who don't sleep with others or flirt with others to get their job or advance in their employment. I applaud anyone who earns their job based on merit, talent, and ability—and not by their looks, personal connections, or off-the-job talents.

I love and commend every one of you who truly cares for others selflessly. I love and commend every one of you who helps others without your being asked and without the expectation of reward. Pat yourselves on the back! You are special!

Just a thought.

Isn't This World Simply Amazing and Scary?

I just finished watching one of those great BBC TV specials. This one was entitled *The Blue Planet*. The filmography of life in the sea is just simply amazing. The sea lives captured on film are simply amazing. I cannot help but overuse the words *simply amazing*. Watching *The Blue Planet* for merely one hour, I felt like I was there, under the sea. I felt as if I was plankton being eaten by sea life. I felt I could be anyone of the trillions of different creatures living in the sea, facing life and death possibly both in the blink of an eye, eating some other creature of the sea, and then moments later being eaten by some larger creature of the sea—life here, life gone.

What amazed me the most watching *The Blue Planet* was how many different life forms exist on this planet, all coexisting side by side with one another and all on the same small planet. I believe if I was wealthy enough to never again have to work, and I chose to spend every waking hour of the rest of my life searching out life forms new to me. I would not live long enough to experience every life form that exists here on this planet. I imagine I would have to live many lifetimes to even entertain the possibility of witnessing every life form on this planet. It is simply amazing so many different life forms coexist on this one rock floating in space. It is so interesting that millions upon millions—if not billions, if not trillions, if not more—varying life forms coexist within this one terrarium we call Earth, a rock that orbits a ball of fiery gas within an obscure solar system within a universe of trillions of such rocks. Sometimes I think it more logical there should be a planet just for whales, a planet just for monkeys, a planet just for insects, and then a planet just for human beings. But here we all are on this one rock, within this one terrarium, coexisting, somehow.

What scared me watching *The Blue Planet* was the same thing that amazed me—how so many different life forms exist on this planet, side by side, with one another. Most life forms on this planet are of the nature that they must feed on other life forms in order to survive; that's kind of scary. We are all made of food, and we all must eat one another to survive. I sometimes wonder whether "something" modified this planet differently from that of other such space rocks so as to be conducive to a specific type of creation that that "something" had the ability to create and then that "something" went wild creating all kinds of variations of what it could create and threw all these creations together on this one rock—in this one terrarium. If true, it could be argued that "something," either intentionally or by way of lack of technological skill, either built into each creation a life span or a life span merely resulted from the creation thereof. That "something" realized its creations could only live for a limited time span and then die. So that "something" questioned, "What to do?" Replication was the most reasonable solution. So that "something" decided to make creations that could self-replicate. Replication was the work-around solution to the inability to perpetuate the creation's existence, the next best thing to perpetual existence was self-replication. But self-replication of trillions of life forms in a small habitat over time has inherent problems that perpetual existence does not; overpopulation if replication overtakes expiration. Anyone who has owned a fish tank with fish that breed has experienced this same problem. The fish grow larger. The fish replicate. The tank is now too small to contain the larger fish population. So what to do? Buy a bigger tank? That may be a good solution for an owner of fish, but what about the terrarium we live within? That would mean creating another Earth-type life-sustaining world and relocating many of the life forms existing on this current planet. Another possible answer is controlling replication. If the trillions of varied life forms necessitate different rates and quantities of replication, then how about making a competition out of it. Instead of creating life forms that draw energy from existing nonlife sources such as the sun, modify the life forms to necessitate their gathering energy to survive by the consumption of one another. Make all life edible and program all life to seek out other life as food to survive, including human beings. This scenario seems to be where we are today. We all chase one another and eat one another. We all consume one another to survive. And it should not escape notice that no one is made so superior within our terrarium as to all other life forms that they themselves cannot be eaten. The case can be made that we, not the moon, are made of cheese. Although human beings have grown to dominate most species on this planet such that we have moved ourselves to the top of the food chain, we still fall prey to those creatures we cannot see—the very small microbial life forms—during our life and upon our deaths. We cannot escape the fact that we like every other creature living within this terrarium Earth are food.

So based on these simple observations, I find this world simply amazing and scary at the same time. And I have to wonder if we are nothing more than entertainment and/or an experiment for some more advanced "something" that looks upon us as no more than a distraction or an ant farm kept on that "something's" equivalent of a mantel for that "something's" amusement.

Just a thought.

Parents' Responsibility to Their Children and the Courts

I find it interesting that some children treat their parents like dirt and the courts do their best to support this foul treatment. Children suing their parents seems to be the new "hip" thing. And there seems to be a lot of lawyers willing to profit off of these suits. And let's face it: our court systems are so messed up (to be generous) that unless you work for the state (judge, prosecutor, etc.), you can lose every dime you saved defending yourself in court. Our court system is supposed to weed out frivolous lawsuits. But does it? It seems there is a lot of what many of us would label as "frivolous" lawsuits that the courts entertain under the guise of "new and questionably arguably viable." It seems to this writer that what we are really witnessing in our legal system is lawyers and proponents getting rich and questionable defendants losing their life savings.

The American "justice" system (it really is not by any means definable as "justice"; it is a "legal" system) has led us to believe we are all innocent until proven guilty. But I do not believe reality bears that out as a valid belief. It appears to me that we are all guilty until proven innocent. And even if we prove our innocence, it can cost us every dime we saved for our retirement. Is that justice? No, that is our legal system. The state uses our tax money to finance its cases. If defendants could use tax money to finance their cases, then maybe it would be a justice system. But that is not the case. And any proponent who wishes to sue in court can do so through the inefficiency and lack of concern for the defendant manifested by the courts; many an innocent defendant will be forced to settle and pay the proponent just to save a little of the hard-earned money the defendant saved over his or her lifetime that the court will syphon out of his or her pocket. That is not justice. That is criminal. That is our legal system.

But I digress. Let us get back to the topic of this thought. I read about a number of cases brought to court by children suing their parents. Just the thought of children suing their parents makes my stomach knot. I find the act simply incredulous. Children, their lawyers, and the courts giving credence to the idea that parents OWE their children beyond food, clothing, shelter, and a safe home— hopefully with love not mandated by the court. Children are alive because their parents created them. If there are any real gods in this world, it is parents; we created the life that is our child. Children live and breathe and grow to become adults because their parents fed, changed, clothed, sheltered, educated, cared for, loved them, and so much more. CHILDREN OWE THEIR PARENTS! Not the other way around. On my sixteenth, seventeenth, and eighteenth birthdays, I bought my parents gifts. Why? I could never understand why they should have to give me gifts for being born. I figured I should be giving them gifts for giving me life! The former may be the norm, but the latter makes more sense when you think about it. Even if my parents hated me and treated me terribly (which they did not), I still owe my parents. My parents don't owe me anything. There are too many snotty, bratty children today that do not appreciate what their parents have done for them. Suing your parents? You should be praising your parents.

If children can sue their parents demanding money and that their personal debts be paid by their parents, then parents should be able to countersue their children for at least eighteen to twenty-one years of childrearing, clothing, food, shelter, heat, vacations, education, toys, doctors, personal care, babysitting, sports, school, and on and on. Think about it!

Just a thought.

Fear

We all know fear. Some claim to be so brave they have never known fear. That is just ignorance, stupidity, or an outright lie. We all have felt fear more than once in our lives. We all will feel fear again and again. We fear failure. We fear not being accepted by our peers and by anyone we need to help us succeed. We fear embarrassment. We fear many things. Most of all, we fear death, because no matter how smart we may become, no matter how much money or fame we may obtain, no matter who we know or what our station in life, we have yet to find a way to defeat death. So no matter what anyone claims, no matter how delusional you may be about fear, the truth is that we all know fear.

But what so many seem to fail to realize is that human beings are not the only species to know fear. Humans have no monopoly on fear. Many species know fear. Our closest friends, our pets know fear. Any dog lover has witnessed his or her best friend suffering in fear of death. I have owned several dogs in my sixty years of life. One of my dogs was an eight-year-old, eighty-four-pound boxer named Sugar Ray. I named my dog in honor of the great boxer Sugar Ray Leonard (hey, Ray, you were fantastic!). Sugar Ray was an amazingly loving and loyal dog. He was constantly by my side 24-7, and Sugar Ray remained more loyal than any human I have known in my life (except my wife, she's the best). At bedtime, it was Sugar Ray's habit to follow me to the bedroom and lie down on the floor next to my bed and only when I turned off the lights to sleep did Sugar Ray lie down in his bed. Sometimes after Sugar Ray has fallen to sleep, I can hear him barking in his sleep, dreaming. And sometimes he has nightmares. Sometimes I hear Sugar Ray whimper and whine frantically in his sleep at night; I know he is having a nightmare, so I call out his name to wake him from his obviously frightening nightmare. Yes, even dogs have nightmares. We all know fear.

So what kind of fear could a dog experience? I cannot say with any certainty. Unlike so many so-called experts who have all the answers, I am not a dog, and so I cannot say with any certainty. I can only extrapolate from my experiences. And I can only then observe how dogs (how my dog) reacts to certain events. I can then only deduce what makes some kind of logical sense from what I observe and what I know of my dog. I am not a scientist who specializes in animal behavior. I am not a religious man who believes he knows everything from voices (his or her own) coming from inside his or her head. But I am a believer that many species think; they don't just instinctively react. I am a believer that many species feel. I am a believer that most species, including humans, are programmed to survive. I am a believer that many species fear death. Not just man, but many species. Dogs fear death. Tortoises fear death. Guinea pigs fear death. Watch how other species react when threatened, and then argue they do not fear death. Now, I mention the aforementioned species only because I own at least one of each, and they are dear to my heart. But I am sure you have owned a dog, a cat, a bird, or some other pet that means the world to you—a pet that you passionately believe feels for you, a pet that knows fear. We all know fear.

So is it a stretch to believe that hamburger feels fear (bad joke, I mean, cows)? Is it a stretch to believe that bacon (bad joke again, I mean, pigs) feel fear? Is it a stretch to believe that chicken (no confusion here, chickens) feel fear? I do not think so, yet we allow the butchering of these animals with little thought whatsoever that panic may be racing in their heads as the dispassionate slaughterhouse killers approach these beings armed with weapons to chop off their heads. Yet we think nothing of the small cages these fearful beings are locked into in numbers too great to allow movement awaiting their impending doom. Yet we care so little that these beings are being bred as food, that pieces of their bodies will be cut off and put between two pieces of bread for us to eat. Yet we feel no disgust that these beings are chopped into little pieces, dressed up, wrapped up into pretty packages with price tags on them and shelved for display at our local grocery store. Yet we think nothing of their babies being torn from their mother's teat. We think nothing of their fear. Yet we all know fear.

Funny how we can humanize other species that we find "cute." Funny how we can humanize other species we call our "pets." Yet if we find other species not so cute or not worthy of being a pet, we label them as "animals" or "objects" and not worthy of compassion. We rationalize these less-than-desirable species as "animals," as instinctual creatures with no cognitive abilities, put on this Earth only as our dinner and/or only to serve us as our slaves. These undesirable, but tasty, species are beneath compassion and/or our respect for their lives and their dignity. Their fear means nothing to us. We feel nothing butchering them. We feel nothing slicing them, dicing them, and packaging them to be displayed in a deli display case. The thought that butchering and eating a living creature may make us evil never crosses our minds while we scrape their remains off our plates into our garbage cans. No, these creatures have no feelings. They are mindless; they are brainless. They are not humans, and they are not our pets. Only humans—and our pets—deserve compassion. Yet we all know fear.

Think outside of the box. Humans are mammals. All mammals have hearts. All mammals have lungs. All mammals eat and defecate. All mammals struggle to survive when attacked. So why is it that we feel fear and other species merely experience the instinct to survive? I contend we both feel fear. All mammals are organic. In other words, we are all food. We can eat cows and pigs and sheep and chickens. But other species can eat us as well. It is not common in today's world, but I have heard of pigs and even our good friends, the dogs, eating humans. In fact, humans can be sliced and diced and chopped up just like cows and pigs and fed to other species like cows or pigs or chickens as food. Today, we are at the top of the food chain. We are a powerful species, so such happenings are not a common event today. But we were more commonly looked upon as a food source many centuries ago. We knew more fear then when the playing field was a little more even. I would not be surprised if our ancestors had greater compassion for other species besides human beings. We share a fear so common to other species today but neglected in respect to other species by years of our being in control of the world. But despite the years of dominance behind us and despite our current control of our environment, we still know fear. We all know fear.

So think. Think what it would be like to be rounded up like cattle and taken to a slaughterhouse knowing your head will be cut off and you will be chopped up, dressed up, priced, and packaged in a deli window. Think what it would be like to have your child taken from you shortly after birth, thrown in a cage with other babies, packed in so tight they have no room to move. Think of your baby being butchered to feed some other species. Think of the fear that would be permeating throughout your every being while all this was happening. Think of the fear going through the mind of your little child—a child barely born to the light of day who is ripped from his or her mother, cold, hungry, alone, and about to die in a horrible way to feed some other species—going to their death at the hand of another species with no compassion shown. We all know fear. Think, and your compassion will be there.

So when you watch a movie about Nazis gassing helpless people, when you watch a movie about aliens attacking Earth and butchering innocent humans, when you hear about dictators butchering a countries' people, when you hear about some crazy guy shooting up a mall, when you or someone you love is ill or elderly and on their deathbed—think about the fear you feel. Think about the fear you know they feel. When a child is kidnapped or missing, think about the fear their parents feel. Think about the fear the child is feeling. Then think too about the many innocent species we share this planet Earth. Think about the many species that do nothing to harm us who we butcher and kill for food and sport. Think about the fear they feel. Think and know that we all know fear.

Just a thought.

We Are Some Creators' Entertaining Pets in an Isolated Terrarium

Throughout history, human beings have given much thought to the big questions of "why" and "how." Religion has its answers to these big questions. Science has its answers to these big questions. The difference between science and religion is science bases its answers on experimentation and fact, while religion makes up the answers to fit what makes it feel empowered and self-important. But ask yourself these questions about the big questions. What if both science and religion got it wrong? Or ask yourself, what if both science and religion got it right? How could they both get it wrong, you ask; or if they both got it right, how could they both get it right? Well, I don't know who is right or wrong. I'm not religious, so I don't pretend to have all the answers. I'm not a scientist, so I haven't done all the necessary research. But like the religious, I'm going to make up an answer, so you religious have to respect my made-up answer if you expect me to respect your made-up answer. You scientists can just humor me. But unlike religion and more like a scientist, I'm going to use some logic to come up with an answer. I'm not claiming it to be the correct answer. I'm just saying, it's "an" answer.

So far as we know, our planet Earth is the only celestial rock in our solar system that harbors life. Heck, our planet Earth is the only celestial rock in the universe that supports life as far as we know. Future exploration of our solar system and beyond may find life elsewhere. I believe it will. But to our current knowledge, we are it. As far as we currently know, thousands and thousands of amazingly different forms of life exist, but only upon this celestial rock we call the planet Earth.

And not only is our planet Earth the only celestial rock harboring life, most life found on this planet Earth is tethered hereto. There may be some bacteria and simple forms of life that can survive off planet Earth—not thrive or reproduce maybe, but survive. But most life forms that we know—what we define as life—are tethered to this rock we call Earth. Some human beings have left the atmosphere of our world. Men and women have rocketed in to space. Heck, dogs, monkeys, and other life born on this Earth have been rocketed in to space. We have even witnessed men rocketing all the way to the moon (yes, men did walk on the moon, you crazy conspiracy theorists). But every living man, woman, dog, or monkey that has left the sanctity of our atmosphere and remained alive has left with a piece of our Earth. Human beings need to take oxygen with them when they leave this Earth. Human beings need to take food with them when they leave this Earth. Human beings need to replicate Earth-like conditions when they rocket away from this Earth, or they will not survive for long, if at all. Space is a dangerous place filled with cosmic rays, solar flares, a lack of gravity, no oxygen, no water readily available, and pressures different from what we need to live and keep our bodies safely functioning. We were created to thrive on the planet Earth. We were not created to thrive in space or on the moon. We were not born to live on an asteroid. We cannot live in the sun. We would be crushed and burned up on the surface of Venus. And Mars . . . well, Mars is a different story. We could make Mars a livable habitat. But we have to create Earth-like conditions for Mars to be a comfortable livable habitat. My point being, we are tethered to this planet Earth.

Earth is like a terrarium. I own two Russian tortoises. I keep them in a small, contained terrarium. My tortoises, Boris and Bullwinkle, never leave their habitat. Everything Boris and Bullwinkle need to survive, I provide for them in their terrarium. I give them fresh water, food, shelter, earth, light, night, and warmth. Everything Boris and Bullwinkle need to survive is within their terrarium. Earth is like a terrarium. We have all the things life needs to survive on our planet Earth. We have water, food, and materials to make shelter, light, night, and warmth. Human beings tend to be more creative and innovative in how we make use of the supplies found in our terrarium Earth more so than Boris and Bullwinkle in their terrarium, but there is a great similarity between our two habitats. True, Boris and Bullwinkle could survive outside their terrarium if they could escape or I set them free. And Boris and Bullwinkle would not need to wear pressurized suits like astronauts, and they could probably find food and water more readily than astronauts could find outside their terrarium Earth. But there is a similarity between the two habitats. Both terrariums are self-contained units that provide the conditions for life, which provide the conditions for the survival of life. Life is more difficult. Survival is more difficult when we try to leave our terrarium, however.

Have you ever questioned why we are made of food? Why is it that all life is eatable by other life? Why must most life forms consume other life forms to survive? The religious will say that all other life forms were made for our use, made for our consumption to survive, made for our use to survive. Science will argue that that is just the way it is: survival of the fittest. The bodies of living organisms are made to consume other living organisms to exact energy needed to continually refurbish and rebuild and energize the consumer. But have you ever questioned why WE are made of food? If we are some higher form of life as the religious claim, godly beings, then why are we made of food, and why are we as eatable as all other life forms on this planet Earth? If we are so special, shouldn't we be made of something other than food? Shouldn't we be more than a possible meal for a wolf, a lion, or rats? It makes me wonder. Doesn't it make you wonder?

I wonder if maybe we do have an intelligent creator. Yes, maybe the religious are right. Maybe there is a god or gods that created us. But maybe the scientists are right too. Maybe evolution is a fact. Maybe survival of the fittest is not only a valid theory but an intended objective of our creators. It seems to me if we are made of food like all other life forms on this planet, if all life forms on this planet are tethered to this planet for their survival—it seems that maybe this was the intent of our creators. Our creators needed a little entertainment, and so they created us and all other life forms on this terrarium

Earth. Our creators created this universe. Our creators created this solar system. Our creators created this Earth—this terrarium—with the conditions to support life as we define it, but our creators did all this with the objective to tether us and all Earth life to this terrarium Earth. Our creators' intent was to keep us tethered to this planet Earth. Our creators' intent was to create thousands and thousands of forms of life and to throw these thousands and thousands of varying forms of life all together inside this contained unit our terrarium Earth and watch what happens for the sport of it all. So we are all made of food. And we all have to eat food to survive. So we all combat one another for survival. So we all combat one another for dominance. And to keep things from getting monotonous and/or boring, we are programmed a limited life span. And we are programmed the will to survive. And we are programmed to reproduce. So we can die. So one creature cannot dominate, or learn too much, and survive forever; but the species can continue through reproduction, always starting over, always relearning—at least to some extent, not taking into consideration collective intelligence.

So think about it. Are we nothing more than some superior being's or beings' pets? Are we nothing more than some superior being's or beings' entertainment? Are we nothing more than tortoises surviving within a terrarium?

Just a thought.

What Is the Meaning of Life, You Ask?

One day I was in my car in the bus loop at my child's school waiting for my child. As usual, my child kept me waiting. Usually, I check my phone messages or the internet news. This day, I did something different: I thought. I looked out the window of my car, and I do not know why, but a tree caught my attention, then the sky, then the movement of things in the wind. And all of a sudden, I had an epiphany.

Life is a tree, growing toward the sky with its leaves gently swaying in a breeze.

Life is flowers blooming on a tree, and then gently falling to the ground like snowflakes from the clouds.

Life is clouds moving and reshaping with the wind, moving round the world, touching everywhere then dispersing and reforming again.

Life is a dog chasing a stick, running happily back to his human, quick as a whip.

Life is a cat cuddling on one's lap, purring and stretching, comfortable and content.

Life is a child running with friends, making no sense, smiling for no reason and having fun without a care or a worry.

Life is wishing to be older, to dream of what one can be—a parent, a spouse, a professional, an athlete, the president.

Life is remembering youth, times gone by, good and bad, exciting and memorable, love found and love lost, memories of many things done and good things accomplished.

Life is a fast car, a short and exciting romance, a roller coaster ride, a fright, a near-tragic escape from death, a glimpse of history or of someone famous, a fleeting but memorable event.

Life is a baby born—that first look, that first touch, that first smile (gas), that first word, that first step, that first talking back, that first day of school, that first time behind the wheel of your car, that first day at college, that first job, that first child, that first grandchild.

Life is your first romance, your first real love, marriage, the realization (s)he is your best friend, knowing (s)he will always be there, family, a home, retirement, a long life, a good life, and love.

Life is experiencing, life is learning, life is realization, life is sharing, life is doing, life is helping, life is knowing, life is exciting, life is long, and then life is short, and life is always unique.

Life is a roller coaster. It begins, and it ends—but, oh, the thrill of the ride. You cannot wait to ride, and when you do, it is over way too soon—but, oh, the thrill of the ride.

The meaning of life has little to do with the before or the after. Life is what is in between the before and the after. The meaning of life is merely what you make of it. Life is not perfect. Some are born with a silver spoon in hand. Some are dealt hardship. Life is what you make of it and sometimes what it makes of you. Regardless of the hand you are dealt with, do not waste the little time you have wishing for things you can never obtain. Do not waste the little time you have disparaging over a bad hand dealt. Find what makes you happy, and do it, live it, be it. Grab a seat on a ride that means the most to you and ride it to the end. Life is short, but life can be sweet. Make it so.

Just a thought.

There Is No Absolute Right or Wrong.
Ask Einstein; It Is All Relative.

Mobs rule the world. It is always mob rule that controls societies, acceptable thoughts, acceptable behaviors, morality, ethics, good and evil, right and wrong. The mob believes it is right about everything. The mob believes it is "modern and enlightened" in its thinking and anyone disagreeing with the mob is ignorant, uninformed, living in the past, living in the dark, evil, and stupid. And hey, why not, "we're the mob, so we are right."

The truth is that most people are sheep. Most people have no opinion of their own about anything. Most people follow along with the loudest voice with the most power that rises out of nowhere but rises above the mob because of charisma and the ability to sway others to his/her way of thinking. Everyone THINKS he/she has original ideas and is at the forefront of innovative thought. Everyone believes they are the "modern" thinkers. Everyone honestly believes they care about what is "right." But what is right? There is no right or wrong—at least not in the absolute sense of the words. Right and wrong is nothing more than what the mob decides it to be once convinced it is beneficial to them to believe something right and/or wrong. And the sheep just follow along, convincing themselves they have always believed what they are being told to believe.

Ray Roddenberry wrote a very prophetic novel many years ago that I am sure many of you have heard of even if you have not read it. *Fahrenheit 451* was a novel that still has great meaning today. If you have not read *Fahrenheit 451*, I suggest you read it. If you are not a reader, I suggest you watch the movie, which is liberally based on the book. I found the movie to be somewhat different from the book, but you should glean the idea Ray Roddenberry was trying to convey from the movie, if not the book. Personally, I think the book better explains the plot than the movie. Anyway, no matter whether you read the book or watch and listen to the movie, pay particular attention to the character Linda Montag and her conversation with her friends whom she invites to her home for some friendly conversation. Read and understand, or listen and understand, to what the women say to each other during their conversation about nothing in particular. Their conversation is very telling. Let me backtrack a little here to talk about the storyline. The basic plot behind *Fahrenheit 451*, as I understand it, is that books have been outlawed because they upset minorities and they make people generally unhappy. The focus on ridding the country of books centers on its believed help for minorities, but the law is thought to help everyone, not just minorities. In this bookless world, people are assumed happier if they do not perceive differences between themselves such that anyone feels inferior or left out. Everyone is to think of themselves the same as everyone else with no controversial thoughts fluttering about in their heads. This law thus makes books illegal to own or read, and the fire department's job is no longer merely to put out fires, but its job description now includes the directive to start fires: to burn any books that are discovered and/or reported as being in the possession of citizens. Linda Montag's friends strongly believe that it is a good thing that books are outlawed. They firmly believe in the "status quo" of their society, and they strongly believe in the legitimacy of their government's book-burning law. Linda and her friends are sheep. They unquestioningly believe what the mob tells them to believe. They believe everything they are told, and they rationalize away any faults in the logic behind the law. To question the mob is wrong. To go along with the mob is right, and what mob believes is right. If asked how they formulated their philosophies, they would "believe" they always thought the way they do, and they would give thought-out reasons as to why book-burning is a "good" thing. Linda and her friends are sheep.

People are sheep. They honestly believe themselves to be free thinkers, but most are no more than followers who adopt the thoughts of others and remember those adopted thoughts as being originated within their own minds. People are sheep. If one researches history, it becomes readily apparent that people cycle through all kinds of thoughts and ideas as to what is good and what is evil, what is right and what is wrong, what is morally acceptable and what is reprehensible. At many times throughout history, same-sex relationships have been considered normal and at many other times throughout history not—and this cycle repeats. In some societies, historically it was considered a precursor to marriage with a woman for a man to have sex with other men prior to marriage. Orgies have been popular in many historical times. There is nothing new about same-sex relationships today except possibly the marrying of same-sex couples. So today's same-sex couples are a "norm" of today. They are the "we have always been progressive thinkers and gay is okay; gay marriage is the same as heterosexual marriage; I've always thought this way." That's what the mob tells us. People are sheep.

The bottom line is that there is no absolute right or wrong. Same-sex relationships, heterosexual relationships, sex with a puppet, none of these acts are of an absolute right or wrong nature.

Right and wrong, morals and ethics, what is acceptable and what is not. These are all concepts invented by humans. They were invented with the purpose of making a society work. They were incorporated into our societies by the mob to force the mob to agree and force the mob to get along, to survival. People are sheep.

There is no absolute right or wrong. There are no absolute right or wrong morals or ethics. What is acceptable and what is not acceptable depends on the mob. People are sheep.

Right and wrong is what the mob forces us to believe it to be, or it is what we the mob agrees it to be. The religious follow their books as if some holy almanac. They follow the rules in their books like a set of commandments dictating right and wrong and the answers to many of life's most difficult questions. The book may read fornication is wrong. The book may read of fathers having sex with their daughters. The book may justify killing innocent babies and taking young girls as sex slaves (concubines). Is it right? Is it wrong? Throughout history, it has been acceptable for adults to have sex with young children. Today that is considered pedophilia and a crime, unless you live in Iran. It was right then. It is wrong now. The mob decided. People are sheep. The times do change, however. The mob does change its mind. But the mob always rules. The mob is always right. People are sheep.

I could go on and on, but I will end here. I will let you think it over. Can you honestly decide what is right and what is wrong? Are you a leader of the mob? Or is the truth that we all have an idea of what WE believe to be right and wrong and we are neither right nor wrong in our assumption of its validity? Just think that the mob may have power. The mob may force you to believe what it dictates or force you to suffer consequences of imprisonment, isolation, embarrassment, loss of power, loss of financial assets, or loss of opportunities. But is the mob right? Not always. There is no absolute right or wrong except maybe Einstein. As Einstein pointed out, it is all relative.

Just a thought.

Fathers Can Be Good Parents Too

Some eighteen years ago, I made a decision to be a "stay-at-home dad." I had just embarked on my law practice several years prior. I graduated from law school in 1990. I took the NY State bar exam and NY State ethics exam, and I was admitted to practice law in January 1991. I decided to go it alone as a solo practitioner, and I opened a law office in my home.

A few years later, I married, and several years after that, my wife and I decided to have our first child. My wife became pregnant and gave birth to our son in December of 1995. I attended every doctor appointment my wife had prior to our son's birth, and I assisted in his birth. My son was born between a late afternoon house closing and an early next morning house closing. Funny story—my wife was in labor some twelve hours, and our son was not born until the early hours of the morning, so I did not get home until about 4:00 a.m. The next day, I had to attend a house closing at a local law firm at 9:00 a.m. I showed up unshaven and in a sweatshirt. The paralegal representing the bank asked me who I was and why I was there. I think she thought I was a bum off the street.

After my son's birth, I spent every moment I could at the hospital until my wife and son could go home. From the moment my wife and son were home, I was involved in every activity from feeding, to burping, to changing diapers, to rocking to sleep. My wife and I worked out a feeding plan where she pumped breast milk, so I could share equally in bottle-feeding our son from day one.

After my wife's maternity leave was over, and she returned to her out-of-the-home job, I continued to run my law practice from my home office but added the pleasure of caring for my son to my daily

110

routine. My law practice was not confined to the home, so when I had to attend a house closing at a another attorney's office, or when I attended proceedings at family court before a judge (I practiced family law early in my career), I took my son with me. I always first asked my clients permission before I brought my son to a house closing or to a court proceeding, and every client, without fail, insisted I bring my son with me. When I walked into other law offices or into court with my son in my arms, men and women came out of nowhere to hold my son and help care for my son while I did my law thing. My son was never a distraction to anyone. I never had a problem giving my all to my client, my work, and my child. I was very impressed that no judge or opposing attorney or client ever complained. Funny story—my son became my ID when entering the court. All the deputies knew me as the father with the baby. I think I may have had an advantage over a female attorney in that I believe very few expected a father to be caring for his child, let alone bringing his child to work. Having my son with me at work never affected repeat business either. Many clients came back because I had my son with me; I think my clients liked the familial image.

My wife and I went on to have two more children (both daughters), three years later and then four years after that. I was no longer able to attend family court with three children (it would not have been fair to my clients or others I worked with to bring an entire family), so I focused my practice on house closings where I could do the majority of the workload within the confines of my home office and give attention to my children as well.

Now, my point behind this thought is not to sing my praises but to make the point that fathers can be good parents too and the side point that working parents can multitask effectively doing their job and caring for their children. This is not for everyone, but it is great if you can. I believe mothers may have a "maternal" instinct, but I also believe fathers may have a "paternal" instinct with equal ability to love and care for their children; I believe this "instinct" is based more on the type of person one is and less on their sex. Our society is changing, and fathers are being accepted as equally loving parents by more and more people, but there still are stereotypes that should be dispelled. One is that it is not natural for fathers to be nurturing parents. I found it came naturally to love and care for my children. I never felt emasculated or embarrassed being the primary caretaker of my children. I never felt lost or confused as to how to care for my children. I did find that many women had problems with a father being the primary caregiver. When my son was less than a year old, I cannot count the number of times women would offer advice thinking I needed advice being I am a man. I never showed it bothered me, although it did, because I was confident I knew as much as they thought they did. In fact, unlike so many of my female counterparts, I always knew the moment my child needed changing or feeding, and I was always able to calm my child when tired, hungry, or upset. Today, twenty-one and eighteen and fourteen years later, I am close with all three of my children. And all three of my children are honor students involved in theater, sports, school politics, community services, as well as being social butterflies with many friends. I think I did okay. And I will never regret that not only did I live my dream to become and practice as an attorney, but I lived my dream to watch and experience my children growing up from infancy until now. That is an experience I know many parents, both moms and dads, are unable to experience due to different working requirements and responsibilities that others may have different than my own.

To all the women who may read this thought, please understand I am only pointing out that men can be good fathers just as equally as women can be good mothers. And please do not refer to us as "Mr. Mom." I know the phrase is meant in good humor with no ill will, but it implies a father pretending to be a mom, something that is not natural to him. I prefer to be referred to merely as a dad.

To all the fathers and mothers who read this thought, please tell others your stories. I know I am not the only father who took the primary role in caring for his children. I know there are a lot of fathers out there who have done the same. I should hear your stories.

Just a thought.

Death, Sadness, and the Meaning of Life

One day, new neighbors riding their bicycles stopped at the end of my driveway to buy lemonade from my daughter. My wife and I introduced ourselves, and they in kind introduced themselves to us. We talked about commonalities we shared, likes and dislikes, and they shared a sad intimacy with us concerning their family. Their son died less than a year ago. Neither my wife nor I asked under what circumstances they lost their son. But we surmised their moving to our neighborhood must have been a result of their son's death as the move was only a month after they said their son had died.

Around that same time we were getting to know our new neighbor, a neighbor we had known for years joined the conversation. She revealed she and her husband are separating. Then not much later, still another neighbor joined the conversation. She is the cousin of another neighbor of ours; that other neighbor was a seventy-year-old woman recovering in a nursing home from still another surgery. (Gloria has since passed on. We miss you Gloria)

All these sad revelations got me thinking about death, sadness, and the meaning of life. My wife lost her mother some years ago. My wife's father passed a few years later. My father passed away just prior to my wife's father's passing. My older brother had a heart transplant several years prior and is still suffering from a blood disorder that necessitated the heart transplant. A good friend of my wife lost her husband to a sudden heart attack not too long ago. A childhood friend of mine lost his younger brother some years ago. I myself had a brush with mortality a couple of years ago.

It is sad that death is a certainty. It is sad that most of us will suffer some if not many illnesses prior to our deaths. It is sad that heart disease and cancer change the lives of so many and take the lives of too many. It is sad that relationships end. It is sad that families break apart and then live apart. I feel sad that I am powerless to do nothing about any of it. I wish I could prevent all death. I wish I could prevent all illnesses. But I cannot. That is not a power I possess. The only ones that come close to possessing such power are those belonging to the medical field.

When I was a little tyke, not yet the age of ten, thoughts of death and illness never entered my mind. I lived every day of my young life as if it was a bright summer day. Youth has a tendency to search out excitement, to learn (at least learn about fun things). Youth has so many dreams of what one can be and what one can do as one grows older. But as I grow older, I think more about things I never thought of as a child. I think about things like, where was I before I was born? What will I be after I die? I know the answers now: I was nowhere before I was born, and I will be in a coffin when I die, but onto life and the living. Will I remain healthy and cognizant until my death? How will I die? I don't mean to imply I obsess about such things, but they enter my thoughts from time to time as I have little doubt they enter the thoughts of most people as they grow older. We all start to become aware of our mortality. We all start to wonder more about the "how" and the "whys."

People search many places for answers. Some people join a religion—the holy book and an invisible god. I choose to search for answers within the realm of life itself, using my five senses. I choose to make no guesses about the "how" and the "whys." I choose not to accept questionable answers handed down generation after generation by questionable sources. Despite the success of many cultures, their cultural success does not make for a philosophical reality.

Sometimes I think of myself as a flower (or maybe a weed). A flower has a beginning, as do I. A flower grows from a seed, as do I. A flower grows from youngling to adulthood, as do I. A flower indelibly grows old and feeble, as will I. A flower is always susceptible to injury, disease, and death throughout its life, as am I. A flower eventually dies, as will I.

I am not suggesting a flower has no purpose. I am not suggesting I have no purpose. Arguably, a flower serves many purposes, not the least of which is to help bees. I think I serve a purpose, part of which is to be a loving husband and friend to my wife—a good role model, caregiver, and father to my children. So what is the meaning to life, sadness, and death?

I cannot help but wonder why we must die. Why must we suffer illness and sadness? What is the meaning of life? Death is something I must accept, and I do. I do not fear it. But I question it. It is sad that so many people lose their mothers, their fathers, their siblings, their children, their friends. There seems no purpose to death except sadness and loss. And why must some people suffer cancer? Why must any of us suffer any kind of illness? Some may suggest illness builds character; it makes you grow as a person. But there are so many ways to build character other than surviving life-debilitating cancers and illnesses. I see no purpose to cancer and illnesses, no rational purpose. These illnesses afflict people indiscriminately; illness is not based on how one has lived one's life. A particular illness does not care whom it afflicts. The good and the bad alike can be afflicted with an illness for no rational reason or purpose.

So what is the meaning of life? I believe the answer to that question is personal to each of us. To me, the meaning of my life is to love my wife and to be a good friend and a good husband to my wife. My purpose is to be there for my wife whenever she may need me. My purpose is to be a friend and confidant. My purpose is to share good times and bad times. My purpose is to be a shoulder to lean on. My purpose is to be a good father to my children. My purpose is to teach my children right from wrong. My purpose is to guide my children to live a good and happy life. My purpose is to provide my children with shelter, clothing, and care and love for all their emotional needs. My purpose is to be a good son to my parents and care for them in their later years as they cared for me in my younger years. My purpose is to be there for my brothers and sisters when they need me and even if they don't need me. My purpose is to be there for my friends when they need me. My purpose is to be there for anyone of the aforementioned when sick, ill, sad, or near death. My purpose is to be there to share in their happy moments and to be there for a shoulder to cry on in sad times. My purpose is to be there when someone I never met needs me, for there are many who have no one else to turn to. There are those who in time of need have no one at hand, and I hope they will return the same kindness for loved ones of mine if needed.

So I will never understand death. I will never understand illness. I will feel sad when I know other people are sad. I will live and die knowing I have a purpose. But I will always wonder about all these things, and I will wonder why.

Just a thought.

Chapter 3

THOUGHTS

Things to Think About

Self-expression is not doing what all the "cool" people are doing.

Professional athletes are exceptional "physical" performers. They are not brain surgeons.

If a politician is rich and his/her country/state/city/town is near bankrupt, you should be a little bit suspicious.

Do not lower your ethics because everyone else have lowered their ethical behavior. But do not let the unethical take advantage of you either.

Comedians are the new politicians.

Theologists believe they are the new scientists.

Politicians may be the new criminals.

What is the world coming to?

Just some random thoughts.

Chapter 4

RELIGION AND PHILOSOPHY

We Are Some Creators' Entertaining
Pets in an Isolated Terrarium

Throughout history, human beings have given much thought to the big questions of "why" and "how." Religion has its answers to these big questions. Science has its answers to these big questions—although science bases its answers on experimentation and fact while religion makes up the answers to fit what makes it feel empowered and self-important. Now ask yourself these two questions about the BIG questions. What if they both got it wrong? Or what if they both got it right? How could they both get it wrong, you might ask, or if they both got it right, how could they both get it right? Well, I don't know who is right or wrong. I'm not religious (although I lean toward being philosophical), so unlike the religious, I don't pretend to have all the answers. I'm not a scientist, so I haven't done all the necessary research and experimentation. But like the religious, I'm going to make up an answer. And like a scientist, I'm going to use some logic to reason my way toward an answer. I'm not claiming my answer to be . . . the correct answer. I am merely suggesting my answer to be . . . an answer.

So far as we know, our planet Earth is the only celestial rock in our solar system that harbors life; we are still waiting on exploration of Jupiter's moons (I cannot wait for that to happen). Heck, our planet Earth is the only celestial rock in the entire universe that supports life as far as we know at this time. Future exploration of our solar system and beyond may find life elsewhere. I believe extraterrestrial life will be found, but to our current knowledge, life on our planet Earth is the only life in our universe. Thousands and thousands of magnificent forms of life in almost every form imaginably possible exist here on this one rock in space, but only upon this one celestial rock we have named the planet Earth.

Not only is our planet Earth the only celestial rock harboring life that we know, most life found on this planet Earth is tethered hereto as well. There may be some bacteria and simple forms of life that can survive off planet Earth—not thrive or reproduce, but survive. But most life forms that we know—what we define as life—are tethered to this rock we call Earth. Some human beings have left the atmosphere of our world. Men and women have rocketed in to space. Heck, dogs, monkeys, and other life born on this Earth have been rocketed in to space—lucky dogs. We have even witnessed men rocketing all the way to the moon. Yes, naysayers, men did walk on the moon! But every man, woman, dog, or monkey that has left the sanctity of our atmosphere has left this planet with a piece of our Earth. Human beings need to take oxygen with them when they leave this Earth. Human beings need to take food with them when they leave this Earth. Human beings need to replicate Earth-like conditions when they rocket away from this Earth, or they will not survive for long, if at all. Space is a dangerous place. Cosmic rays, solar flares, the lack of an Earth-type gravity or any gravity, no oxygen, no readily available water (although that may be found elsewhere than Earth), and pressure differences that mean life or death to us. We were created to live and thrive on this planet Earth, not in space, not on the moon, not on an asteroid, definitely not in the sun, not on Venus (too much pressure on that lady), and Mars . . . well, Mars is a different story. We could make Mars a viable habitat for human beings—artificially or possibly terrareformed—but we have to create Earth-like conditions on Mars for Mars to be a viable habitat for human life. My point being, we are tethered to this planet Earth—our prison, our home, our terrarium.

Earth is like a terrarium. I own two Russian tortoises. I keep them in a small, contained terrarium. My tortoises, Boris and Bullwinkle, never leave their habitat. Everything Boris and Bullwinkle need to survive, I provide for them within their terrarium. I give them fresh water, food, shelter, earth, light, night, and warmth on a daily basis. Everything Boris and Bullwinkle need to survive is contained within their terrarium. Earth is like a terrarium. We have all the things life existing here on Earth needs to survive. We have water, food, light, night, and warmth and items to make shelter to protect us and keep us safe. Human beings tend to be more creative and innovative in how we make use of the supplies found in our terrarium Earth than Boris and Bullwinkle in their terrarium, but there is a great similarity between our two habitats. It is true, Boris and Bullwinkle could survive outside their terrarium if they could escape or if I set them free—under the right conditions, they would survive. Boris and Bullwinkle would not need to wear pressurized suits like astronauts, and they could probably find food and water more readily than astronauts could find outside of their terrarium Earth. But there is a similarity between the two habitats. Both terrariums are self-contained units that provide the conditions for life, which provide the conditions for the survival of life. Life is more difficult—survival is more difficult—for all concerned, however, when we try to leave our terrarium.

Have you ever pondered why we are made of food? Why is it that all life is eatable by other life? Why must most life forms need to consume other life forms to survive? The religious will say that all other life forms were made for our use as food, clothing, and tools of labor—made for our consumption and use to aid our ability to survive. Science will argue that a multitude of life forms came into existence based on their environment and those that proved the fittest and those that adapted best to their particular environment survive. Science argues survival of the fittest while religion argues survival by the will of god. But no matter science or religion as your basis for or being, the truth still remains the bodies of living organisms are made to consume other living organisms to exact energy needed to continually refurbish and rebuild and energize the organism doing the consuming. Have you ever questioned why we are made of food? If we are supposedly some higher form of life as the religious claim, if we are godly beings, then why are me made of food? Why are we as eatable as most any other life form on this planet Earth? If we are so special, shouldn't we be made of something other than food? Shouldn't we be more than a possible meal for a wolf, a lion, or rats? It makes me wonder. Doesn't it make you wonder? Thinking of myself being eaten by some animal makes me think of myself as a meal and not a god-favored being.

Still, I wonder, if maybe, we do have an intelligent creator. Yes, maybe the religious are right. Maybe there is a god or gods that created us. But maybe the scientists are right too. Maybe evolution is a fact. Maybe survival of the fittest is not only a valid theory but an intended objective of our creators. It seems to me if we are made of food like all other life forms on this planet. If all life forms on this planet are tethered to this planet for their survival, it seems that maybe this was the intent of our creators. Our creators needed a little entertainment, and so they created us and all other life forms on this terrarium Earth. Our creators created this universe. Our creators created this solar system. Our creators created this Earth—this terrarium—with the conditions to support life as we define life, but our creators did all this with the objective to tether us and all earthly life to this terrarium Earth. Our creator's intent was to keep us tethered to this planet Earth. Our creator's intent was to create thousands and thousands of forms of life and to throw these thousands and thousands of varying forms of life all together inside this contained unit—our terrarium Earth—for the purpose of watching and experiencing what would happen as we interact. So we are all made of food. And we all have to eat food to survive. So we all combat one another for survival. So we all combat one another for dominance. And to keep things from getting monotonous and/or boring, our creator has programmed into all of us a limited life span with reproductive capabilities to continue and vary the entertainment. And we are programmed with the will to survive so we do not give up the fight; we will entertain. And we are programmed to reproduce so species can lose one battle but live on to fight anew. So we can die when we grow too smart and too boring and one creature cannot dominate forever, or learn too much and survive too long, but the species can continue by reproducing bringing forth more combatants and more entertainment—the game always starting over, the players always relearning from a fresh slate, at least to some extent, not taking into account the collective intelligence of man and many other species, which merely makes the entertainment grow in interest.

So think about what I just wrote, and ask yourself—are we superior beings, or are we the pets of superior beings living in a terrarium? Are we merely entertainment for superior beings? Are we nothing greater than tortoises surviving within a terrarium?

Just a thought.

Are We Not Educated Enough as a Society to Realize How Dangerous Believers of Invisible Beings Can Be?

Arguably, there are more educated people in the world today—relative to the overall world population—than days gone by, but this does not mean people on average are any smarter. More people than not still believe in invisible supernatural beings watching over and interacting with their daily lives. Is believing something someone told you that lacks all common sense a smart thing? Would you believe me if I told you I am the Son of God? Yet someone tells you a man that lived (maybe) some two thousand years ago was the Son of God and you just believe them? You don't do a little research? Would you believe me if I told you the Easter bunny was real and he lays chocolate eggs? I doubt you would, but then my statement would lack logic. Do you see where I am going with this?

Religion does not dominate our morals; religion is not the creator of morals. (Wo)man is the creator of morals. The good needs only believe and do good to be good. Religion has no monopoly on morals and/or our being good and kind to our neighbors; it is (wo)man and not religious belief in invisible gods that monopolizes good.

Doctors save lives, not religion. The next time you feel the need to thank a god for the successful results of your surgery, I suggest you ask yourself—if your god could have healed you, why did you beg your surgeon to perform the operation? If your god can save you, cut out the middleman and just pray. I dare you, but I DO NOT suggest you take me up on my dare because your god will desert you unlike your surgeon who will save you. Thank your surgeon, not your invisible, noninteractive god.

Love is also something worth taking a look at. I believe people who sincerely love others do so because they care about others, not out of fear of hell nor dreams of heaven, but out of a sincere concern and compassion for someone else. If you love others merely because you believe this is what your god wants and it is your ticket to heaven and a pass out of hell, then you are selfish, self-centered, and not loving even in the manner your god wishes you to love. True love is compassion no matter a promise of reward or punishment; true love is reality.

We will always find hate and judgment and separation amongst groups who believe THEY know and are special above all other groups because of their beliefs in beings that do not exist. It is more difficult yet more rewarding to love and care for others ONLY BECAUSE— than to do so out of fear of damnation or dreams of paradise.

Paradise can be found within the mind. Love and concern for others is not religiously based but thoughtfully based within ourselves independent of our beliefs of creation. Miracles are performed by people just like us (doctors, nurses) who care so much about helping others that they study, research, and attempt to perform repairs on our bodies. If one truly believes in a deity, not a doctor as the one responsible for saving lives than do not go to a doctor. No deity ACTS through a doctor; that belief is false justification for believing in an invisible deity. A doctor acts alone and deserves all our thanks for saving lives. A doctor saved my life and I thank him gratefully, sincerely and I thank only him and his medical staff. No god saved my life; no prayer saved my life. If I had merely prayed to be saved, I would have bled to death. Too often doctors and their medical staff are taken for granted. Do not take medical staff for granted. Many of us owe these good people so much.

We take for granted explanations and stories handed down to us by parents and others in our social groups and in our schools and in our communities. The killer in Ohio who years back said he was afraid to show he was a Muslim and afraid to pray in public is one of those people. He was no one special. His false beliefs made him no one special. His beliefs led to his believing persecution or torment by others of other beliefs, and so he lashed out as his prophet claimed he should. All God-fearing religions have a creator as the basis of their beliefs. The three major religions of our world today are based upon the beliefs of the Hebrews. MEN created these religions, not gods. Governments and powerful people grew these religions, not gods. Rome grew Christianity. Arab nations grew Islam. The popular religions of today are no more real, no more fact-based than the popular religions of days gone by. Zeus and the gods of Olympus; Odin and the Norse gods; the god Nike, who is now merely a shoe—all were and are as viable as the god of Christianity, Judaism, and Islam. The current viable god(s) are only more credible because YOU believe in them.

Goodness and kindness and the concern for others are within you because you want them to be, not because you join a religious club. Give yourself credit for the kind acts you perform. Give others credit for the kind acts they perform. Thank medical staff for all the things they do to prolong and save lives; don't demand they do so; thank them for doing so. Know that YOU and YOUR NEIGHBORS are the basis of love and charity, not invisible nonexistent beings. If more of us think with our feet planted solidly on the ground and not with our heads in the clouds, far fewer bad things will happen, and we will have that much less to fight among ourselves about.

I thank you all for being YOU.

Just a thought.

Realist Versus Religious

The main difference between myself—a realist (aka atheist)—and the religious status quo came to me in a thought today, and I can convey that difference very simply and succinctly: I AM A GOOD, LOVING PERSON JUST BECAUSE I THINK IT RIGHT TO BE SO WHILE THE RELIGIOUS DO IT BECAUSE OF FEAR OF AND THE EXPECTATION OF REWARD FROM THEIR GOD.

I am faithful to my wife because I care about my wife and I care about her feelings and my never wanting to hurt her, not because a god may punish me. I stay with my wife, and never stray, and together we raise our children because I love them all—not because a god may punish me. I help my neighbors in time of need and when I believe they could use a little help even if I am not asked, not out of a belief of some afterlife reward and not out of a belief that some god will later shine down good favors upon me in return.

If I die tomorrow, and I will die sometime, on my deathbed, I will be thankful for the reward of my wife's love and my children's love and the time I was able to spend with them. I will die a happy man with a little bit of sadness, knowing so many people lived their lives out of fear and expectations of reward from a nonexistent being in a nonexistent afterlife.

It is sad to realize that so many people "act" good for the wrong reasons. No one should "act" or pretend to be good. Everyone should strive to "be" good for goodness's sake. The feeling of being good for its sake alone is so much better, and its lifetime reward is so much more real.

Just a thought.

The Qur'an Is a Comic Book

I have read NUMEROUS passages from the Qur'an, and I have easily come to the determination that it is nothing more than a comic book written by an insane, crazed child about the age of ten. The content of the Qur'an must be interpreted in its entirety and not cherry-picked as done by such either ignorant or OIL MOTIVATED presidents. For nearly every so-called peaceful passage in the Qur'an thereafter follows an explanatory passage of hate or definition that specifies peace as being for Muslims only. The Qur'an is chock full of HATE for Jews and Christians alike. And not to merely raise the Jews and Christians onto a lonely pedestal of hate, the Muslims are only too anxious to add ALL infidels to their aim of hatred.

READ THE QUR'AN! I cannot emphasis this enough! There are too many bleeding hearts in America and other Western nations who do not read, but wait for the movie to come out or for someone to tell them what to think. Know the movie is always written, directed, and produced by those whose message is wanted to be believed and not necessarily—and usually never—the truth. READ! And read materials by different authors from different sources and avoid those sources, which are motivated to fool you into believing something other than the truth. MOSTLY—READ THE QUR'AN itself! And READ THE HADITH! The Hadith is just as important to Muslims—and infidels to know the truth—as is the Qur'an.

I guarantee, when you read the Qur'an, it will not read as a symphony that will bring you to tears as some Muslims claim. But the Qur'an will bring a logically reasoning, peace-loving human being to emotions of laughter, sadness for those killed by strict followers of Islam; fear for the safety and happiness of Jews and Christians;

and finally, anger for all the hatred the book teaches. And after reading the Qur'an, do not be fooled as some may try to fool you into believing Muslims believe the Qur'an is not to be read literally or that many of the passages of the Qur'an no longer are followed—that they were of and for a day gone by, because any teacher of Islam will tell you the book is the word of god and is ageless and its message is meant to transgress time itself. Muslims will tell you that Muhammad is to be held up as the model man that all men of yesterday, today, and tomorrow should emulate: Muhammad, a crazed and insane childlike warlord who believed himself (or at least wanted others to believe) to be the voice of god. Muhammad who conveniently had an answer from god whenever a situation arose that required he explain his actions. Muhammad who had the "blessings" of "his" god to have sex with nine-year-old girls, to own slaves, to sleep with other men's wives, to kill anyone who would not agree with him, who taught his people to hate Jews, who refused to tolerate others from practicing their own religious beliefs, who subjugated anyone not Muslim as well as anyone Muslim or not who was born with a vagina, Muhammad who waged war on all who he did not control and stole their gold, possessions, and women and children. Muhammad a model man? Hardly! Muhammad was an insane, sex-crazed pedophile. Muhammad's favorite wife was a nine-year-old child, who still played on swings, who had not even menstruated yet when he married the child, model man? Hardly!

READ THE QUR'AN! You will find it is not a book like the Torah or the Bible. I am not a fan of the Torah or the Bible either. Both are books of fables, myths, and customs of a group of people who wish to declare themselves as special as and more informed than all others in our world, no different than the story books about the Gods of Olympus. BUT neither the Torah nor the Bible rise to the heights of hate or insane childish and incomprehensible nonsense as does the Qur'an. The Qur'an is an obvious rip off of both the Torah and the Bible but interpreted by Muhammad to justify his arguably evil acts. The Qur'an is a rewrite of both the Torah and the Bible but rewritten so as to make Muhammad a king on Earth and again to justify his arguably evil acts. The Qur'an is obviously written by the mind of a child who must have his way—a male child who must dominate ALL others and who must dominate women who he is afraid of. Many in Muhammad's time believed he was insane, and they were right. READ THE QUR'AN, and you will understand the truth.

Remember, as you read the comic book the Qur'an, that not all religions are created equal. Not all religions are about peace. Religions are nothing more than philosophies built on superstition and ignorance to explain life and its purpose. Religions have no exclusive rights to morals or the determination of what is good, evil, right, or wrong. Men and women decide what is right and wrong, good or evil. Time helps us decide what is right or wrong, good or evil. Religions are locked in the past, locked in day's gone by. Time gives us knowledge. Time gives us answers to questions. To be a truthful and morally helpful philosophy, a religion must evolve over time; it must take into consideration the new truths we learn, the answers revealed to us by science and progress. But religion takes none of that into consideration. Religion is stagnant. Religion lives in the past—the past where the sun revolves around the flat Earth, the past where slavery is acceptable, the past where marrying girls under ten years old is acceptable, the past where tolerance of others is unacceptable, the past where equal rights of men and women do not exist.

Read the comic book the Qur'an, and you will discover that it is, in fact, a comic book but with an evil hateful message as bad as Hitler's Mein Kampf, and you will discover that Muhammad is no more a model man than was Adolf Hitler.

This said, this does not mean all Muslims are bad, nor Christians nor Jews. I speak only of the Qur'an, not all the followers of Islam. The problem as I see it is so many people follow religious beliefs thrown at them by parents, their societies, their countries, and they follow these philosophies blindly. So many people never take the time to examine what they are taught in an independent light. There are many good Muslims, Christians, and Jews. My wife is Jewish, and I know her to be the most loving and caring person. My extended family is Catholic, and I know them to be good people. But because they are good people does not make the religions they follow good philosophies. Because they are good people does not change the origin of their religious faiths. Truth is truth, and history is history. Let us throw away the horrible books of the past and live good lives in the present together.

Just at thought.

Islam Is a Religion Based on Fraud, Violence, and Fantasy

Islam is not alone in this truth, but what makes Islam worse than some of the other major religions is that it is built on violence and its false prophet is a crazed woman demeaning pedophile who hated the Jews and barely tolerated the Christians. The Qur'an is a hateful book instructing its Arabic followers to hate and kill Jews and Christians. The Qur'an sanctions war against disbelievers of Islam. Unlike the Bible (another book of fables), the Qur'an preaches violence against nonbelievers and whomever it decides is an enemy. The Qur'an advocates conquering and controlling the world. Now, I am not going to convince hard-core Muslims to see the truth, and I will never get most Muslims to see reality, and even many ignorant non-Muslims will read these words and see hatred, not truth. But reality can be a bitch. Although truth and reality are just what the words infer them to be—truth and reality.

I'm not going to list all the evils and crazed behaviors and self-serving mannerisms of the war hawk Muhammad. You can research it for yourself as I have. But I dare you to put the truth where your mouth is and do the research as I have. Don't just condemn my words as hateful. Islam is hateful. Calling a philosophy birthed on hatred and suppression of others anything but that is a crime. So don't turn a blind eye, and believe Islam is good and peaceful. Research the Qur'an; research Islamic history. And don't give me that "Christianity was bad too" crap. You're right—it was/is. The Vatican is bad. If you truly read the Bible as you may claim, the Israelites were killers as well. PLEASE DO READ, RESEARCH. But you will find a very violent women abusing MAN in Muhammad that you will not find in crazy Joseph Smith or self-proclaimed son of god Jesus. What you will find about Muhammad is that Muhammad is no different than other so-called gods and prophets in that he was a self-delusional individual who heard voices and saw people no one else could hear or see—convenient for him, I will say. Of course, the same claim of self-proclaimed special closeness to god was made by Joseph Smith and so many others. What you will find that sets Muhammad apart from the other so-called prophets is a violent man who held women in low esteem as chattel and who justified every act no matter how bad as a revelation of god, even killing others. Digressing a bit, I find it amazing so many simple minds believe men like him and follow him and hold him up as a godlike figure beyond criticism. Apparently, facts, reality, and truth mean nothing when it comes to explaining the whys and the hows for many too lazy to research or even see the obvious. Why do so many people question their auto mechanic charging them an exorbitant bill for a car repair, yet they take another human being's word that he spoke to god? I find that unbelievably crazy.

While Jesus may have been considered crazy by his brothers and sisters, at least Jesus did not wage war on those Jews and Gentiles who did not believe he was the son of god. Jesus did not kill other people and proclaim god told him all those who will not believe him and follow him deserve to die. Jesus preached of a heaven not of this earth. Jesus did not preach to conquer this earth. Jesus preached this earthly world is Cesar's and heaven is god's—to each their own. Jesus did not rally his followers to conquer Rome. Jesus preached conversion to his faith by choice and peaceful means. Muhammad decided killing people who did not want to believe his false claims of godhood was his God-given right—given him privately through revelations—by god/Allah himself. Jesus also did not marry and have sex with nine-year-old children, like some so-called prophets. Moses did not take numerous wives and keep a harem unto him, like some prophets. Abraham did not marry his adopted son's ex-wife and add her to his stable of wives—like some prophets. Would you force your wife to cover her face and body when in public? Would you allow your husband to marry three other women besides you and not lay claim for the same or that you are the only one? Would you allow your husband to exercise complete control over your coming and going from your home? It's up to him if you go out into public? Do you believe women cannot be witness to their own rape? If not, but you think Islam is okay, ask the many rape victims imprisoned for claiming to be raped but unable to find four male witnesses to prove their claims. Ask these same women how adultery can be levied against them, causing their imprisonment or death if their valid claim of rape cannot be proven by male witnesses. And then, thank Muhammad and Islam for their imprisonment.

There are many fake religions in the world today. I can easily show the lies and craziness of all of them. But craziness and lies are okay if harmless. If you want to believe in invisible winged creatures, be my guest. But if your religion is based on killing my Jewish and Christian friends as well as atheists and realists and any other non-Muslim philosophies or even other Muslims, then I have no tolerance for you and your evil, nasty, hateful philosophy. If your religion is based on subjugating my daughters and my sisters, then I have no tolerance for you and your evil, nasty, hateful philosophy.

If you, the reader, do enough research, you will find how so many of the major popular religions are all tied together. Their histories are linked. How? Why? Because they are all tales created in local areas where many groups lived and worked and shared ideas and influenced one another. And the common thread among them all is usually some crazed individual with charisma and/or a propensity to violence who either charmed the simple or overpowered the weak. The common thread among them is a delusional individual who draws on the insecurities of a group of people and convinces this group THEY are better than everyone else if only they believe and follow him and HIS rules. Have more self-respect for yourself than that. Have more respect for your neighbor than that. Have more respect for women than Islam. Have more respect for those who are of different countries, different ethnicities, and different races.

But don't take my word about Islam. RESEARCH! But do your research with an open mind, which means look at a fair number of objective sources—not just sources that praise Allah and Islam. If you research enough of the right resources, what you will find interesting is how fair-minded one religion will be about the other. That is one religion, even factions within the same religion, will usually be willing to point out the flaws and inconsistencies that the other religion or faction of its own will gloss over—or conveniently forget—about its own.

Just a thought.

Simple Proof There Is No Soul

Many people, religious and not, claim we all have a soul, but they make said claim without a shred of proof. I am sorry to say, there is no such thing as a soul—literally, at least; figuratively, arguably yes. The brain is often confused as being a separate entity from the mind or a "soul" although the truth is the brain is mind and soul. Our brains are what we think and what we describe and believe to be us. Look what happens when someone's brain is injured. They cannot think clearly or they cannot speak, or they cannot walk. Was their soul damaged along with their brain? No. Well, yes. It all depends on how you define the soul, and there are only two ways to define the soul. Either the soul is just a fun way to describe your brain having rhythm, or the soul is a separate entity that survives your brain's death. I agree with the former, but not the latter. If your soul survives your death, then how you think should not change at any time during your lifetime, no matter when you are young, old or damaged. But the way you think does change over your lifetime. You know next to nothing when born and quite a lot more before you die, assuming your brain is undamaged. But if you suffer from Alzheimer or dementia or aphasia or some other brain injury or deficiency later in life, the way you think does change. What do those who believe in a soul surviving the body believe? That your soul will separate from your brain at death and all of a sudden revert to some preordained preferred stage of thinking in your life? I don't think so. So I am sorry to disappoint the disillusioned, but there is no soul—only a brain, so take care of your brain, and your soul will be fine.

Just a thought.

The Nature of Existence: Sin and Free Will

I watched an episode entitled "Sin and Free Will" from a Netflix series entitled *The Nature of Existence*. It confirmed in my mind that human beings are crazy—especially religious human beings. If not for the fact that religious fanatics dominate the world, I would merely laugh at what I heard and saw of this Netflix telecast. But there are so many human "animals" that I cannot help but feel depressed for, knowing that rational logical thought falls into a distant third place to irrational, egotistical, simpleminded religious thought. As an example, I picture in my mind the image of a Hasidic Jew. Why, because this is merely one example of ridiculousness and craziness practiced by otherwise intelligent human beings. He is merely one of millions of examples I could have chosen. I picture a Hasidic Jew as a man believing he must dress a certain way and he must wear a beard and his hair a certain way to be considered "good" within his philosophy. To me, that is crazy and ridiculous. You should watch and listen to this Netflix series as it may help you understand just how crazy people can be. When people talk crazy and irrational while believing within their own minds that they are speaking rationally and logically, I have to pause and think—"Oh my stars, does (s)he really believe that? Did (s)he really say that? So watch and listen, but if you watch and listen, you must try to think rationally and logically about what you see and hear, not emotionally. Too often in life, people merely rationalize away the wrongs they have been taught and the wrongs they see and hear on a daily basis and people never apply logic and valid reasoning to what they have learned in their past or what they see and hear in the present. I could go into a thirty-page commentary on this topic, but I will merely sum it up in a few words. Human beings are one variation of billions of life forms on this planet, and we are no more "godly" than any of the other life forms on this planet. Human beings delude themselves into believing they are second only to a god that is made in man's image. This makes human beings less in tune with reality than even less intelligent of our other planetary species we share this world with. Dressing a certain way, bending one's knees, facing east rather than west, mumbling rehearsed prayers to no one, growing or not growing a beard, makes no difference in one's position or status in reality. Is it not extremely interesting that animals do not dress up and fold their paws together and beg the great mouse god to give them cheese? We as human beings have the free will to be crazy, and we have the free will to sin and the free will to define sin, but do we have to be so crazy? Let's use our free will to be rational and logical and a little less crazy.

Just a thought.

Be Proud You Are a Realist (Atheist)

ARE YOU AFRAID TO ADMIT YOU ARE A RATIONAL HUMAN BEING PROUD OF YOUR INTELLIGENCE? If not, then I dare you to read this "thought" out loud to anyone and everyone you know. Atheism—or what I believe is more accurately referable to as "realism"—is not merely believing in reality itself; it is not merely being logical in your thought processes. It is so much more; it is thinking—really thinking—not merely repeating what you are told to think. It is caring for others, as well as being honest, not merely to others but honest to yourself, and it is being proud to unabashedly proclaim you have both feet firmly planted on the ground, and it is being proud knowing you are brave enough and strong enough to live each day without feeling the need to make up some fantastic explanation of why you exist and without feeling the need to live someone else's fantastical explanation of invisible winged angels living in clouds, kneeling daily before a bearded man (not woman) wearing sandals, who happens to look like you.

You should not feel shame or embarrassment that you believe in facts! You should not feel the need to tell someone who believes in mythical beings that they "might be right." You should be strong enough in your convictions to tell them they can believe what they want, but you believe in truth, facts, and you believe in reality, not fiction! Be proud you believe in reality and know that "faith" in old stories told are not equal to facts and reality. Remember that just as "God" is truth to the religious, "science" is truth to realists, and we have just as much right to proclaim our beliefs and disbeliefs as the religious. If we hide our beliefs, we are not being respectful to the religious; we are being disrespectful to ourselves.

You should be proud to say to anyone and everyone that you did not vote for a lying, wife-cheating, crooked businessman for president, and you should be proud to look your philosophy in its face proudly and honestly able to proclaim you stood for and you voted for your beliefs—proud that you put your vote where you mouth is by refusing to vote for a man who lacks kindness, a man who lacks concern for others, a man who fails to show love for all races, equality for women, and concern for the poor. Be proud you are unlike the hypocritical religious right who claim to have a monopoly on ethics and love and kindness yet vote into the presidency and into Congress men who fit the description of their biblical devil.

You should be proud to say to anyone and everyone that you refused to vote for into the office of the presidency at any time during your life a man who had a reputation as a drug user, a drinker, and used his family and political pull to get out of active service yet as commander in chief sent innocent men into battle to fight for his and his friends' corporate welfare, making his friends richer while your friends lost life and/or limbs. You are a realist.

You should be proud to say to anyone and everyone that it was your DOCTOR and his/her medical staff that saved your life and not some cloud-sitting, sandal-wearing nonexistent being that was made up by desert people who died centuries ago. Your doctors studied hard and worked hard and sacrificed much to learn how to save your life, so it would be insulting to them to give your thanks to the wind and not them who saved you. Be proud that you appreciate your real savior(s)—the men and women who saved your life—and be proud you let them know it was them, not some invisible being that you know saved your life. And for those confused patients who believe it was an invisible guiding hand that saved you, tell them the next time they need serious medical attention, just pray and cut out the middleman, and tell us how that works out for them.

Religions are but philosophies that are but subjective thoughts collected and followed by groups with the intent of defining not only one's daily life but the understanding of one's existence. Be proud you are not lazy and that you are brave enough to not give up the search for the truth. Be proud you do not stray from the path of logic and blindly wander down a road pointed out by some delusional person who demands you to believe some story told them as a child, and even more sadly for some, a story told them as an adult. Be proud you can think for yourself and you do not blindly regurgitate false information as fact! Be proud you are a good person for goodness's sake and not merely because you hope to earn a ticket to fantasy island or a free pass out of a pit of fire. Even those who believe in the unbelievable should know that being good is only good if one is good for goodness's sake; no one is truly good if they act good hoping for a reward. And you should know that being good has nothing to do with religion and the belief in winged creatures. Being good has to do with your concern for others despite yourself, and religion has no monopoly on good. Take a look at all the so-called religious souls, and count how many are divorced, cheating, lying, and breaking every rule of morality when it suits them best.

Be proud you do not watch FOX News or believe any of the "spin" from Bill O'Reilly or any of the rhetoric of Sean Hannity. If the fans of FOX News would take even a few minutes of their time to research the so-called "facts" FOX newscasters spew on TV and in books, they would discover lies told, and they would glean personal agendas from these politically and financially motivated hate-mongers and charlatans. And they may decide that these rich religious claimants really care for no one but themselves and their own wallets. Be proud you see through the spin and rhetoric and the hate they spew daily while claiming to be "good Christians." And always keep asking yourself these questions while listening to the spin and the rhetoric. Was Jesus ever known to be a hater and a liar? Was Jesus ever known to cheat people at business? Did Jesus ever cheat on his wife (yes, he was married)? Would Jesus have approved of Drumpf (I love you John Oliver), Hannity, or O'Reilly?

Be proud, and show how proud you are of YOUR faith, your philosophy. Be proud that you are a good person who cares for your family and others without the expectation of reward or fear of punishment during life or after death. Know you have just as much right to proclaim you pride in THESE beliefs, which are the beliefs of you the REALIST; you have just as much right to proclaim your pride in your beliefs, beliefs including that today's current and most widely practiced religions are based on nothing more than made-up stories by desert people who died centuries ago. Know you have just as much right as the currently popular religious groups to be proud of the tenets of your belief as they proclaim to be proud of the tenets of their philosophies. And always know the religious owe you as much respect to live and proclaim your beliefs as they claim you owe them.

Just a thought.

Have You Ever Thought That Evil Is God's Intent?

It would explain a lot. Some of the richest men and women in the world earned their fortunes performing what many of us would believe to be evil acts, and how about those celebrities and athletes? Many of the rich and famous seem to have a lot of skeletons in their closets. Well, the skeletons used to be kept in the closet; nowadays those skeletons seem to be right out where everyone can see them and proudly displayed.

So why would God create the world with evil intent? Why would God's intent be evil if the faithful followers of god-fearing religion are supposed to be God's chosen ones? Why would God's intent be evil if the meek are supposed to inherit the Earth? I don't know, but ask yourself this question, "Why does evil rule the world?" Why don't the meek, the humble, the poor, and the pious rule the world? If an omnipotent God exists, I have to believe the answer is it's God's will. Or it can be argued a god—or better yet, a creator or creators, created life on this planet Earth merely for its entertainment.

What if we are born of said creators and said creators live in a fourth spatial dimension—a dimension we of the inferior third dimension cannot perceive given our limited abilities of perception. We cannot perceive the higher fourth dimension because the ability to perceive a fourth spatial dimension is not programmed into our DNA. But despite our inability to perceive our creators and the higher dimension, they exist within here and all around us. And from this higher dimension, our creators are watching us. Our creators, bored after living since before the dawn of what we define as time, are amusing themselves by watching us live and die, kill and be killed, eat and be eaten. Our creators are stark raving mad bored, so they need us as entertainment. And if we are merely entertainment, do you think a church-, temple-, or mosque-going law-abiding nice guy or gal is going to be exciting entertainment? Our creators love danger, death, murder, cheating, lying, stealing, adultery, hatred, slavery, war, violence, sickness, and disease. Are not those the very keys to our movie and television entertainment? It would certainly explain a lot, wouldn't it?

Think about our planet Earth—a solitary rock moving throughout dark space. Think about how our planet exists within a solar system where no other life has been found. Yet on this one space rock, millions of species of life are all competing for survival. We are all coexisting; we are all competing for limited resources and for the control and the continued existence of our respective species. Think about it. What excitement this must be for a bored bunch of creators. These creators can sit back or whatever their intellect containment units do to relax, and they can observe our planet, and they can live vicariously through all the evil and terrible events that occur here on our violent little space rock. What fun we must be. What entertainment we must be. What evil intent our creators must have in mind for us for their personal amusement.

So the next time you think about being a "good" person—a good Christian, Jew, Muslim, Hindu, or whatever—wonder whether our creators care less about you being good than they do about you being "bad." Bad is more exciting, and it is in our nature to want to be bad at least now and then. Deny it all you want, but you are lying to yourself if you do. So think about what our creators may really want you to do; maybe they want you to be the bad boy or the bad girl. Maybe our creators want you to start a war or just do something really rotten. It doesn't mean the creators will reward you for being evil. But they might. Look at all the billionaires and historically famous who have lived rewarding lives by being bad. But whether the creators reward you or not, know they will be watching you. And as long as you are part of some act that is entertaining, you will survive; you will be taken care of. You will serve a purpose. Think about it. It just might explain some things.

Just a thought.

What If God Was a Man or a Woman?

What if God turns out to be a man or a woman? I am merely asking, "What if?" Many pretend to know the answers to the questions of how, when, and why. Others strongly believe they know the answers to the questions of how, when, and why. Still others make no claim to know the answers to such questions but restlessly search to answer these questions of how, when, and why. And still some others just do not know the answers and they have no belief they ever will know the answers. Me, I have no answers, but I am proposing a "what if." What if God was a man or a woman?

There can be no question that science and technology has advanced at incredible rates in a short period of time. Once man and woman decided religion was not the final word to their existence, science and technology began to flourish. We live in a technological age today only dreamed of a mere two hundred years ago. We fly around the world and think no more of flying than walking. We drive automobiles that protect us from foul weather and house more amenities than you can pack on a mule. We make use of personal computers that fit in the palm of our hands that connect us with other computers and, hence, other people around the world. We can communicate with anyone anywhere in the world in seconds. We have running water in our homes and can buy our food at a local supermarket instead of hunting it down. We have trained ourselves to heal wounds and cure illnesses. We can replace a person's heart with a new heart; I know this firsthand by way of my brother and his heart transplant. We can give artificial limbs to the handicapped. We (not me, but other men) have walked on the moon (yes, conspiracy theorists, men have walked on the moon). We have explored the atom, and we have explored the universe—the big and the small. The things that men and women have accomplished to this point in time—things taken for granted by many of us—are incredible accomplishments that only the species of men and women have accomplished, incredible things, and we are not yet done accomplishing the spectacular as a species.

The world we live in today could only have been dreamed of by men and women some years before. The world of the future can only be a world we dream of today, but with everything accomplished to date, almost anything seems possible now. Men and women and science have been able to clone life. Men and women have split the atom (for good and for bad). It does not seem impossible that someday in the future, men and women may create life. And someday, much further in the future, it may be possible that men and women may create a universe. Imagine a universe of our creation, complete with current rules of physics—or maybe our own man/woman made rules of physics. Imagine that.

Many current physicists such as Michio Kaku have proposed that our universe may be merely one universe amongst thousands. And some of those other universes may run by a different set of rules than our own. And some of those other universes may run by the same set of rules as our own, but whether the same rules of physics apply to other universes or not, the idea remains plausible that we may be but one universe of many universes—one universe of thousands of universes all consisting of life similar to our own, life forms like us.

The current accepted belief of physicists regarding the creation of the universe is labeled the big bang. It is believed the universe was incredibly compact and exploded or expanded (for lack of a better way of describing the event) into existence (like a balloon filling with air), and the universe is still expanding, still growing today.

Now here is where my "what if" comes into the picture. What if men and women (no different than us) existing in a universe (no different than ours) were so technologically advanced that they created our universe billions of years ago? The most intelligent men and women of that time and universe, working in a lab, were able to create a tiny universe that held all the information needed to expand

and grow into the universe we live in today. What if those men and women using some catalyst jump-started our universe into motion—to become the universe it is today? This would mean that men and women—no different than ourselves other than being far superior technologically and intellectually—created us. In effect, one could say, "We created ourselves." Or one could say, "Human kind cloned itself and its universe."

What happened to our creators is another thought experiment. The creation of our universe could have meant the destruction of their universe; our current universe could have engulfed their universe seconds after its creation. Or they could have been intelligent enough to push our newly created universe into another spatial dimension to join the many previously existing universes as suggested by Michio Kaku. Our creators could be dead and gone unless they conquered death, which is a technological possibility for such an advanced race of men and women. Who knows, they could even have the means to watch and study us—and maybe they are watching and studying us at this very moment. But again, that is another thought for another time.

So think about it. What if we created ourselves?

Just a "what if" thought.

When I Was Sick, It Was the Doctor
Who Saved Me, Not God

How many times have you heard someone say, "Thank you, God. You saved my life."

Someone comes down with a terrible illness—cancer, for example—or a tragedy befalls them, an auto accident causing a spinal injury that potentially takes away the ability to ever walk again. That person is admitted to a hospital. A medical team of doctors and nurses and so many others heal them, make them "whole" again. And the words, "Thank you for saving me, God," are uttered.

It was not god who saved this person; it was not god who cured that person. It was a medical team of doctors, nurses, and so many others who saved these people. **It was a medical team of doctors, nurses, and so many others who cured these people.** Yet the credit for saving this person and/or curing that person is so often given to an invisible being that does not exist. So often the words are uttered by someone that the medical team was no more than "an instrument through which god worked his wonders." Reality check, people, that is not what went down. It was without a doubt the doctors, nurses, and the rest of their medical team that saved and/or cured that person. No god worked through them. Just a medical team that misses out the credit if they cured or saved the life of someone and/or are blamed if they fail in the attempt to cure and/or save the life of someone—someone who obviously could not cure or save themselves. So often the medical team rarely gets the full credit for saving and/or curing someone who cannot save or cure themselves.

On behalf of doctors, nurses, and their medical staff everywhere, I find it insulting to the medical team to give credit to mythical creatures that do not exist. Credit should be given to whom credit is due. Let me ask the religious this question, "Why does god have to work though someone else to perform his miracles?" Is not god powerful enough to perform miracles first hand? And let me ask another question, "If god is responsible for saving and/or curing an injured party, is not god then responsible for injuring the injured party?" If the god in question is so powerful that he can save and/or cure someone, doesn't it make sense that that same god is powerful enough to prevent the harm from ever occurring? And if said god is so powerful and omnipotent, why does he let the injury happen in the first place? The religious might say we should not question the will of god, but shouldn't we? Shouldn't we at least ask him why? Or a better question to ask is of us, and that question is, "Isn't there something wrong with this belief that a god is saving Timmy's life?" If a man or woman had it in their power to prevent harm befalling someone, wouldn't we expect they would use that power to help prevent the occurrence of harm to someone? And if a man or woman had the power to cure someone, wouldn't we expect they would cure the injured party right away, without delay? Yet the religious seem to give allowance for their god's actions and inactions. It seems their god is allowed great cruelty, great cruelty that we would not tolerate from man or woman. I find this religious line of thought very curious. It seems that excuses are made to justify the insane illogical behavior of a religion's supposed god. Could it be that the illogical behavior exists because there is no Christian, Jewish, Muslim, or fill-in-the-blank manlike god?

Think about it. If the religious so strongly believe a god will save or cure them, then maybe they do not need doctors or hospitals. Maybe they should leave the medical teams to those of us with so little faith, and they can just sit home and pray to be saved. I wonder if a record was kept of those who avoided doctors and hospitals and only prayed for cures, and a record was kept of those who sought out doctors and a medical team for help, which record would record the most survivors and the most cured. I have no doubt it would be those who sought out medical help, so give credit where credit is due. Thank you, Doctor, for saving my life.

Just a thought.

Death Is a Fearful Reality We All Must Face

I had not thought about death much in my younger years, but it is a topic that I pause to think about more often these days upon my sixtieth orbit of the sun. What got me seriously thinking about death recently was something my wife spontaneously blurted out in my presence. My wife quietly said, "I don't want to die." She made this known to me with tears streaming down her face and a fearful look in her eyes. I could only look at my wife in surprise and ask myself, "What upset my wife so much that today of all days she is fearful of death?"

This day my wife received a telephone call from a close friend who painfully announced the friend's husband of many years died of a sudden heart attack at the relatively young age of fifty-eight. I met the man recently, and although I cannot say I ever spoke with him more than that two times in brief conversations, he struck me as a very nice man and a loving husband. He left three children and a loving wife behind him. My wife took his death to heart as she is good friends with his widow and she knew him to be a good man, husband, and father. And I'll tell you a lot of people must have loved this man because the line of visitors to his wake snaked around the building.

But I think what set my wife over the edge, beyond sympathy and compassion, is the awareness that she, having just turned fifty years of age at that time, is herself at risk of death given she is no longer a young woman in her twenties, thirties, or even forties—not that fifty is the end of life. Most men and women live well into their seventies and eighties, but fifty is a milestone for many of us—a milestone that gets us thinking about our mortality. As we age well into our middle and later middle years, we witness more of our friends and their parents suffering with issues of bad health, some with cancer and heart disease. My brother who is just four years older than myself (I am sixty) was diagnosed with a rare blood disorder when he was no older than fifty-four, which ended his work career and nearly took his life. If not for a heart transplant, he would not be here with us today. And even with the heart transplant, the underlying disorder that necessitated a heart transplant has not and cannot be cured. The disorder is manageable, but something he must live with for the rest of his life, which I hope to be a long one.

I myself came to grips with my own mortality just some years ago. One day, I was struck with abdominal pain that felt like I swallowed a boulder, and I suffered with it from midnight that day until 8:00 a.m. the next day. I was unable to sleep all night due to the pain. I did not want to wake my wife, so I writhed on the floor and/or paced the floor all night. In the morning, I tried to have a bowel movement, hoping that would solve my problem. Instead, I lost what looked like a quart or more of blood. I decided then to tell my wife that maybe I should see our doctor. As we got ready to leave for the hospital, I passed out. I quickly came to, but my wife telephoned an ambulance, and I was taken to our hospital. In the hospital, I received several blood transfusions, and I was constantly connected to IVs in both arms. The doctor who performed the endoscopy was not available until Monday, and I was admitted Saturday morning, so I lay in the hospital bed hooked up to machines and IVs with blood tests every eight hours—no food, urinating in a bottle, and/orally restrained from leaving my bed for any reason. I did convince the medical staff I could shower, and they agreed as long as my wife assisted me. That was a mistake. I passed out and fell on my wife. I awoke to eight arms wearing white coats reaching down to pick up my naked body. To me, at the time, me naked on the floor looking up at a bunch of doctors seemed funny. To my wife, it was scary. I was eventually diagnosed with a bleeding ulcer and scheduled for a procedure to seal what the doctor told me was a "quarter-sized" hole in my duodenum. Afterward, my blood count was still in the low twenties, and the medical staff was concerned enough that they would not entertain my release. Then the medical staff discovered my heart rate was far below normal (in the forties or fifties?), and they expressed concern about my heart rate. I was put through all kinds of extensive tests and was examined with all kinds of expensive machines. It was only six days in the hospital, but I remember that my resolve was starting to wear, and I chanted for about an hour one night, "I'm never going home." I called the night nurse to my room, and I demanded to be released so I could go home. The doctors talked me out of my going home, but I was becoming very depressed about my situation. I began to believe that I was going to die. It seemed to me that whenever I thought the medical staff had solved one problem and I would be told I would be going home soon, they found some other reason, or issue with me, that was to keep me there a while longer. Finally, the staff felt I was fit enough, and I was released. I celebrated with the medical staff and nearly jumped out the window just to get out of the building. On a side note, the medical staff was the most wonderful and caring group of people, and I feel extremely fortunate they were there to make be well again. It is easy to take medical care for granted. It is easy to take medical procedures and operations for granted. I could have died if they were not there to help me. I could not have healed myself. If my bleeding ulcer had hit me some two hundred years ago, I probably would be dead. We take medical help way to casually. I am very thankful.

When I got home, I had several panic attacks. I had never before felt the shadow of death, but now the fear of death had made itself known to me. A realization set in that I am mortal after all, and I can die. Unfamiliar thoughts filled my head that my now being fifty-five years of age, I have lived more than half my life. This, coupled with living through my brother's illness and his much closer encounter with death, brought a new outlook on all the other many deaths of friends and family I have experienced to this point in my life. I think, for me anyway, it is the deaths closest to me that bring forth the realization of my own mortality.

The truth to life is that life ends in death. Death is a certainty—maybe not a welcome one, but it is certain. It is difficult to experience the death of people we know, and it is difficult knowing that we ourselves will die someday. People create all kinds of philosophies to handle their fear of death. Religion is used by many as a way to ease their fear of death. The belief of a life after death makes death seem less final; it makes life that ends in death seem more purposeful. I personally am not a believer in life after death. I believe death is final, but that does not mean I fear death any more or any less. My personal experience has made me realize how precious life is while it is. I believe that while I live, I should live life to my fullest potential. And when my time comes to an end, I must accept death. I will have no choice in the matter. I believe once I die, I am gone. And once I am gone, I no longer exist. And once I no longer exist, there is no remorse, no regret, and no pain. Death is inevitable, but life is livable, so live while you live. Handle your fear of death in any way that lessens your fear, but live your life to its fullest.

Just a thought.

Why Reincarnation Is Irrational and Illogical

Reincarnation is an age-old belief that dates back as far as the creation of many popular religions. In fact, reincarnation is itself a religion or at least an intricate piece of many popular religions. Reincarnation is the religious or philosophical concept that the soul or spirit, after death, begins a new life in a new body that may be human, animal, or spiritual depending on the moral quality of the previous life's actions. This doctrine is a central tenet of the Indian religions—such as, Hinduism, Jainism, Buddhism, and Sikhism. It is also a common belief of religions—such as, Druidism, Spiritism, Theosophy, and Eckankar. There is even a possible argument that the story of Jesus and the story of his resurrection is a form of rein-carnation—a belief in reincarnation may be where the Jesus fable of resurrection was birthed.

But does reincarnation make sense? Is it logical? Is it rational? Is it realistic? My answer is "no."

To begin with, there is no proof that anyone has reincarnated from a previous life. Science cannot prove it; religion has not proved it. Oh, those who believe in reincarnation would have you believe that a soul travels from one body to another. That a soul contains the essence of the man, but all memory is wiped clean in the new body. An easy explanation (excuse) as to why those who wish to prove or disprove reincarnation cannot. But then that brings up the age-old argument of the irrational being, the religious faithful: "If you can-not disprove something, then there is always the possibility that that something is true. Hence, a belief in reincarnation can only mean reincarnation is true unless someone can prove otherwise." But the "truth" is that is a ridiculous and fallacious argument. It is no more valid an argument than to say, "You did not see Fred jump off a fif-ty-story building and hit the cement. So how do you know he did not survive?" Believe me, Fred is dead.

Think about this scenario if you will. If I were to tell you I lived before in another body and who I am today is the reincarnation of that earlier life, you might be curious enough to ask a few questions. For the sake of this scenario, I hope so. First question, "How do I know I am reincarnated?" Second question, "What led me to that conclusion—that is, what proof do I have that I am reincarnated?" I cannot think of a single logical answer to either question. Can you? I suppose I could answer, "I have dreams of a past life." But then who doesn't dream? I suppose I could answer, "I was hypnotized, and in my hypnotic state, I revealed a past life that I couldn't have known unless I lived it." Is any of that reasonable to believe? Is any of that within the realm of proof? No, it is not. It is pure imagination and/ or wishful thinking. That is where most religious thoughts and most mystic dreams are birthed. In one's head. In one's imagination. In one's hopes and out of one's fears. There is no more proof of reincar-nation today than there is of a religion's manlike god. All who believe in reincarnation as well as all who believe in organized popular reli-gions today believe in fables created by men long dead. I find it a little sad. I find it sad that so many people are so afraid of dying, so afraid of their mortality, so afraid that they must make up a fantasy to salve their fear. I find it sad so many people cannot face the reality of their life and our world. I find it so sad so many people cannot face their not being special. I find it so sad so many people are so afraid of reality that they create fictions like reincarnation and man-gods ruling over heavenly afterlives.

Now, once again, think about the possibility of my being rein-carnated, and think about this as well. There are about 7 billion human beings in the world today. I tell you, I was reincarnated from a previous life I lived in the year 500 BCE. Some sources put the world population at that time at about 100 million. Now that means about 6.9 billion new human bodies have been created since I previ-ously inhabited another body prior to my current body. Where did all the NEW souls come from? Am I just one of 100 million souls reincarnated from 500 BCE? If I am, then what about the other souls? They could not have been reincarnated. The other souls must be new souls. So how do we know who was reincarnated and who was newly created? If reincarnation exists for everyone, then new souls are being created that have yet to live a second life. Why are new souls constantly being created? And are new souls going to continually be created? And what purpose does reincarnation serve anyway? Some may argue to prove oneself over and over again until they reach a stage of being worthy of a heavenly existence. So I am to believe some heavenly god constantly creates new souls and tests these new souls by reincarnating only those who failed to prove worthy of heaven the first time? How long is the creation and testing going to go on? Is there a population limit? Will heaven eventually up the standard of acceptance or stop accepting applicants? The whole idea is rather ridiculous.

Reincarnation, like all man-god religions, is a man-made concept to ease one's fear of one's mortality and to aid one's acceptance of their meritocracy. If human kind wants to aspire to godlike status, if human beings wish to believe they have a greater purpose than all other life forms, if men and women aspire to live forever—then they should stop believing in ridiculous, made-up, and improvable concepts such as reincarnation and man-god religion and search for the real truth. Search for the answers. Don't be lazy. Don't make up the answers. Research how to extend human life. Support and contribute to scientists and medical researchers searching for answers how to save, cure, and extend lives. Join the search for our beginnings. Join the "real" world. For this is the only world you have. You have not been reincarnated from a previous life. You will not be reincarnated into a new life. The life you are living now is the only life you have and the only life you will ever have. Make the best of your life. Be happy with your life. Make this a better world for you and everyone else. Stop making excuses. Stop claiming this world is bad and we all need to die, be reincarnated or whatever, to make it to a better world, a heaven; heaven does not exist except possibly on this planet and for you only during your lifetime.

Just a thought.

Every Religion Believes It Is the Right Faith Following the Correct Beliefs

One of the many things I find disturbing about organized religions is that each individual religion presents itself as right; each religion claims to be the correct answer to life with no chance of being wrong. And of course, it follows that all nonmembers are, without a doubt, wrong. It doesn't have to be said; it just naturally can be inferred.

It appears to me that anyone not included in the club is less than perfect and obviously following a path toward philosophical error and possibly damnation. There can be no room for error according to the established religions, so everyone must join their club or be looked upon unfavorably. A religion presents itself as the one true correct philosophy, and unless we are onboard, we are flawed; we are wrong. And in the eyes of the established religions, they do not have to prove the very foundations of their philosophies to demand all to become members. They believe the very fact their clubs have existed for hundreds and/or thousands of years makes them right. Just like the once held belief of many religious groups that the sun revolves around the Earth, a belief by many for thousands of years, time makes it right. Their belief has earned tenure. Facts, truth, reality—all are meaningless to the major religions. But faith—yes, faith is the only credible key. How often do you hear that the key to eternal life is "faith"? The established religions claim to be right about everything they say, preach, and do—despite their having no logical foundation to their claims, despite no foundation in reality, despite no proof for the vary base their philosophy rests upon. Facts and logic appear meaningless. Just have faith, little one, and eternal life will be yours.

Believe what we say although we cannot prove anything we say; just know we are right. We are the only ones with the true answers to life and an eternal existence. Join our club, and you too will find heaven. We won't pressure you to join our faith, but if you want to succeed in our community and get work and live forever, you should consider joining.

I find it very insulting that the Jewish philosophy claims they are "the chosen ones." This implies anyone not Jewish is less than special as a human being—that merely being born Jewish makes you a favorite of the god. I do not like the inference that I am less special, less significant than other human beings just because I am not Jewish. My wife is Jewish, and I love her, along with my children—more than any other human beings on this planet—and to me they are special, but not because they are Jewish. They are special because of who they are and who they are to me.

I find it very insulting that the Christian philosophy infers I must be baptized and become a member of their club or risk the fiery pits of some place they call hell. I was raised a Catholic, but I quickly realized I was no more or no less special as a human being than the next guy, Catholic or not. This is another example of a group claiming their barbaric ritual (one they created—it was not god sent) is the only way to "salvation." Just because I do not believe in bearded men with wings living in clouds should not mean I am going to some fiery hell upon my death to be tortured forever. Heck, we should be applauded for not believing in bearded men living in clouds. Isn't that kind of comic book-like in its storyline? And what is the deal with hell anyway? To me, hell appears to be an obvious scare tactic to recruit members. And where is this hell anyway? According to religious history, it's located below the Earth's surface . . . No, wait, now it's at the center of the Earth . . . No, wait, now it's in another dimension? Damn, that science—the more science reveals about our world, the further away religion moves its hell.

So what is it that really irks me about the established religions claims of being the true and only answer to life's questions? It's the evil that comes from their claims. People are favored in jobs, communities, politics, clubs, friendships, and more, merely because they are

Jewish, Catholic, Muslim, or whatever. Legislation is skewed one way or the other based on the erroneous religious beliefs of legislators, lobbyists, and special-interest groups. Public schools are brought into the fray because of the many teachers who want all children to be raised believing in their same erroneously held beliefs. Religious philosophies are forced on men, women, and children who fear arguing; otherwise it will cost them friends, jobs, and a chance at a better life. Even the courts and the Supreme Court of the United States are affected by the religious beliefs of the constituents. There is no one and nothing that is not touched, that is not affected, by the erroneous beliefs of these flawed religious philosophies. And the irony is that this country of the US created a Constitution to keep this from happening—a Constitution that is consistently ignored by the legislative branch, the executive branch, and the judicial branch of this country. Watching a past Republican presidential debate, I consistently witnessed debaters—Mitt Romney, especially—try to turn fellow Republican Ron Paul's respect for the US Constitution into a joke. The real joke is that not enough people realize Ron Paul's respect for the US Constitution shows him as someone who respects the core of this country's beliefs, and one of those core beliefs is separation of church and state. Oh, but to paraphrase a past president, "We all believe in god." No, we don't! And even those who do believe in a god do not believe in the same god, or at least not in the same way—else they would be of the same philosophy and belong to the same religious club.

I suggest we all search for the real truth. I suggest we search for reality. Do not get lost in the erroneous philosophies of the major religions. Do not make up your own religion. Do not believe the voices in your head. Especially, do not believe the voices in other people's heads. Think for yourself. Discuss your thoughts and your beliefs with others. But research, study, read, and discuss your thoughts and your beliefs with a little logic. Search for real answers. And if you live your entire life without ever finding the answers to the "big" questions, just remember you are not alone. The major religions do not have the answers either; they just pretend to have the answers or self-delude themselves into believing they have the answers. Know that no one religious group is any better off or better prepared for death than you.

Know the truth that when people with no answers to questions of great importance stop looking for answers to those questions, the answers will never be found. Keep looking.

Just a thought.

Many Religions Claim Man Is Made in God's Image

The Judeo-Christian faiths claim man is made in their god's image. Have you ever really thought about this claim? We are made in god's image. That means not only do we look like god, but the reverse is true as well: god looks like us. Makes sense, right? Think about it.

For god to look like us, god must have the same body parts as us. God must not just be a holographic image of us but a complete replica; he must have the same internal organs as us. If not, why would he have the same outside appearance as us? Ask yourself these questions. Does not a mouth have teeth, a tongue, and connect to a throat? Does not a throat lead to a stomach and intestines and an anus? If god has all these similarly human parts and god and humans look alike, surely god also has a heart, lungs, and a brain. This makes sense, does it not? If your answer to my question is no, then you have to admit god does not look like us and that we are not made in god's image.

Now think a little deeper. If god has a mouth with teeth and a tongue all leading to a stomach, then does it not seem logical that god eats? And if god eats, what does god eat? Does god eat chicken, burgers, tacos? The Jewish faith might argue god eats kosher. Catholics might argue god eats fish and no meat on Fridays. But why does god need to eat? Is he not god? And if god eats, where does he shop for his food? Does god shop at the local God's supermarket? I suppose he could just wish for food, and it would appear, but why should he have to wish for food? Is he not god? Why should god have to eat? For us mere mortals, if we don't eat, we die. Does that mean god can die if he doesn't eat? I thought god was immortal and has lived forever. And I don't know about god, but after I eat a little too much, I get gas and eventually, I poop. Does god belch now and then? Oh, yeah . . . that's thunder. And does god poop? If he does, where does he do his business? Does god poop in the godly toilet? Or does that explain the asteroids orbiting our solar system. You may think I am being insulting in my choice of questions, but I truly believe these are legitimate questions to religion's claim that we are made in god's image.

And to continue the bodily comparisons, why would god need a heart and lungs? Why should an immortal being living somewhere in space need a heart and lungs? Don't both organs require oxygen to function as intended? Modern science, which even the major religions will admit, has proven oxygen is a gas that is included in our atmosphere and our atmosphere is a thin layer surrounding our planet. I think we all agree that if a man or woman leaves this planet's atmosphere, as astronauts do, man still remains tethered to the Earth via oxygen he brings with him and/or her. Is god tethered to the Earth? Does god carry oxygen tanks along with him so he can breathe when he travels through space? I assume god no longer lives on Earth as the major religions have moved heaven from the clouds of Earth to some realm or dimension that is unseen or unreachable by man; religion has continually sold god's house and moved god into a different neighborhood whenever science proves god's current home is nonexistent. God's constantly being on the run brings me to another question. Why does god feel he needs to hide from us? Why does god flee whenever science gets closer to heaven?

But I digress. Let's get back to the bodily organs we supposedly share. If god has lungs like us, why does god need lungs? If I stop breathing, I die. Does this mean god can die from lack of oxygen? I thought god could never die. If god has a heart like us, why does god need a heart? Does blood and oxygen run through his godly veins? What if god's heart stops? Can god have a heart attack?

And how can we not talk about sexual organs. As humans seem so completely preoccupied with their sexual organs, how can we not ask why god has a penis and testicles? Why does god need a penis? Why does god need testicles? I guess if god eats, he does need a way to relieve liquid waste, but why a penis? Isn't a penis shaped the way it is so it can find its way into a female's vagina? And isn't the purpose of inserting a penis into a vagina to release testicular sperm into the female for the purpose of reproduction? And if god has a penis, does god get horny? Does god have a girlfriend or a wife? The Bible says man should not fornicate. Historically, and even in many religious cultures today, man is not allowed to have sex outside of marriage (not that this tenet stops even the most faithful), so I assume either god masturbates or he is married and has regular sex with his wife. But that would mean there is a Mrs. God. I thought there was only "one" god. Oh, but I guess that is up for interpretation, right? Look at the Christian religion. They believe in "one" god, yet they claim Jesus is the son of god. Wouldn't that make Jesus a god or at least a demigod? Oh, this is all too confusing. If only I had faith.

So think about what I just wrote. Think of your own analogies. And when you have thought it over awhile, ask yourself if man is made in god's image.

Just a thought.

If God Exists and Heaven Is the
Goal, Why Fight Death?

I find it interesting that many religious followers believe the ultimate goal is heaven, life after death, and yet they fight tooth and nail to avoid death. Why is that? If the ultimate goal for the religious is heaven, if the ultimate goal for the religious is sitting at the right hand of god—why fight to prolong one's existence on this Earth? Why not let nature take its course and go to god when called? This desire to live and prolong one's life is an obvious contradiction to the religious proclamation that heaven is the ultimate goal: to leave this life and be with god should be a desirable objective.

I understand that some religious faithful believe suicide to be a sin against god. I can appreciate that as a tenet of one's faith—so long as they do not project their belief on to others who do not follow their faith. But suicide aside, why do the religious fight death? Why do they cling to life as much as any proclaimed atheist? An atheist clinging to life, I can understand. An atheist believes in life here on Earth only; an atheist does not believe in an afterlife. So to an atheist, death is final. But why do the religious cling to life with equal passion? Do not the religious have "faith" in their own faith? Are the religious fearful of the afterlife? Do not the religious want to meet and live with their god? The religious claim the ultimate goal in their existence is to be with their god. So why delay? If god comes calling, should they not answer the call?

I have heard arguments that god has a plan for "his" people. And a sudden death caused by natural causes, or by an environmental disaster—such as a typhoon, earthquake, hurricane, or tornado—or even by fault of another human being or by accident, all are part of god's plan. It is common amongst the religious to say after a death that, "Her death is all part of god's plan." Or speaking of the recently departed that, "They are in heaven with their maker now. Now they are at peace in a better world." But if the religious truly believe these words, then why do they do everything possible to prevent death? By attempting to prevent a natural death, is not the religious going against the will of god? Did not god create man and all his weaknesses? Does not god's plan call for all people to eventually die? Is it not contradictory to say "It is god's will" and in the same breath say "God intervened through doctors or men to save a life?" Is it not men who intervene and prevent god's will from coming about? Doctors are men and women, not god. And should not the religious do everything in their power to make god's will be done? But they do not. To paraphrase a fight game expression, "The religious talk the talk but don't walk the walk."

Is not the alternate argument as follows: any artificial intervention by man to prevent death is in contradiction and in conflict with god's plan? If the religious truly believe life and death is god's plan, then why seek medical help when ill? If a person has a bad heart, why seek a heart transplant? Is not a bad heart god's way of saying, "I am ready for you to sit by my side? Come to a better place. Be with me in heaven." If you blow out your knee, why repair it? Is it not god's will you blew out your knee? Maybe god's plan is for you to live your life with a bad knee. Yet the religious seek medical help. When our children are very young, they come down with fevers and infections and many sicknesses. But we don't say, "It is in god's hands." We seek help from our pediatricians, men and women trained to prevent natural death. We seek the help of surgeons, men and women trained to repair that which nature injured and/or broke, trained to save lives from passing on to god's kingdom. We seek cures to illness with man-made medicines. Why? Is not illness god's way of saying, "It is your time to be with me"? And should not the religious want their child to go to heaven as soon as god calls for them? Is it not selfish to contradict god's calling to keep an ill child here with us?

When natural disasters strike, why protect ourselves from them? Why build retaining walls to keep out floods? Why seek shelter from tornadoes? Is not a natural disaster god's way of bringing us home to him? Isn't it part of god's plan? God created nature, did he not? If god has a plan and god created the Earth, are not natural disasters part of his plan? And would not an "all-knowing being" be aware that tornadoes, earthquakes, hurricanes, and other natural disasters will cause loss of human life? I would think the religious want to expedite their way into heaven. Why wait if god is calling? Why ignore god's calling? Why run from god's call? Do they fear death? Do they fear god? Does life actually mean more to them than the opportunity to be in heaven with their god?

There are many contradictions in the religious expression of desirability for heaven and their claim that life here on Earth has less value than heaven. I challenge the religious to live up to their claims. Do not seek medical help when sick, injured, and/or dying. Do not partake of vaccines. Do not hide from natural disasters. Accept your god, and go to him when called. Or change your pronouncements of a better world after life on Earth and admit you would rather remain here on Earth. Admit you do not believe in life after death and this life here on Earth is the only life you will ever live.

If the religious cannot follow through on their own beliefs of an afterlife, if the religious choose to fight death in an attempt to prolong their life here on Earth—then they should admit they doubt the entire concept of heaven and an afterlife. The religious should give credit where credit is due. We owe so much for our prolonged lives to the medical profession. We owe so much for our survival in this life to human beings who search for knowledge to aid in our survival, our repair, and the lengthening of our lifespans. If not for human beings willing to train themselves beyond memorization of a few prayers, if not for human beings willing to train themselves in how the human body works and how to repair it, if not for human beings willing to teach themselves how to manipulate the elements of the Earth to better our lives, if not for these individuals—god would take so many more of us to heaven on a daily basis.

The religious cannot have it both ways. I have no doubt, however, someone religious will manufacture a counterargument similar to the following: "God works through the doctors. God works through scientists and engineers." But they cannot have it both ways. The religious cannot claim that their god calls them to heaven when their time is at hand—that their god calls them by illness, accident, injury, or what may, and then in the same breath say, "God saved me through the hands of a surgeon." Not true, not a valid explanation. Either god is calling or god is not calling. If you believe in a godly plan, then accept your fate. If not then seek medical help. The first is god's plan. The latter is human intervention. I advised seeking the latter if you wish to continue existing.

If god exists and heaven is your goal, then do not fight death. Embrace your god. Embrace his heaven. Embrace his plan. Ignore the ignorant scientists and engineers and doctors who fight to save and prolong life. Ignore those who fight to make life safer and easier. Ignore the ignorant that fight for life here on Earth. If you truly believe your own religious faith and its claim of an afterlife, embrace it and leave life to those who embrace life here on Earth. But I caution you. You do so at great risk that your religious beliefs are fantasy and your life will be over.

Just a thought.

I Am Jesus Son of God, and I Am Resurrected

The time has come once again to reveal my presence to man. Many of my other creations knew my identity at the date of my earthly conception, but man does not recognize truth as readily, so I must make my pronouncement. I came once before. I was born to woman in the town of Bethlehem on the West Bank, some six miles south of Jerusalem. I lived with my earthly mother and her husband until I decided the time was right to preach the word of my father, our lord in heaven. I befriended, and taught the truth to, followers who carried on my teachings well past the time of my earthly departure. I allowed my own people to be instrumental in my death—a death meant to bring attention to our God—and so all would know who I was and how much my father loves them. I rose from the dead three days thereafter. I shook off my earthly body and revealed my spiritual self to my closest followers, so they would have no doubt who I was, and so they would spread the word of God my father throughout the world.

Christianity, as my new Judaism is called, has thrived since my departure. So I now return to the world of man to reveal the final stages of God our father's plan. It is time to believe or not believe. Faith is the only word of worth. You must believe I am who I say I am with as much faith and fervor as those faithful believed in me when I came as and in the body Jesus the carpenter. I now come to you as and in the body of Gregory the lawyer. I will reveal more of the father's plan as time goes on, but you must have faith and believe in me and believe in our father. Do not doubt, for doubt means lack of faith. And no faith means ignorance of the truth—ignorance of God and the light and the way.

Throw off the shackles of your science. Believe in the words of your fathers and their prophets of long ago. Believe in the books of God—the Bible, the Talmud. Know I am the word. And as when I came before, believe in me, and you believed in me then believe in me now.

And if you believe me not, prove me wrong. But to consider to prove me wrong is to lack faith in God our father.

If Jesus was born today, would you believe he was the son of god?

Just a thought.

Does God Know He Is Here?

Have you ever wondered what it would be like to be god? Have you ever wondered what it would be like to be a supreme being that exists alone within himself—a being that has existed for all time and before time, a being that knows he will exist for all time and after time, a being who is all wise, a being who knows everything, a being that cannot be judged, a being that cannot be challenged, a being who is always awake and never sleeps.

If you were a god, what would you think? What would you do? Do you think you would eventually become bored? I mean, you already know everything and you have lived a very long time. Do you think you might become depressed? Do you think it might be lonely being a god?

I think being a god cannot be easy. A god may ponder all the aforementioned thoughts I wrote, and a god may wonder what it would be like to be a man. How would god feel being a man? How would god think if a man? If god became a man and blanked his memory that he was once god, would god believe that god existed? Would god have faith that god is there as god expects man should? Would god fear death? Would god make the right choices in life? Would god choose good over evil? Might god then question himself and ponder that maybe this is the one scenario even he may not have the answers? What is it like to be a man?

Now imagine god thought about becoming a man. Imagine god acting on his thought and god becoming a man. God is all-powerful. God could take the form of man and be born to woman with the appearance of having a human father. For all we know, god did. For all we know, god walks amongst us as a man this very day. God could be out there somewhere looking and acting like any other man. We fail to see him as god because he is god and god can do and be whatever he wants. God can allow us to see or not to see whatever he wishes, and maybe god wishes us to only see him, not as God, but as a man.

What if god walks amongst as a man, but god has no knowledge that he is god? What I mean to say is, what if god intentionally stripped his conscious mind of all memory that he is god? The reason why he would do this, you ask? So he, god, can experience what it is to be a man. How best to experience being a man with all man's failings and weaknesses and strengths than to believe you are a man and not god? So god acts on his ponder, and now god walks amongst us as a man. Yet god does not know he is god. God believes he is man.

What kind of man—or woman—do you think god might be if god acted on this thought to be a man? When I say man, I really mean human being; god could be a woman. Do you think god would choose the spotlight? Would god choose to be a politician, a celebrity, a religious leader, or maybe a lawyer? God forbid, a lawyer? Or do you think god would choose to be a small, meek man. A man barely noticed by other men, so as to observe mankind and not be observed by mankind so much. So as to suffer the domination of other stronger men and the evils of the world and to appreciate how the meek feel? Is god walking amongst this very day? Are you god?

Just a thought.

Chapter 5

POLITICAL

The Real Definition of Royalty
is Bloodthirsty Butcher

This is one thing wrong with America! The interest Americans show in royalty is absolutely ludicrous and un-American. To the royalty admiring people amongst us—you do realize there was a war with a monarchy to end a monarchy as our controlling government? Americans preoccupied with the rich royalty, glorifying them and treating royalty as a privileged class to be admired should read a little history. Monarchies were created by force by bloodthirsty wars where thousands were killed—men, women, and children—so a few who then would call themselves royalty could take control of everyone's land, belongings, and to make slaves of everyone not of their inner circle. YES, America, African Americans were not the only slaves throughout history; they are just the ones we talk about here in America. EVERY NATIONALITY you can think of at one time or another HAD slaves and/or were slaves—slaves of a few ruthless barbarians who forced their way into control of the greater populous. The entire indigenous American populations, both North and South, were destroyed mercilessly by the Spanish and other European nations just so they could take their gold and silver (and later cotton and other valuables). And the Native Americans were made into the slaves, the ones that were not butchered, of the Europeans— their land, their culture, their pride, their women, their lives decimated for their GOLD, their children's futures decimated as well. All throughout history, this has been the case. And these women who called themselves "princesses" (I use the term *princess* loosely) are the descendants of mercenaries, killers, rapists, butchers, and thieves.

They are not to be admired. No one should teach their daughters to be a princess is a good thing, because it is NOT.

Given this misplaced admiration, I am not surprised Americans voted for a KING as their president—a rich, spoiled, merciless, woman-hating, gold-loving tyrant. How far we have NOT come in two hundred plus years. The Republicans mention our forefathers regularly, yet I doubt our forefathers would mention them regularly. If our forefathers were alive today, our current Congress, our current president, his cabinet, his Benedict Arnold mouth-pieces would not be viewed in a positive light. No, America, "royalty"—princesses, princes, kings, and queens—are not good role models. This commentary is my opinion and my opinion only.

Just a thought.

It's Time to Become a Nation of Peace, Not War

Since World War II, our nation, these United States, have become an unrelenting war machine. Our nation has become an imperialistic power bent on controlling the world and the world economy through military supremacy and nuclear threat. We are the only nation to have used nuclear weapons on another nation, and we are the only nation to repeatedly threaten their use (that maybe changing with the development of North Korea). Throughout these years, our people have been brainwashed by our leaders—leaders who have increasingly come from the ranks of the military or corporate elite. We have been convinced our current militaristic society is necessary for our survival. THIS IS NOT TRUE!

Even former President Eisenhower, a general of great importance in World War II, believed the Pentagon (created during World War II) should have been dismantled early post-World War II. The Cold War that came about when the Soviet Union attained its own atom bomb was a fabrication by the military out of paranoia of the possibility of the ultimate end to all life or at least civilization as we know it (never justified). Even the American statesman Henry L. Stimpson at that time, out of fear of a Cold War, wanted the military machine that he saw the Pentagon would become, to be dismantled along with our military forces, and he and others wanted to share our nuclear secrets with the world—all with the intent to avoid a Cold War. Stimpson lost that argument. The Cold War began and thrived, to our detriment and to the detriment of the world at large. The Cold War finally ended during Ronald Reagan's term as president, but it almost did not come to an end despite the difficult task of ending undertaken solely by Mikhail Gorbachev the then-leader of the "Evil Empire" of the Soviet Union. Yes, it was Gorbachev, not Ronald Reagan, who brought about the end of the Soviet Union and the Cold War. Ronald Regan did his utmost to continue the Cold War until he and his political career were caught in the headlights of the Iran Contra Affair, which left him no choice but to go along with Gorbachev so as to draw attention away from his war-hawking regime. As a side note, I find it interesting and dumbfounding that Reagan could be involved in such a blatant illegal act as providing funds to the Contras in violation of Congress and US law and remain president while a few years later Republican politicians would attempt impeachment of Democrat President Bill Clinton because of a White House blow job. Politics always win out over the people's welfare and US law.

We are a nation that claims to be THE NATION OF PEACE, yet WE are the nation that has historically supported dictators. We are the nation starting "preemptive" wars. We are the nation with military bases in some 130 countries around the world. How would we react with a Chinese or Russian military base in our country? How would we react with a North Korean military presence in Canada or Cuba aiming weapons at our border? I believe such a scenario was before us, and the issue was answered by President Kennedy and our nation in the year 1962.

As the former Soviet Union began disarming and withdrawing from its satellite neighbors and allowing the dismantling of the Berlin Wall, effectively ending the Cold War, the United States responded by illegally attacking Panama. As a former Soviet ambassador said to a former US ambassador at that time, it looks like YOU are now the threatening power. When Gorbachev began lessening the quantity and strength of his country's nuclear arsenal, George H. W. Bush responded in kind—by retiring antiquated tactical weapons that the Pentagon no longer saw as feasible to our war effort. In other words, the Pentagon did not respond in kind or in good faith. The Pentagon and our president talked about how much they wanted to end the Cold War, but did they really? Actions speak louder than words.

We live in a nation today that tells us to FEAR THE WORLD. A nation that tells us but for our beloved Pentagon all us would be dead by nuclear attack and/or overrun by militaristic countries such as China, Russia, North Korea—the list goes on. The TRUTH—OUR LEADERS ARE OUR WORST enemies. We live in a military-run system of government. We work within an economy that thrives on the proliferation of the military and the production of weapons of mass and conventional destruction. Our elected leaders would rather cut spending of the tax dollars they take from us the middle class (the rich are proportionally, if not totally, exempt) on programs such as Medicare, Medicaid, and Social Security—programs WE (NOT THEY, THE RICH) pay more than our fair share for—than cut spending on an unnecessary, militaristic machine run by the Pentagon, which does nothing to protect us and everything to subjugate us and the world on behalf of survival of the Pentagon and the military machine itself as well as corporate America which IS/ARE OUR POLITICAL LEADERS. We need entitlements such as Medicare, Medicaid, and Social Security to assist us in times of need, to assist the poor and helpless in our society. We do not need excessive spending on a self-perpetuating military machine and the Pentagon, which does nothing but start wars to justify its own existence and give us nothing in return—not peace, just war and fear.

We need to divorce our country from these rich corporate politicians that make up our current Congress/Senate, executive branch, and judicial branch, and we need to close down the Pentagon and become the nation we claim to be—A NATION OF PEACE. Currently, we are not a nation of peace; we are an imperialistic empire that uses military force to control its people, the world, and our economy as well as the world economy. We should not be the police of the world and not because as some believe that the world should take care of itself; the world WANTS TO take care of itself. We should not be the police of the world because we claim to be a nation of peace, not war, and being the police of the world states otherwise. STOP and THINK. What nation is attacking us? What nation is threatening us? And then stop and think, who is really threatening who and why? It is THIS nation that is threatening the world. It is this nation that is bringing other nations into a world of fear where they feel it necessary to arm themselves to defend themselves against a possible "preemptive" attack by us if our economy and our Pentagon should so deem it helpful to the survival of the Pentagon and the flourishing of our economy and the survival of our 5 percent rich.

END THE WAR MACHINE. END THE PENTAGON. ELECT MIDDLE-CLASS POLITICIANS who strive to help US, not the rich. END this war machine that strives to perpetuate the Pentagon's war machine and the rich corporation's asset build-up—all of which is done at our expense and all of which is done at the expense of PEACE in our country and peace in the world.

PEACE begins at home. Peace is a civilian economy run by most of us, not just a few of us. Peace is not born from weapons contracts. Peace is negotiating with our neighbors on an even table in good faith, not by threats of war and economic destruction. To truly be the model nation of peace we claim to be, we must be a nation of peace not war. Currently, we are not a nation of peace; we are a nation of war. Only we can change our nation. This commentary is my opinion and my opinion only.

Just a thought.

War . . . What Is It Good For?

War . . . what is it good for? I am positive you have heard that phrase before. It's even a popular song sung by Edwin Starr. So what is war good for? Well, apparently, there are millions throughout history who think war is good for something. Not me. I think war is good for nothing, but then as usual, I'm in the minority. Today people praise war. People shout for war. At my son's high school graduation, one of the speakers presiding over the ceremony at one point asked all students going to a four-year school to stand up. There was a small applause. He then asked all students going to a technical school to stand up. Again, there was a small applause. He then asked the small number of students going into the military to stand up, and then he asked everyone in the audience to stand up and applaud, and the entire room (except for me) stood on their feet screaming applause. Why, because the two or three high school graduates were going to defend our lives from terrorists? Really, they are going to defend me from whom? What is the real truth here? These naive high school graduates are enlisting in the military to most likely fight as mercenaries for corporate and political greed. This is my opinion only and should not be taken as the truth. I do not know any of the graduates, and I do not know what battles—if any—they will be involved in if they do, in fact, enlist in the military and if they do, in fact, fight in a battle. I also have no proof or inside information regarding the military and the military's modus operandi. It is my opinion, however, that the USA is not involved in any legitimate war today. In my opinion, men and women enlisting in our military are subject to battles where they may shoot and kill but merely to take control or maintain control of worldwide assets for the corporate elite in this country.

It is definitely not the 'sixties anymore. In the 'sixties, people were screaming and protesting for peace. The sixties are long gone, and now everyone—at least here in war-hawk America—everyone is shouting for war. It doesn't matter what the reason or where the reason arises. Americans scream for war. Americans want to be involved in every war in the world. Apparently, only Americans know what is best for the rest of the much-older world. Americans are right about everything. America is land of the free and home of the brave, so why shouldn't Americans dictate their policies to the world and police the world as well to make sure our policies are carried through to fruition? I think that question should be asked again and answered differently. Why shouldn't Americans dictate their policies to the world and police the world as well to make sure our policies are carried through to fruition? Because Americans are not as free as they think. America is not the land of the free and home of the brave. America is land of the lied to and the land of the ignorant. America is the land of those who believe just about anything they are told, and America has become a police state. Freedoms are disappearing quicker than a Muslim can bow down to pray. Americans are oblivious to their true state of being; they believe they have more freedom today than yesterday, and that is far from true. We are spied upon by government with impunity. We are taxed to the teeth by government. We are lied to by government. When government tells us they are giving us a tax break, they are giving themselves and their rich friends' tax breaks, not you and me. If you want to become rich today, become a politician, then you can take bribes from corporations and foreign powers and use ignorant poor people to die in battles fighting for your personal riches under the guise of freedom fighting.

And here is an interesting thought: centuries ago, when wars were "declared" and when wars were fought, the leaders, the kings, the generals, the very men who started the wars, were also engaged in the wars. Today our leaders in the executive branch and Congress, and even our high-ranking generals, start the wars but send naive "patriots" into battle to fight the war and risk life and limb for them.

While our soldiers are risking their lives, our president, Congress, and generals are sitting in their ivory towers protected by bodyguards sipping champagne, eating caviar, vacationing, and living in the lap of luxury. And if the war plans do not work out as expected for anyone of these leaders, who do you think escapes the wrath of the victorious opposition? Not the soldier. Not the civilians on either side of the conflict. Our fearless leaders, of course, because we all know government cannot function without our fearless leaders. And we all know that soldiers and civilians are EXPENDABLE. That is the sad truth. Face it, and believe it.

The world leaders of today are cowards living off the blood sweat and tears of naive and many times impoverished souls who join the military for all the wrong reasons. They join to fight for freedom, and they are actually fighting for corporate wallets. I have to believe many young men and women join the military because they are poor and unskilled to do anything else. I have to believe many young men and women join the military because they are poor and the military entices them to join by offering a paid education. Education is expensive, and you cannot beat a paid education with a military background on your résumé when job hunting. And unfortunately, I have to believe some men and women join the military because they like the legalized excuse and license to shoot and kill people. I feel for those men and women who feel forced to join the military because they feel they have no other job choices, and I feel for the naive. I don't feel sorry for those men and women who enlist to get and education because they are only putting their own needs above the lives and welfare of others if engaged in battles of questionable legitimacy. I definitely feel nothing by anger toward those men and women looking for an opportunity to do battle for battle's sake. War is not and should not be a game.

It amazes me how many people want to become involved in the military and fight wars or at least encourage others to do so. Even on our civilian streets, this bloodthirsty desire for war is evident. Take a good look at our men and women in blue. The police are armed like the military. The police are armed like soldiers. The police act like soldiers and treat us civilians like enemy soldiers. Many police departments are not merely equipped to handle domestic affairs and traffic control. A lot of police departments have tanks and body armor and weapons of incredible power. And you cannot convince me the police do not break the same laws we must uphold. I get the impression being a cop means one no longer has to abide by the same rules. And forget about the words "To protect and serve" written on the side of many police vehicles. Call for a cop if you are in trouble, and start your stopwatch to time how long it takes for them to show up. Take note of how unconcerned they are about your predicament when they arrive. Note how many cops show up. Then take note of when a cop needs the assistance of another cop. Take note of the multitude of cops that fly out of seemingly nowhere to aid their "brother officer." Take note of the violence and quickness to shoot, harm, and kill anyone they perceive as acting negative or threatening to another cop. It doesn't seem to me that cops "protect and serve" the public. It appears to me more like cops protect and serve themselves. Just the use of the words "brotherhood of police" by cops, I find as insulting to the general public. If cops don't want to work to protect civilians, if civilians are a distance second to cops as goes that "protect and serve," then maybe that cop should not be a police officer. I thought the idea behind "protect and serve" was about police putting civilians first, not themselves. I thought police were supposed to be brave men and women who cared about the average Joe and Sue and put their lives on the line for us. I was very disillusioned in my belief about what the police stand for. Cops put themselves first. That is evident from the very bad, condescending behavior they exhibit whenever they interact with the rest of us. And just as men and women in blue armor put themselves first before our safety, our government leaders put themselves first.

So the next time you find yourselves shouting "Let's go to war"; the next time you find yourself praising mercenaries fighting corporate battles for overseas assets and land, THINK and ask yourself, "Is there a valid reason for this war? Who profits from this war? Are our leaders so sure of the need for this war that they are willing to go to battle alongside our soldiers?" Many of our government leaders fought in the Revolutionary War, and many of our Congressional leaders fought in the Civil War. Why is it that none of today's leader's fight in the wars they start? So ask our leaders many questions as to why it is necessary to send our sons and our daughters overseas to fight a war. Ask our leaders to *prove* this war they want our soldiers to fight is more than a facade for political gain and/or corporate power.

War . . . what is it good for? As the song goes, war is good for absolutely nothing.

Just a thought.

We Must Be Responsible.
We Must Exercise Our Power.

Why do the majority of Americans refuse to nominate candidates from either party who have no or little baggage going into an election for president? For those who hate candidates like Hillary Clinton and those who hate candidates like Donald Drumpf, who is to blame for their party nominations? There were many other candidates to select from in the 2016 presidential election, especially on the Republican side. I could easily have seen myself voting for Democrat Bernie Sanders or Republican John Kasich. And I could easily see so much less hate and espionage resorted to in this term's election if those two seasoned politicians were the candidates nominated to represent their parties as candidates for the presidency.

Remember, we do have a say and as well a part in the fault of who is selected as our candidates for office. Party politics have changed drastically since the 'sixties. I find it incredible the number of people who post-nomination claim they hate both chosen candidates, and yet an overwhelming majority of voters chose these two candidates as the representatives of their respective Republican and Democratic parties. If so many Republicans and Democrats do not like the candidates they have chosen, then they have only themselves and their parties to blame—as well as their fellow Republicans and Democrats, respectively. And if they did not vote for a candidate or they voted for a nonviable candidate instead of one of the party favorites, again they have only themselves to blame. Maybe it is time to become an independent?

But no matter your party of choice—it is always the right time to vote! Not voting and leaving the candidate choice solely to others is capitulation of your power to be a part of the selection process. Not voting or throwing away your vote on a nonelectable candidate is a poor excuse to blame others for the choice others are brave enough to make. Voting is the one power we have that can influence so much in our and others' lives that it should not be wasted by writing in your mother-in-law or some other nonviable candidate as some Republicans (Bush) stated they would do or did. It is no different than not voting at all. Yes, sometimes the choice must be made between the lesser of two evils. THAT IS THE ADULT thing to do; that is the responsible thing to do; that is the right thing to do. We give the president a lot of power. The president gets to choose many individuals to help exercise and implement that power. We have to take this and ALL elections seriously. We have to vote!

Just a thought.

We Live in a Sexist World!

When will the world wake up and admit it believes women are inferior to ANY man. Most people are in denial. Men AND WOMEN are in denial. Even many women believe themselves inferior to men. It is not sexual equipment of birth that defines the intellect and the integrity and the compassion and the abilities and the fitness to lead this world. If any of us believe that, then we condemn our daughters upon birth to second-class citizenship. I like to think of myself as an intelligent—not smart, but intelligent person (there is a difference), but I do not kid myself, believing I am more intelligent than someone else merely because of the sexual equipment born to me.

On behalf of myself, my wife, my daughters, my mother, my sisters, and all the women I know—I take offense to any philosophy in this world whether it defines itself as religion or custom or government that denigrates and subjugates and pins women down into a second-class position merely because they are not men, merely because they have no penis and they can give birth to children. How is that inferior? I live in the United States of America—a country that has fought for women's rights, a country that has fought for the freedom and equal rights of all men and all women, a country that commenced with certain beliefs of the freedom of people and rule by the people, a country that has grown to implement and expand on those beliefs of a country by the people for the people. I do not believe in tolerating any country, any philosophy, any religion, any cultural customs, and any foreign government's directive that impinges on our United States Constitution and our form of government and our civil rights—for all our people. I do not believe in tolerating antiquated beliefs that women should be under the control of men as some religions, cultures, and philosophies so dictate. I do not believe in treating women as anything but equal. I believe the recent 2016 presidential election brought out the true feelings of many in not only this country but most of this world. Many men AND WOMEN in this world believe a woman is a less serious and an inferior candidate to lead any government.

I believe the bar had been set so low for Donald Trump (a man?) in the 2016 election that Trump could shoot the pope and not lose a single follower. I believe the bar had been set so high for Hillary Clinton in the 2016 election that she could cure cancer and she would still be referred to as that "nasty woman" by the many woman haters (and that group includes men and women). I believe this country was prepared in 2008 to vote a black man into the office of the presidency—reluctantly by some—for the wrong reasons by some but a progressive move nonetheless. But despite the progress made with race equality, I believe there still are less people in this country prepared to vote a woman into office, and among these unprepared groups are included not only men as expected, but unexpectedly many women. In my opinion, of the two major party candidates who ran for president in the 2016 election, there was only one clear choice, and that was Hillary Clinton. I saw no cogent argument to the contrary. But look who won the election—a man.

I am not a Democrat. I am not a Republican. I was not a supporter of Hillary Clinton until the final two candidates were announced. I am a rational voter. I am a lover of our Constitution and our Bill of Rights. I believe in equal and fair civil rights for ALL Americans. Ideally, I believe in what this country claims it stands for of equality for ALL. The intent behind my presidential vote in the 2016 election was to elect an individual who I hoped would put the GOOD OF ALL before merely the good for me and the good for the few. Unfortunately, there are many, many people in this world—men AND WOMEN, who kid themselves as to the reasons why they will not vote for a woman as president. The truth is easy to HEAR by the very words that spewed from the mouth of the male candidate and now elected president. WE LIVE IN A SEXIST WORLD!

I hoped that if Hilary Clinton had been elected president that she would have changed the mind-set of the sexist and vanquish the weak excuses and justifications against voting for a female president. I hoped her term in office and her actions therein would alleviate any doubts men and women have about a female leader. These hopes of mine will go unanswered for some time yet. But there still is a future, and I will not lose hope. I hope my daughters and your daughters and the daughters throughout this country and throughout the world will someday live a future where they no longer find themselves in servitude to their fathers and their brothers. I hope ALL women will learn to have pride in themselves and, if necessary, make a stand for themselves and shout to the world for themselves and others like themselves that they are not second-class citizens merely by way of the sexual equipment of their birth. EQUALITY is not merely a word; it is an ACTION! Believe it, and believe in it!

Just a thought.

All Lives Matter!

I am so tired of black and white Americans claiming that only "black" lives matter and the poor argument that it has a special meaning over the preferred phrase "all" lives matter because of our history of slavery. Slavery had existed since before prostitution, which makes IT the oldest institution in human history. People these days like to gloss over history and pretend that only black-skinned people have been slaves, and they like to make us all believe that slavery only existed in the United States and our country would not exist but for our black slaves. WRONG! Read history! The United States did not invent slavery, but they did end it! And not all of the states legalized slavery!

I deplore slavery as much as the next man and woman, but I deplore lies as well. I have little doubt that researching far enough back in my family history, I could discover an ancestor who was someone's slave. White men and women, Oriental men and women, Hispanic men and women, Indian (east and west) men and women have all been slaves throughout history and at one time or another historically. Black American slaves just happen to have been more recent in time and within our homeland the United States. But not all of America had slaves. Not all of America built its success, created its inventions, modernized its technology on the backs of slaves. The most successful states were slave-free. In truth, much of America and many, many Americans gave their lives and risked their careers and lives to free America's slaves. More white Americans died in the American Civil War than any other war this country fought—fighting to free black Americans. These brave white men deserve credit for ending the institution of slavery, which had existed century after century in civilization after civilization—INCLUDING BLACK civilizations that also held others as slaves which is a fact conveniently glossed over and/or forgotten today.

Our fallen and honorable white heroes who fought to free slaves and make all men and women free in America are forgotten by so many black Americans today. Our politicians—who we know usually live just to line their own pockets with $$$ wealth $$$—risked their careers to free black slaves and to have them recognized as free men and women and citizens of this country. Yet so many black Americans today blame anyone who has white skin for every problem in their life and label everything bad in their life as a result of racism, and so many black Americans blame anyone with white skin just because they are white. Sounds like racism to me! Not reverse racism—which is a silly reference—just plain, old racism! Most of white America came to this country after slavery was outlawed, and so these white Americans never had anything to do with slavery. Most of the Americans living in the free states did not own slaves even when slavery was legal. Most Americans living in states that owned slaves did not own slaves; they were dirt- poor farmers.

If we as human beings truly believe that all men and women are created equal and should be treated equally, then we should do more than give this belief lip service. Stop praising kings and queens—they are no better than anyone else. They are just born privileged, and their babies are no cuter than yours or mine. Stop praising the rich; they tend to be people who do almost anything—no matter how hurtful to the rest of us—to amass $$$ a fortune $$$ at our expense, and they tend to amass it in disgusting excess. Stop allowing our politicians to make fortunes at our expense; they don't deserve it. And they are bending the laws to line their pockets at our expense, and they are sending our children into battles in foreign lands to line their pockets at the expense of our children's lives and limbs. Stop praising actors as if they are gods; they are overpaid thespians who contribute nothing. Stop praising professional athletes; they are also overpaid, and they also contribute nothing. I can find something to entertain myself if actors and athletes disappear tomorrow, so can you.

Respect yourself. Respect your spouse, your parents, your siblings, your children, your family. Respect your friends. Respect your neighbors. Respect all peoples no matter their sex, religion, race, color, or philosophy—as long as their philosophy is not one of subjugation and hate. Prove you are not a racist by coming to the defense of someone who does not look like you! I challenge the Black Lives Matter group to come to the defense of white people hurt by black people; that would prove to me you are not a racist. Just defending people that look like you and ignoring the plight of people that don't look like you leads me to believe you are hypocritical racist liars. To be truly equal, to truly live what one says and claims, one must do what one says and what one claims!

Respect, love, peace, equality, and truth are more than words— they are actions! LIVE THEM!

Just a thought.

I'm Coming Out as a Mr. Potato Head

I'm coming out as a Mr. Potato Head, and I expect equal treatment in the eyes of the law and society. No longer will I hide my inner feelings. I have always wanted to be a potato since I was a child. I remember times as a child, sitting at the dinner table, and just staring at the potato on my plate. Wishing I too was a potato. I cannot remember when I didn't feel like a potato. I like sitting on the coach and watching TV for endless hours at a time. I like to stare blankly off into space. I love ketchup and butter!

It is very disturbing to me that people make fun of me or stare at me when I dress myself up in ketchup or when I walk outside merely covered in a thick soothing coat of deep, dark gravy. And oh, how I love French women—tall, thin, greasy French women all smothered in ketchup. It's not fair. Men and women can make love. Men and men and women and women can make love. Men can make love

to goats, and women can make love to dogs. So . . . why cannot I make love to mashed potatoes?

Some say my wanting to be a Mr. Potato Head is unnatural. But I say, who are you to judge my lif style! I'm not hurting anyone. It's none of their business that I love HASH browns . . . in more ways than one. I don't criticize their lifestyle choices. This is my lifestyle choice. Who is anyone else to judge? What gives someone else the right to judge my life choices?

And who are you naysayers who say I cannot marry another potato. There have been Mr. and Mrs. Potato Heads for many years now. You must live under a rock if you've never seen the movie *Toy Story*. And just because I cannot have a baby with another potato does not mean we can't adopt a little spud. Potatoes make great parents! Again, *Toy Story*—the potato heads and the aliens!

So I'm coming out today. I'm coming out a potato and I'm proud!

Just a thought.

Do You Think This Truck Owner Loves Guns?

I was caught behind this truck in stop-and-go traffic today, and so to amuse myself, I read the many bumper sticker "notifications" on his truck. I find it a little scary when someone wants to shout to the world via words and pictures on their vehicle what I saw and read today on the back of this truck.

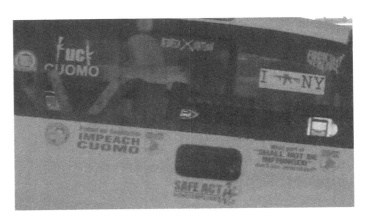

In the top corner was a bumper sticker with a picture of the continental United States with the words "Fuck Off We're Full" filling the boundaries of our great country. Then below that was a sticker that I'm not exactly sure what it is supposed to say, but it shows words and a picture of an assault weapon as follows: "I (picture of gun) NY. To the left of that is a sticker. Redneck (guns crossed in an X) nation. And to the left of that is a sticker: "Fuck Cuomo"—with guns used as the *F* and *K* in *Fuck*.

The other three stickers not on the rear window of the truck did not bother me as much as the four aforementioned stickers on the rear window of the truck. I expected to see a Donald Trump for president bumper sticker on the truck too, but I did not see one.

I can only imagine what anyone who would display these bumper stickers on their vehicle is like as a person, and it is a little scary to me to imagine.

Why are guns and hateful words so popular in this country? Guns kill; they serve no other purpose. Words like *fuck* used as they are to signify hate and anger are sad. At least show some intelligence, and use more creative words than a word used to describe a sexual act. Is your vocabulary that limited?

The aforementioned is merely my opinion based on my observation and . . .

Just a thought.

There Is No Excuse for Killing! No Excuse!

I believe there should be no excuse for killing, yet people—secular and religious—find an excuse or reason why killing is acceptable and/or excusable. On a newscast recently, I watched/listened to a couple of religious preachers preaching how much of a good thing it was that "homos" and "pedophiles" were killed in the Orlando attack. Listening to these so-called preachers, I understood them to be saying that the Bible preaches death to homosexuals and so homosexuals deserve to be killed. The Bible makes it right—the Bible, a fairy-tale book written by a group of unenlightened, not-living-in-reality people. And how is it that being homosexual makes one a pedophile? Homosexual and pedophile are two distinctly different animals.

Now, I do not believe in same-sex marriage. I believe marriage is about a man and a woman pledging to stay together and have children of their own they will raise together. And before you say—no, wait a minute—what about a man and a woman marrying and choosing not to have children or what about a man and woman marrying who cannot have children and adopt? Life is not perfect. It was never meant to be, unless those among the religious believe their god is fallible. There will always be excep-

tions. And it is not some made-up god that decides right or wrong. It is ourselves collectively as a species—collectively if we wish to live together, individually if we choose not to live together in harmony. Marriage was invented many years ago, and it was and has been about children and keeping a couples own children with their own parents, supposedly setting us apart from many other species that have sex and leave their offspring or eat their offspring if the chance and/or opportunity arise. I believe marriage between a man and a woman makes logical, rational sense as compared to same-sex marriage, and I believe same-sex marriage is different than the marriage between a man and a woman, but that is my heartfelt belief—and my personal belief—but not one I thrust on anyone else. It is not for me to decide the definition of and lawfulness of marriage and who it may and/ or may not be between. I am merely one heartfelt belief amongst many who deserve to believe what I believe without being dictated to that I have to believe what others want me to believe. But what is allowable, and what is not allowable are decisions the society we live in must decide, and we must abide by its decision if we wish to live in harmony. And no matter what society decides regarding the rights pertaining to marriage, no one should rightfully or excusably be put to death because of their sexual beliefs.

I believe marriage between a man and a woman who have children of their own is more than sex. I believe marriage between a man and a man or a woman and a woman is about sex. I love my brothers. I love my father. But I don't want to have sex with any of them. I love my wife, and I want to have sex with my wife. Same-sex relationships need to be honest that it is not merely love for another person but the desire to have sex with their own sex that motivates them to have same-sex relationships. This is merely my opinion. I am not saying that is bad, and I am not saying that is good. It is merely being honest. And honesty is something most people in this world avoid whenever possible. Just like most people get involved in specific causes, not because they are right or wrong or worthy of their intervention, but because the outcome of such specific causes affect them personally. More of us should make judgments of right and wrong based on objective rational thinking rather than personal interests. More problems would be solved that way. But I doubt that will ever come to be. Most people tend to be selfish and self-centered and only interested in themselves and their own lives and how anything and everything merely affects them and their lives.

There should be more people fighting for causes that don't affect them directly: black Americans arguing against black crime and admitting there is more black-on-white than white-on-black crime in America; Muslims fighting for the rights of women; rich people fighting for aid to the poor and doing their fair share, not merely giving up heated seats in their fifth BMW; poor people being grateful and advocating to other poor people to be grateful for help they receive but do not deserve by some unseen godly right. I didn't mention white people here because they are one color of people that has many within their fold fighting for others not like them, yet they are constantly maligned as if all white people are rich and drive a BMW. I am not suggesting that white people are superior to all other colors; they are not. There are just as many ignorant and bad white people—probably more as they are greater in numbers in this country. I am merely pointing out how there are many white people who are never given credit for trying to make this country a more equal and level playing field for all. And I do recognize there are many black, Hispanic, Asian, and Native Americans who also selflessly work for the equality of ALL.

But I digress. Let's get back to the original topic. I believe all killing is wrong. There is no universal right or wrong. All right and wrong is species and culturally and nationally determined. But despite that acknowledgment, I still believe all killing is wrong. There is no excuse to kill. If I am shot tomorrow by someone who hates my viewpoint and has such a low tolerance for objective discourse and varied opinions, and I die, killing that person will not bring me back to life. Killing that person will not make right my life being ended sooner rather than later. Killing the killer will only duplicate a killing that had no excuse in the first place. I am not suggesting I am above killing if the right circumstances presented themselves. I am as flawed as anyone else. I am only saying I believe killing to be wrong.

Guns are meant to kill, not to save lives or defend lives. Why cannot people admit the real purpose for guns? Why do so many people fight for the right to own a device, the purpose of which is to kill another human being? The Second Amendment to the US Constitution is praised and defended with more gusto than the existence of a manlike god. Why? Shouldn't we be more interested in defending the First, the Fourth, the Thirteenth, the Fourteenth, the Fifteenth, and the Nineteenth Amendments—not to mention all others before the Second Amendment? Both arguments that guns are primarily meant to save lives and defend lives are irrational and wrong, but then so are most people irrational and wrong. We are not that far advanced morally, ethically, or in the love for our neighbor than insects, our pets, and other such species that our species label as dumb animals. At least most other species are honest and open in how they conduct their lives. They kill because they wish to eat and survive. Our species should at least admit that we kill other thinking and loving species with no concern whatsoever for the other species. We also kill for food and for survival, but we label other species as unfeeling or religiously put on Earth for our domination. We show no respect for other species whatsoever. We kill their parents; we kill their babies; we breed them to eat them. Maybe our species should admit it has a problem in that our species glorifies killing—as long as it is not us specifically—as long as it is someone or something else. Maybe then we will all realize that we are not smarter than the average bear but mean and self-centered and desirous of owning a gun so we can kill someone or we can kill another species. Maybe if we can admit we have a problem. Maybe if we can admit other species are not objects and they want to live as much as we do. Maybe if we can admit guns are merely instruments to kill, not to save lives or defend lives. Maybe then, we can admit to ourselves that there is NO EXCUSE TO KILL.

Just a thought.

Regarding the Japanese Group Demanding President Obama Apologize for the Dropping of the Atomic Bombs on Japan Near the End of World War II, I Say, "NO!"

I am a pacifist through and through. I think the horror that was a result of two atomic bombs dropped on two of Japan's major cities was something that should never have happened and hopefully never will be repeated.

But Japan attacked the United States. Japan started a war against our people. Japan owes the United States an apology for starting a war against the United States. The United States owes no apology. It may be argued that the atomic bombs were unnecessary. It may be argued that the war was over. But Japan did not surrender before the bombs were dropped. Germany was done, but Japan was defiant.

Years ago, I spoke with some former war veterans who stood steadfast behind the decision to drop the atomic bombs on Japan. These soldiers believed that the alternative was a land assault on the shores of Japan that would have resulted in possibly the deaths of near a million American soldiers—possibly their lives, their fellow soldiers' lives, their friends' lives. The atomic bombs saved American lives.

I am not proud the US government dropped two atomic bombs on Japanese cities. No, I am not happy of the suffering and death that resulted from the bombing of Japanese civilians. But America did not start the war, and Japan did not want to surrender. Japan owes the United States an apology. The United States owes the Japanese no apology whatsoever.

Just a thought.

Abortion Rights, Fair for Women . . .
Not Fair for Men

I am pro choice pertaining to abortion. It is a choice I am not completely comfortable with because I cherish all life, and I do believe life begins at conception. I believe the Supreme Court's reasoning that life does not begin at conception is flawed and illogical. However, I also believe some arguments of pro-life advocates to be flawed as well. Nearly all pro-life advocates advocate specific exceptions to abortion. The pro-life advocates use the argument that life begins at conception and life is a God-given miracle and that no man or woman has a right to terminate the life of a child unborn or otherwise. Pro-life advocates argue that the unborn child has a right to live and abortion is murder. Yet if exceptions are allowable, then pro-life advocates do not really believe in their own argument. It is not the fault of the unborn if its father raped its mother. The unborn child is faultless, innocent of all crimes. So if pro-life advocates really believe abortion is murder, there can be no exceptions.

I understand, however, why so many believe there should be certain exceptions to abortion and why both sides of the debate believe in those exceptions. It seems horrible to force a woman to birth a child conceived by forcible raped committed upon her; it is horrible. But it is also not the child's fault; the child did not choose its parents or its manner of conception. A child conceived by way of rape is a terrible thing for all involved—mother and child.

Regarding a woman's right within her own body, I believe a woman should have the right to decide the fate of her bodily functions; others should not be allowed to force a woman to conceive a child. Yet I also believe the law governing a woman's right to decide

208

the fate of her unborn child is unfair to the father by allowing the mother to solely make the choice whether their child shall live or die. I find it incredible that the courts should rule that only the mother be allowed to decide the fate of a couple's unborn child and then mandate that—both parents—are responsible for that child upon its birth.

I believe the right to abortion should remain in effect for the above-stated reasons and more but with the following changes and nonchanges made to the law. It is plain to see, at least to me, that men and women and the courts they adjudicate are sickened by the thought of aborting a child, and that is why the court decided a child can only be aborted prior to its taking on a very human appearance—the first trimester argument. That way, the courts, and both men and women, can feel they are not killing a living child but that they are merely disposing of a nonentity. I think if we are honest about this, we can admit abortion is, in fact, killing a human child, and it does not matter the age of the unborn child when it is aborted, because life begins at conception. The unborn child is a living human being if nine months old or if nine seconds old. Would you say a person dying of heart disease is not a person even though (s)he is being healed by heart surgery? A fetus is a living being developing a heart and lungs and arms and legs; why is developing any different than healing? I do not see a difference, but then if we are to advocate abortion, then we must pick a stage in development that we can agree is less repugnant to abort than another—that stage being one where the fetus appears less human.

So that is the nonchange: abort a child early in its early development before it begins to look too human. The change to the current abortion law that I propose would be as follows: both the father and the mother shall have the right to decide whether to abort or birth the child. The mother, however, shall have the final say if the parents cannot agree on birth or abortion. But—and this is the big *but*—if the father wants to abort the unborn child and the mother wants to birth the child, the mother can birth the child but the father shall not be responsible for the child upon its birth. The father shall not be responsible for child support and/or anything else regarding the upbringing, welfare, care, and expense for and of the child. It shall be as if the child had no father. The father shall be required to sign a legally binding document relinquishing all rights in and to the child in perpetuity. This is not a perfect solution to abortion and both a mother and a father's rights thereto; it does not address the situation where a father wants the child to be birthed and the mother chooses to abort the child. But then life is not perfect nor fair, and I believe the woman should have the right to decide the fate of what happens to her own body in any event, but I also believe the father has shared 50 percent of the makeup of the couple's child, and the father should have more than a minor say in the birth of their child.

Just a thought.

Is Being Black and a Celebrity a Pass for Rape?

I ask this of the black community and of society in general. I do not know whether Bill Cosby is guilty of multiple counts of rape. I was not there when any of the alleged incidents took place. I am not any of the women making said claims against Mr. Cosby. I am not Bill Cosby. But I have my doubts as to his innocence given the number of women coming forward with accusations against Mr. Cosby. I have my doubts as to his innocence given the testimony and evidence presented some years ago wherein it appears Mr. Cosby admits guilt to such actions or something similar regarding at least one of the women who have come forward.

So I ask again. Is being a black-skinned American and a celebrity a pass for rape? I hear very little to no outrage by the black community. In fact, it appears Mr. Cosby is receiving a lot of support, even if some of it is silent support, but support nonetheless. If a white-skinned American raped a black-skinned American, the black community would be in an uproar. The streets would be crowded with protesters—rioting and looting—all those great American acts of indignation. Yet the black community seems insultingly silent regarding the claims made against Mr. Cosby. In fact, some are all too ready to defend him.

Equality in America and/or any place on this Earth must be defined and interpreted the same for all or it does not exist. Equality is blindness to color, sex, age, religion, philosophy, size, health, yada yada yada. And yet equality is not what many people in reality really seem to want. It seems most people really want superiority rather than equality, and it does not matter one's color, sex, age, religion, philosophy, size, health, yada yada yada. If equality is what we all truly want, then Bill Cosby should be reviled for such revolting acts because of said revolting acts and not given a pass by people that look like Bill Cosby. ALL LIVES MATTER!

Ask yourself this question: How many men are in jail for raping ONE WOMAN? And then ask yourself the follow-up question: How long of a prison sentence are they serving? Then look at what Mr. Cosby has admitted to having done wrong. And look at the allegations of the multiple times he committed such wrong doing. Then ask yourself, how is it fair that Bill Cosby, just because he is black and a celebrity, appears to be given a pass for committing multiple crimes. Ask yourself, how is it fair Bill Cosby, just because he is a celebrity, is given a pass for committing multiple crimes AND other noncelebrities, black and white, are in prison and reviled by us all for committing said crime and for committing said crime only ONCE.

Racism is alive and well in America today, but white Americans have no monopoly on such hatred. In fact, I contend there is an argument to claim there are more black American racists than white American racists. Racism is hatred born of self-interest and dislikes for those not the same as oneself; racism is pegging someone as being something in particular merely because of a characteristic they share with others pegged as a group.

So while all his high-priced celebrity lawyers defend the poor, kind, gentle, elderly Mr. Cosby against allegations some of which Mr. Cosby seems to have admitted to have occurred, think about equality and what equality means. Think about the women who have lived with the pain of being treated like an object, as a receptacle for a man's unwanted sperm and sexual touches and bodily invasion. Think about your daughters, your sisters, your mothers, your aunts, your baby girls. Think about all the years that have passed, all the lives affected by one man who is now accused of allegedly committing vile sexual acts against helpless drugged women multiple times and his having never being punished therefore. Now think about the noncelebrities, black and white, spending years and for many of them lifetimes in prison, in a small, cagelike cell, for doing the same thing Mr. Cosby is accused of doing. Think of the prison time caged like animals these noncelebrities must do as punishment of committing rape only ONCE. Think, and again ask yourself, is being black and a celebrity a pass for rape?

This is my opinion and my opinion only. I make no allegations or judgment as to the guilt of Bill Cosby. My commentary is based on allegations made and news reports as to admissions or statements made by Bill Cosby. And I focus on Mr. Cosby's color because it seems there is an undercurrent of fear in this country to prosecute well-known black-skinned Americans for fear of being labeled a racist.

Just a thought.

Antipolitically Correct Signs Draw Attention

I am against religious displays on or at public schools and government establishments, but privately owned restaurants are something else. I am a realist (aka an atheist), but I have no problem with any restaurant, chain, or singular in nature, promoting Christmas or Hanukkah or Diwali or Rosh Hashanah or whatever. This is America. There is separation of church and state, but there is also freedom of expression of one's beliefs. It is not appropriate when the state promotes one religious philosophy over another, but I believe it is appropriate for private enterprise to promote its personal beliefs. Private enterprise may alienate certain customers from patronizing its establishment(s), but they should be free to make that business decision, and we should be free to patronize their competitors if we are upset with their personal displays of their religious philosophies. Separation of church and state is meant to protect our freedoms to express our philosophies; it is to keep the state from curtailing our freedoms and to prevent one group's philosophy from being forced upon us. But separation of church and state should not go so far as to have the opposite effect, so proudly wear your yamaka. Proudly wear your cross; proudly wear your vermilion mark; and proudly wear your shahada necklace

Just a thought.

Media Distortion in America: A Personal Distortion-Based Thereon

Two scenarios—neither one true.

SCENARIO ONE—it's a nice sunny Fourth of July holiday, at a black church in South Carolina. About one hundred African Americans are gathering to worship their Lord on the same day that coincidentally coincides with America's Independence Day. All the parishioners are in a happy celebratory mood as they exit the church. Little Jayden is laughing and playing with his brother Michael as they exit the church with their mom and dad. Jayden turns to Michael and says, "Look, I have a firecracker." The two boys light and set off the fireworks. Then all hell breaks loose. A policeman happened by at the exact moment little Jayden and Michael set off the firecracker, a police car driven by a white cop. The white cop comes to the immediate conclusion and firmly believes someone has fired a gun directed at him. What else could he think when looking at African Americans coming out of a church? The white cop calls for backup. In a flash, twenty cop cars are on the scene at the church—all driven by white cops. Without hesitation, All thirty-nine cops pull their weapons, aim, and shoot Jayden and Michael as well as half of the unsuspecting and innocent churchgoers—blood, gore, and dead bodies are everywhere. No cop yelled halt. No cop looked for a gun. No cop was threatened in any way. All thirty-nine white cops shot first and never asked questions. Soon the news media shows up on the scene. And only then do the white cops report the tragic happening to their superiors. The official story is reported by the cops that . . . several guns were found on the scene. The first white cop was driving by the church and heard multiple gunshots; several hit his patrol car. Evidence of bullet damage was found in the side door of his patrol car. The cop called for backup and waited for backup to arrive. When the other patrol cars arrived, more gunshots rang out; the cops felt their lives were threatened. The cops claimed churchgoers were heard yelling, "Death to pigs, death to the white bastards." The cops claim they only did what they needed to do to protect themselves and control the situation.

SCENARIO TWO—we are in front of a bank. There is yelling and screaming. Five white men are holding up the bank; this is a bank in a predominately African American neighborhood. Two bank tellers have been shot and killed. One African American bank customer has been able to elude the white robbers, hide, and call the police on his cell phone. The African American customer tells the police what is happening and where it is happening. A white cop is taking the customer's call. The white cop says to the customer, "You sound black. Is this a black bank?" The panicked customer, fearful for his life and that of all others in the bank, pleads for help. The white cop tells him, he'll dispatch a car when one is available. A half hour later, a patrol car with two white cops arrives at the bank. The white cops walk into the bank and find the five white bank robbers punching customers, eating McDonalds while doing so, and that some of the men are molesting female customers. The bank robbers seem in no hurry to escape. The two white cops stop to grab a doughnut. The one white cop remarks to anyone who can hear, "Oh, crap, I left my gun in the patrol car." The other cop shouts, "Darn it, I dropped my gun." The white robbers run out of the bank to effect their escape. One of the white cops winks at the robbers as the robbers run out of the bank. Then the cop, who dropped his gun, picks up the gun, and both cops run out of the bank after the escaping men. Outside of the bank, out of sight of all within the bank, the white cops whisper to the white robbers, "We won't stop you. Those blacks deserved to be robbed. We never saw you. Get out of here quick." As a sign of appreciation, the white robbers throw a bag of cash to the officers, who pocket the cash. The cops' official report would be . . . The cops were called to the scene and arrived within minutes of the call for help. The cops rushed in to the bank and, at their personal risk, confronted the rob-bers—all who were black—but were outnumbered and outgunned. The robbers shouted, "Death to pigs," at the cops and fired rocket launchers at the cops and ran out of the bank, effecting a clean get-away. One hour later, ten black men were found and arrested for the robbery. The alleged bank robbers were found in a church, hiding from capture; they also were found with an empty bank moneybag. The money was never found. But a white judge, a white prosecutor, and an all-white jury found all ten African Americans guilty of felony murder and ten men are now on death row.

These two scenarios are not real. Both they are just that . . . sce-narios of possible events. Both scenarios are of events that are untrue and never happened. But these two scenarios are not so farfetched as to what the media and some people in the black community would like everyone to believe. Some people would like us to believe all white cops are bad. All white cops are out to put churchgoing African Americans in jail—all white cops treat white people favorably, even allowing white people to commit crimes, while persecuting innocent black people just because they are black. Some would like us to believe that ALL white people are evil, that all white people are racist, that all white people once owned slaves and are now responsible for every misfortune that befalls anyone who is black. Some people would like us to believe all African Americans are churchgoing, loving, caring people—people who love white people, people who cannot be racist because only white people can be racist. Some people would like us to believe that black Americans do not commit crimes—that ALL black people are sweet innocent people but for their being framed by evil white people.

The truth is something else. There are no slave owners in America today. Proclaiming white people racist and responsible for slavery is itself racist. A large percentage of white people living in America today arrived in this country post slavery. People in this country labeled "white" are no more prejudice against other races than people in this country labeled "black"—racism. Racism is itself color-blind. Racism is not a personal attribute belonging only to white people. Crime is not a personal attribute related merely to white people. People of all colors, race, religion, nationality commit crimes. Poverty does not excuse criminal behavior. Poverty was not, and is not, an excuse for white people; and poverty was not, and is not, an excuse for black people. Larger numbers of black people in jail does not necessarily mean a legal system favorable to whites. It might just mean more criminals are black. ALL LIVES MATTER! Not just black lives. Equality is just that: equality. Not favoritism. And no African Americans do not deserve to be treated better than white Americans because slavery existed in this country over a 150 years ago. Each American is an individual. Each American is equal to every other American—at least under the eyes of the law; it should be. Stop blaming white babies for all the problems of black adults. Stop apologizing for slavery when you were never a master, but you were only a caring human being. Stop blaming everyone else for your troubles. We all have troubles, and there are many, many poor white people as well as every other color of poor. Stop making up stories of racism because they sell. If the media is going to report white-on-black crime as white-on-black crime, then the media should also equally report black-on-white crime as black on white crime—but the media rarely reports racial crimes equally. Come on America. Stop putting money first. Put people first. And black Americans who think of themselves as "black" and not Americans should stop going to "black" churches and black clubs, and stop blaming white people for all your woes. If white people went to "white" churches and white clubs, they would be labeled racist. Yet for "black" Americans to do so, it is just being true to your heritage? To be nonracist, to be equal, means not just white people but all people see no color. It means white, black, brown, yellow, and red people see no color. I will not apologize for slavery. I had nothing to do with slavery. I will feel sorry for those who were slaves. I will not feel guilty for all the woes of black Americans. I grew up poor, and no black American felt sorry for me. I will feel sorry for anyone who is poor, no matter their color. And when white, brown, red, and yellow Americans are shot by the cops, I will continue to ask where are the protesters. Where are the black, white, brown, red, and yellow protestors? I have yet to see them, and it seems because not enough Americans believe ALL LIVES MATTER. Come on, let's get real, America.

Just a thought.

Is Media the Real Bad Guy in America Today?

I strongly believe the media should share in the responsibility for the attacks and murders of two New York City police officers. Two police officers sitting in their patrol car . . . called to protect a neighborhood already ripe with criminal intent and mischief. Two innocent family men shot to death in cold blood by an arguably cowardly and sick black man—"allegedly" because they were cops and not black—"possibly and possibly allegedly." Yes, prior to that incident and for some time, NYC "peaceful" protestors were shouting, "We want dead cops." But come on, they didn't really mean it. They were just yelling shouting death to cops for fun, right? All these protestors had done besides protest an issue that arguably did not exist—that is, most white cops are out to kill black men. All these protestors did is drive fear into police, politicians, and rich white and rich black politicians and media to hold back the police from stopping criminals who are black skinned, and it appears instill in others the desire to kill police. The result of this media-driven hysteria was two dead police officers. The result of this media-driven hysteria, mothers and fathers and wives and sisters and brothers and children have now lost their sons, their husbands, their brothers, their fathers.

I have said it many times before, and I will say it again. I am not a fan of cops, but I am not a fan of lies, selfishness, and murder as well, and so we NEED police. We need policing. We are NOT a self-controlled society. There are a lot of bad cops. I believe there are more bad cops than good police officers. That said, policing millions of self-centered, self-interested people is a difficult job—a job I would not want. Police have to keep peace amongst a country of insane people who are ALL INNOCENT no matter what crime they commit.

So many people, no matter their financial station in life, refuse to believe we NEED police to keep the many lowlifes in line; we need police to protect law-abiding citizens from being robbed, bullied, threatened, and/or killed by individuals who care so little about the lives and livelihood of others. How many incidents have the media reported where the media have turned criminals into victims and the police into villains? How many black celebrities have used the media and how many black politically visible individuals have used the media to turn police encounters such as Brown (seen robbing a store on video) and Garner (allegedly illegally selling cigarettes and resisting arrest) to incite hatred within the "black" community against ALL in the "white" community? Many! The media is making $$money$$, and celebrities and politicians are promoting themselves by creating a nonexistent issue with little to no concern for us (us being of all colors). I have witnessed many white Americans standing with black Americans in causes aiding the "black" community, but I see very few black Americans standing with white Americans when black Americans commit crimes against white Americans. Why is that? Maybe, just maybe, because the media portrays white people as evil and responsible for everything wrong in the black community. And maybe the media doesn't care to report black-on-white crime or the police treating white civilians equally as terrible as they treat black civilians because it doesn't sell; it doesn't make the media any money. Shouldn't the media be reporting events of equal effect and equal concern to all? But then that doesn't sell; the media sells sensationalism. The media sells stories that raise anger, hate, or powerful emotions in people. The media sells only what it knows will make it money.

I believe the media shares a large proportion of the blame for the number of violent protests, the violence in Ferguson, and the death of the two NYC police officers. Racism $$sells$$. Racism $$sells$$. Shame on you, media. Shame on all Americans, black and white, that buy into the crap the media thrusts at us. Shame on anyone making money by exaggerating events and inferring said events are everyday occurrences. It does none of us any good creating hate and mistrust amongst us. STOP. LOOK. THINK. Look at each other, and tell me that white guy over there is trying to make your life hell merely because you're black. Most of us "white" guys are just trying to make a living for ourselves. I don't hate you because your skin is black. If I hate you at all, it is because I think you're an A&*H%*E for the same reasons I think some white-skinned guy is an Aand*and*LE . It is the most ridiculous paranoid nonsense that some people believe media inferences that "white" people are out to make "black" people miserable while showering kindness on all other "white" people. The media creates and perpetuates racism. I cannot believe cops are collectively thinking, "Today looks like a great day to arrest or shoot some black guy." I do believe cops are collectively thinking most of us are bad guys, and they must act aggressively and authoritatively with a condescending and insulting attitude whenever they interact with us. I am certain cops see criminals in all colors. I agree cops are condescending, egotistical bullies, and they act as thugs when interacting with us often. But I also believe cops are like that with people of all colors. The reason we learn about stories like the Brown and Garner incidents is, because the media likes to report incidents gone bad in which the cops are white and alleged criminal(s) are black, racism sells. Racism against black Americans sells. There are stories to be told about cops (white and black) having bad interactions with "white" criminals, but these stories rarely make the big time in the media.

Hate is not a problem solved by more hate. People need to stop blaming others for their problems. Stop looking for a scapegoat. Take responsibility for your actions. Do not let the media bring you to hate others. Know that the media survives on selling sensationalism—hate, anger sells. If a man commits a crime, it does not mean we share the blame because we are of the same color, religion, or nationality of that man. If a man resists arrest and something goes wrong as a result of his wrongful reaction to his arrest, it is not an attack on us because we are of the same color, religion, or nationality of that man. We are all individuals! Equality means we stop characterizing ourselves as separate groups at war with each other; equality means we stop forming groups where we alienate others we consider different from ourselves. THAT IS RACISM! I am not evil or naive.

I do not believe you are evil or naive. I am an individual. You are an individual. I am not white or black. You are not white or black. I am not a cracker or a nigger. You are not a cracker or a nigger. I am not a racist. You are not a racist. I have never been a slave or a slave owner. You have never been a slave or a slave owner. I am not rich. You may be, I don't know. I am a man. I am a father. I am a husband. I am a son. I am a brother. I am a neighbor. I may be a friend. I like all people except those who dislike me or are nasty or hateful to me. I do not wish harm or a bad life on anyone. I am human. You are human. I agree I am no better than you. BUT I AM ALSO JUST AS GOOD AS YOU. And I wish to be treated no less than you expect to be treated yourself. Let's ignore the hate spewed by the media.

Think of when was the last time you experienced a story told by FOX News or CNN or the new media politicians—comedians (hereinafter referred to collectively as the "media")—that was a "nice" story with a positive message. And if you can remember one, make note of that one and when you saw it, and count the number of "nasty" stories heard in between that nice story and the next nice story. I expect the number of nasty stories you count will be rather large. WHY? Why must "news" always be about nasty stories? News doesn't have to always be bad news, but it usually is bad news. Why? Because bad news—"nasty"—sells; nice news does not sell. Nice bores people. Nasty gets everyone's blood boiling. People come out of the cracks in the walls to yell and scream and write nasty comments about each other when incited by a nasty story put out there by the media. Race is one of the biggest sellers today, despite its smaller stature in today's America.

Out of all the encounters between white and black in America, what encounters do the media focus on? Do I really need to tell you? And does it matter if the media is accurate about the encounter being racism? It doesn't appear so from what I have witnessed. Just as long as the media can spin a tale that enough people will bite upon, and once blood is tasted, the sheep turn into a swarm of sharks who don't care what they are biting—only that everyone else is biting so why not me too? I want to be part of the frenzy; I want to be part of the mob. It's sad, but most people are sheep, usually angry sheep that viciously bite without thinking for themselves—all the while convincing themselves they have thought it out and it has always been their original thought.

So where is the media coverage of all the nice encounters between black and white in America? The nice encounters between nice black-skinned Americans and nice white-skinned Americans who respect one another. And yes, that is most of America. There are a lot of nice black Americans, and there are a lot of nice white Americans. None of who are anywhere near close to racist. Most Americans are nowhere near racist. But niceness doesn't sell. Black and white Americans befriending each other doesn't sell. A black American saves a white family. A white American saves a black family. These kinds of stories are out there waiting to be told, waiting to be heard. And sometimes they are covered by the media, but race is usually not mentioned in those stories, and those stories are quickly forgotten and few between despite the fact that they happen often. Yet if a bad encounter happens between a white American and a black American, it often is told as a tale of racism EVEN THOUGH something besides race may have caused the bad encounter. Remember, we are all human beings. Our skin color is not the only feature that defines us. Our ethnic background is not the only feature that defines us. We are not merely "black" Americans, nor are we merely "white" Americans. We are Americans; we are brothers and sisters and mothers and fathers and sons and daughters. We are so much more than merely a color. Look inside yourself, and look inside others. And when negative encounters occur between us, judge honestly and fairly and not with predisposed beliefs.

But again, remember why the media exists; its primary purpose is not to inform but to make money. Remember, niceness between the races doesn't sell, but racism does sell. And if the media can concoct a story of racism and hate, or the media can find one or two or three bad examples relative to the millions of good examples of Americans living in America today, they will, and the media will report it to us ad nauseum.

So should the media be held accountable for its actions? Should the media be pulled out from behind the protective wall of rights they claim when they blatantly display an agenda to incite hate and mistrust amongst Americans? If the media truly wants to present news that is fair and balanced, news that is not meant to incite anger, but news meant to report and inform, shouldn't they be presenting "nice" equally with "nasty"?

Just a thought.

Isn't It Time to Repeal an Amendment That's Only Nature Is to Kill?

Isn't it time to seriously think about repealing, not upholding, the Second Amendment to the United States Constitution? Are we not beyond killing each other yet? Is it so important that every man, woman, and childlike adult be armed to the teeth? Is anyone being saved by anyone else wearing or owning an armory on their property? I don't think so!

Is defending an outdated, outmoded idea worth the loss of innocent lives? Is defending the Second Constitutional Amendment worth losing the lives of our daughters to jealous, angry husbands and/or boyfriends? Or losing our grandchildren to crazed maniacs? Is demanding the right to own a device that's sole purpose is to kill more important than the lives of our sons, daughters, friends, and neighbors?

Is a neighborhood armory or hometown militia even capable of winning a battle against a tyrannous government armed with the most sophisticated weapons as well as vast Armies, Navies, and an Air Force? This is not the year 1776.

Childlike men and women as well as money run Congress. Childlike men and women are the NRA. Hateful, violent, killers, and potential killers love to own as many weapons as possible. They know weapons kill. Weapons are not made for peace-loving people. Weapons are made for killers—people unafraid to kill, although likely afraid to be shot themselves. These are some of the same people who are turning red with anger and thoughts of killing me at this very moment as they read this commentary, and they are, thus, only proving my point.

REPEAL THE SECOND CONSTITUTIONAL AMENDMENT! REPEAL. REPEAL. REPEAL IT!

Just a thought.

I Have to Commend Former President Obama

President Obama made me so happy as our current president. I could not help but feel empathy, hope, and anger when President Obama spoke about the Oregon college campus shootings and what we as a nation should be doing about guns. I have to agree with the president. If I understood correctly the meaning of his every word, the president seemed visibly impassioned and hurt by what was another tragedy where innocent lives were lost at the sorry end of a gun wielded by another crazed gunner. I support the president and his passion and his concerns for the safety of us all. I did keep his feelings about guns in the forefront of my mind when I cast my 2016 presidential vote.

No matter what the NRA may say, I do not believe the NRA cares who dies by gunfire. I do believe the NRA cares only that every American is afforded the right to own, carry, and use any weapon of their choice. I do believe the NRA believes every American should be able to own any weapon no matter how powerful and no matter how over qualified a weapon may be for its intended purpose. I do believe the NRA is looking for large penis alternatives. I do believe the NRA is looking for weaponized ego enhancers. I do not believe most people who claim they own guns to protect and defend. I do believe most people own guns because they like to kill things, and if that thing is a purpose, all the better. GUNS ARE ALL ABOUT KILLING! This is my opinion, like it or not.

Abused spouses die by gunfire. Children die by gunfire. Innocents unknown to the shooter die by gunfire. My friends and your friends die by gunfire. My relatives and your relatives die by gunfire. No one is SAVED by gunfire. The too-often-used argument that guns will only be in the hands of the "bad" if not also in the hands of the "good" is hogwash. Almost all gun holders are bad with bad intentions. Guns are meant to kill, not save lives.

None of us are any safer because our neighbors are armed. Do you think the world is safer when more nuclear weapons are held by more countries? Mass shootings are not prevented by the NRA and its policies and its lobbyists. Mass shootings have not been prevented by our upholding and interpreting the meaning of the Second Amendment that we can all own and carry weapons. Our nation is not free of terrorists because our neighbor John Smith down the street has an armory in his basement. In fact, a lot of us are a little bit afraid of why John Smith has an armory in his basement.

We as a nation are not starving because there are not enough hunters equipped with rapid-fire weapons out making Swiss cheese out of our food. We will not die of boredom as a nation if we do not have guns to shoot at targets WITH PICTURES OF PEOPLE ON THEM.

We do not need guns except in extreme circumstances of war. Ask your forefathers what they thought about that! And even then, owning and using guns is nothing to be proud about. Weapons used to defend should not be glorified. War is nothing to be proud of.

STAND BEHIND FORMER PRESIDENT BARACK OBAMA. VOTE OUT GUN LOBBING CANDIDATES in the next election and ALL elections no matter how big or how small the office—whether a general, national, or local election. Vote for peace and safety and common sense for your family and the families of others. No more guns.

Just a thought.

Who Is the Real Monster on This Planet? Is It Animal or Man?

I just finished watching an old black-an-white horror film entitled *The Creature from the Black Lagoon*. I watched this film when I was a child, and loving old films like I do, I watched it again. But as a child, when I watched the creature interacting with the lead characters, I saw hero scientists fighting off a mindless killing machine—a monster, a killer. Now, many years later, watching the film as a fifty-eight-year-old adult, I looked at the creature a little differently. Today I saw a money-hungry, fame-seeking entrepreneur, along with a number of scientists doing his bidding so as not to lose their paychecks attack, harass and chase down a creature who would have left them alone but for their harassment of the creature. Granted the

 creature was not totally innocent as unprovoked it attacked two employees of one of the scientists prior to its being attacked by the entrepreneur and his crew. But to me, the message remains the same. Man provokes and instigates violence on other species while claiming to have a God-given right to do so unchallenged and with impunity.

Man (men and women) have no more "absolute" right to kill, enslave, and torture other species than other species have to do so to man. Man justifies the many terrible things man does to other species by claiming to be made in some creator's image and as the creator's favorite to be endowed with rights and powers given by said creator to do as man pleases to any of the other species on this planet. This is just delusional humankind justifying man's terrible acts to be committed on a daily basis against any and every other species that man feels it needs to act upon.

As an example, man corrals chickens and other fowl, caging them in containment areas with little to no space between each bird in filthy cages with the intended purpose of their later being slaughtered. The children of these fowl are slaughtered as well; no age is exempt. And it may seem odd to refer to their offspring as children, but they are their children. Chickens aren't the only species we cage and breed as food. Cattle are kept in buildings and eventually run through a process where their heads are unmercifully cut off their bodies and their bodies sliced and diced like paper by scissors. Animals are hung upside down in slaughterhouses, slit down their middles, and left to drain of blood—just food to be prepared for our stomachs. These species and many more of species like them butchered and then packaged and labeled and dressed up like Christmas presents to be displayed behind glass in a food store to then be bought and eaten with potatoes on the side.

What if your family, your children, your babies were caged and slaughtered and wrapped and bowed and sold in supermarkets by other species sold to be eaten. You would cry—monstrous!

What if you and your family were put in cages in human zoos and exhibited naked while fed from a trough and hosed down to be cleaned and gawked at by the peering eyes of other species as you had sex with your mate and/or relieved yourself after a meal. Oh, for some reason, mankind believes man has the God-given right to demean, cage, enslave, and eat other species; the God-given right to torture other species; the God-given right to be evil and call himself divine. Man is not divine. Man is just another animal, another species of life on this planet. And many times, mankind is not the kindest species in the kingdom. Very often, mankind is more like a T-Rex in the age of the dinosaurs. Mankind is a predator; mankind is a killer. Mankind is not special or divine as mankind would like to believe mankind to be.

But mankind is intelligent. Mankind has proved to be more intelligent than most if not all species on this planet. Mankind has visited the moon, built amazing civilizations and wondrous tools. However, despite man's intelligence, mankind has not proved man to be any less a monster than man depicts *The Creature of the Black Lagoon*. One could argue that other less-intelligent species can be forgiven for some of the evils they commit upon other species because they don't know any better. What is man's excuse if mankind is so intelligent? Maybe mankind has no excuse. Maybe out of all the species on this planet, the real monster on this planet is man.

Just a thought.

I Am Proud to Be Who and What I Am

RACE

I am proud to be African American, but don't call me black. I am proud of my African heritage, and I am unashamed to celebrate my pride. I have African American churches and African American clubs and African-American organizations, and my sports heroes are all African American, and my celebrity idols are all African American. I am African American and proud of it. I'm not racist; I'm just proud of who I am.

I am proud to be European American, but don't call me white. I am proud of my European heritage, and I am unashamed to celebrate my pride. I have European American churches and European American clubs and European American organizations, and my sports heroes are all European American, and my celebrity idols are all European American. I am European American and proud of it. I'm not a racist; I'm just proud of who I am.

SEXUAL ORIENTATION

I am proud to be homosexual, but don't call me a homo. I am proud of my sexual orientation, and I am unashamed to celebrate my pride. I march in gay parades, and I belong to gay clubs and gay organizations, and my sports heroes are all gay, and my celebrity idols are all gay. I am gay and proud of it.

I am proud to be heterosexual, but don't call me homophobic. I am proud of my sexual orientation, and I am unashamed to celebrate my pride. I march in heterosexual parades, and I belong to heterosexual clubs and heterosexual organizations, and my sports heroes are all heterosexual, and my celebrity idols are all heterosexual. I am heterosexual and proud of it.

SEXUAL IDENTITY

I am proud to be a woman. I am proud of my sex, and I demand to be treated equality—no more, no less. I vote for women politicians because they are female like me. I'm proud of women and what we can accomplish.

Now read this:

I am proud to be a man. I am proud of my sex, and I demand to be treated equality—no more, no less. I vote for male politicians because they are male like me. I'm proud of men and what we can accomplish.

HYPOCRISY

There is hypocrisy in America. Equality means equality—just that, nothing more, nothing less. Equality does not mean those as perceived to be treated unjustly are to be favored in every event, conflict, and happening of the day. Equality means equality, not overcompensation for perceived past faults of others. Equality is not the reality in America today. Very often, just being a European American heterosexual male in America means to be automatically labeled racist, sexist, homophobic, and white. The most unfairly treated group in America today is arguably the European heterosexual male. These men are grouped together and labeled as "white." They can be fodder of African-American comedians while the most innocent of jokes made of African-Americans by a European-American comedian is met with a public whipping and a career-ending result. To show any pride in one's sexual orientation is only acceptable if one is homosexual. To be a heterosexual with pride is equated with "homophobia." To be a European-American male is to be open to constant insults and being portrayed on television and in movies as the bumbling idiotic father, the cowardly male, and evil villain while the African American men; and women and European American women are portrayed as good, kind, intelligent saviors of the day.

Merely because an individual is considered a member of a group considered the largest group in America does not make that individual racist, sexist, and/or homophobic. And it does not obligate that individual to be representative of said group. Equality is about individuality and the rights of all individuals to be treated as individuals, not as members of a group. Racism, sexism, and sexual phobia run across ALL GROUPS and can be found of ANY INDIVIDUAL in America. And it usually is! Racism knows no color; there are many racist African Americans even though they are regularly ignored and/or considered acceptable by America. Sexual phobia knows no boundaries. Sexism favors neither one sex nor the other. So if you are going to celebrate who and what you are, if you are going to proclaim pride in whom and what you are, everyone else not like you should be allowed to do so as well. A person is no more racist, sexual phobic, or sexist than an African American, a homosexual, and/or a woman just because that person is male and of European descent. European Americans have just as much right to be proud of who and what they are as anyone else. All former immigrants to this great land we call America have the right to proclaim pride in their national and ethnic backgrounds. If your group believes it can belong to exclusive clubs special to your identity, then all other groups should be able to do the same. We all have the same right to not to be grouped and labeled by others. Think about it!

Just a thought.

World Shocked at Enduring Racism, Gun Violence in USA

Is it true? Is the USA a cesspool of racism and gun-toting Old-West Clint Eastwood wannabes? I say yes, but yes with an accusation directed back at China and other finger pointers. Yes, there is racism in the USA. But not just racism against blacks; there is also racism against whites. The trouble is that racism against whites does not sell papers or airtime. And just because a white man commits a racist act against a black individual that does not mean ALL white men are racist. To infer that is racism. And just because a black man commits a racist act against a white individual that does not mean ALL black men are racist. To infer that is racism. The trouble with this country is $$money$$ comes before equality and humanity. Racism against blacks sells. No one cares if a black man kills a white man. It is insulting to me, and I have no doubt it is insulting to other men and women born with white skin to be grouped together as racist when someone who is white like us but not us commits a racist act against someone who is not white. I abhor acts of hate and violence against anyone no matter race, creed, religion, sex, and/or color. I look at every man, woman, and child with the same expectations that they be kind, friendly, and treat me as I hope to treat them with similar kindness and equality. So I do not like being labeled a racist because I am white-skinned any more than I believe a black man or woman likes being labeled in a negative way purely because of the color of their skin.

As far as racism in the USA, we are a unique country in that we have a very diverse group of people living here. Many other countries do not have the same level of diversity that we have here and so no diversity issues arise. Many other countries do have diverse cultures, religious backgrounds, ethnic differences, and they have problems similar and/or worse than our own. Look at the recent genocide in Africa. Look at the many Asian nations attempts to kill minorities living in their countries. Look at the Muslim world and how it treats non-Muslims and women and other Muslims not of their own religious denomination, and China who may like to finger-point is no saint when it comes to racism and subjugation. Even though China may have a valid claim about our racial issues, China is no country to sit in judgment. I think China needs to address its human rights issues as well as its issues with other cultures, religions, and races before it addresses our problems. China is a dictatorial nation that TELLS its people how to act, live, and breathe; China is no nation to criticize other nations.

As far as any allegation about our country's obsession with guns, I agree with anyone and everyone who takes issue with this country's love of guns. Guns kill; guns do not save lives. To argue we need guns to protect ourselves from criminals who own guns is a false argument lacking of logic and circular in nature. We do not need guns. We do not need to kill except possibly in defense if our nation is attacked. And a small cache of guns owned by private citizens is not going to protect us from a government like ours that is harboring nuclear missiles amongst other weapons of enormous power and of which we have no defense. The argument is ridiculous. The court's interpretation of the Second Amendment is ridiculous and antiquated. We did not have a standing military at the enactment of the Second Amendment; we do now. Why do people in this country love to kill? Why do people in this country love to own devices that extinguish life? We do not need guns. The rest of the world arguing the USA is obsessed with guns, and a violent nation, therefore, is right. We would be a less violent country and a safer country if guns were not worn like jewelry. We should not be happy and proud to own weapons that kill people. This is not the Old West. And the Old West wasn't as pretty a picture as Hollywood history showed us, and so many people seem to believe it to have been. Even the use of weapons in war is terrible—sometimes necessary, but terrible. We should not be happy and proud about being involved in wars. Wars are horrible; men, women, and children die. We should be reluctant to kill, and if we do kill, we should do so only in self-defense. After all is said and done, we should be sad we ever had to defend ourselves, not proud. My opinion regarding ownership of guns in this country . . . We do not need them; they are not necessary. They are only good for death, destruction, and evil.

PS, regarding a recent mass shooting at a church, I applaud the survivors and family members of the victims of the church massacre who spoke out at the defendant's bail hearing for the kindness and goodwill and good heart they spoke toward the accused. If one of my family members were one of his victims, I do not know if I could have displayed as much compassion as did they. I hope all the best for the survivors and all who knew and lost friends, family, and loved ones.

Just a thought.

Kate Middleton, Prince William Welcome Baby Girl! WHY DO AMERICANS CARE?

WHY DOES ANYONE CARE? I cannot believe the pomp and ceremony. I cannot believe the press given this event. I cannot believe the interest some people in the American public have in some overprivileged rich people giving birth to some to-be overprivileged, rich child. What is wrong with your sense of pride and sense of self-worth and your belief in equality in life? Are you not Americans?

There is nothing special about Middleton or William. Their baby was not born of an immaculate conception. William stuck his penis in Kate just like any other man does to any other woman to fertilize her egg resulting in the birth of a child. God wasn't shining a light down on Kate's womb smiling all the while and thinking to himself, "Oh, this is the most wondrous baby in the world. I love this child so much more than all those other schmucks and their bastard offspring." What is wrong with you, people? Is this baby the new baby Jesus?

What you rightfully need to celebrate is the birth of your own children and that of your children's children, not the birth of a child of some rich overprivileged people. I could not help but laugh when I saw a picture of British citizens celebrating in the streets the birth of their "prince's" child. It made me sad—sad to think that so many people allow themselves to be subjugated to strangers because of their wealth and power. Sad to think that so many people allow strangers to be showered with THEIR hard-earned money, allow strangers privileges and power they deny themselves just because these strangers are born to other strangers who grabbed money, privilege, and power from the weaker for themselves—all the while labeling themselves gods, kings, princes, and princesses. How can anyone celebrate a monarchy? How can anyone support a monarchy? How can anyone believe some stranger is better than themselves, their relatives, their friends, and neighbors—merely because that stranger was born into power and money?

And even sadder than the British are the Americans who feel the same way. What is wrong with you? Didn't we free ourselves of the British monarchy centuries ago? Do you realize what a "prince, a princess, a king, a queen, a duke, a duchess" is in reality? They are rulers. They are strangers born of other strangers who subjugated multitudes of people while amassing a fortune and a grand lifestyle at the expense of the masses. They are no better, no different, than you. They have two legs, two arms, and an anus. They eat, breathe, and crap. They are born, and they will die. They are no better than you. So why celebrate them as if they are special? Why allow them the perpetual privileges and wealth they and their offspring continue to enjoy but never earn?

If the British have no self-respect, that is something of a problem for the British. But we are Americans. Don't you as Americans respect yourselves? Don't you respect your freedom, your form of government, your equality to all other men and women? Don't you realize that if anyone is special in this world, it is YOU, YOUR SPOUSE, YOUR CHILDREN, YOUR FRIENDS AND RELATIVES—ALL MORE SPECIAL than some empowered, spoiled, overprivileged rich people calling themselves princes and princesses. Have a little self-respect. Be a real American.

Just a thought.

The Pledge of Allegiance Is Unconstitutional

This is how the pledge presently reads:

> I pledge Allegiance to the flag
> of the United States of America
> and to the Republic for which it stands,
> one nation under God, indivisible,
> with Liberty and Justice for all.

This is how I propose the pledge should read:

> I pledge Allegiance to the flag
> of the United States of America
> and to the Republic for which it stands,
> one nation under the **Constitution
> of the people**, indivisible,
> with Liberty and Justice for all.

"God" is the Judo/Christian god, not the Hindu gods or the secular god or the American Indian gods. Pledging allegiance to the god of one or more religions is in contradiction to the basic tenets of our nation. The First Amendment (Amendment I) to the United States Constitution prohibits the making of any law respecting an establishment of religion . . . And yet our courts request witnesses to swear to one religion's god. And yet our public schools request our children to stand and swear allegiance to one religion's god.

When you or your children are asked to pledge allegiance to the flag, I suggest you and your children recite my rendition of the pledge and place a loud verbal emphasis on the words "**Constitution of the people**" when others recite "under God." Be a patriot when you recite the Pledge, and honor our Constitution, not the god of yours or someone else's religion.

Just a thought.

Guilty Until Proven Innocent!

How often have we heard the words "innocent until proven guilty"? Are not those words the words that are supposed to define our justice system? Well, to begin with, we do not have a justice system in the USA. We have a "legal" system. And in our legal system, a charged party is "guilty until proven innocent." To be innocent until proven guilty, one would be free from imprisonment, free from police and judicial harassment and confinement. But that is not how our legal system works.

If a person is charged with a crime, said person is typically restrained by the police and jailed until arraigned. How is this innocent until proven guilty?

Then the said charged person pleads innocent, or sometimes the court will force a plea of innocent on the now-defendant. A request for bail is held. Why a request for bail? Because the "innocent until proven guilty" defendant must prove (s)he is not a flight risk and said defendant is really considered more guilty than innocent even at this early stage. If the defendant can afford the bail, (s)he is out of jail but restrained in ability to travel either by bail restrictions or the fear of loss of life savings. Is this innocent until proven guilty? If the defendant cannot afford the bail, it is back to jail. A defendant can spend a long time in jail waiting for "justice" from a coldhearted court that itself goes home to dinner every night and sleeps in a warm bed. Is this innocent until proven guilty?

Then a trial commences. The defendant must hire an overpriced attorney and could lose a lifetime of savings paying some guy to "prove" his or her innocence. I thought the court was supposed to prove his or her guilt? Is this innocent until proven guilty? And at trial, it seems the prosecutor is intent on winning, which means nothing good for the defendant. And many judges seem to side more so with the prosecution and the police than the defense. Is this justice? I thought the court and the prosecutor were supposed to look for truth, justice, and the "American way." Is not the search for the truth even if you lose the case what justice is supposed to be all about? But no, the defendant must fight TO PROVE HIS OR HER INNOCENCE. The defendant must fight with his or her life savings against a bottomless pit of money and resources available to the prosecution, the court, and the police. Is this justice? No! The prosecution may claim it has the burden of proof, that the prosecution must prove the defendant guilty. But what appears happening as I see it is the prosecution is being charged with confirming the defendant's guilt. In reality, isn't the defendant being charged with proving his or her innocence?

The truth be told, if charged with a crime, you are **GUILTY UNTIL PROVEN INNOCENT**!

Just a thought.

Golden Globes 2015:
Jeremy Renner Criticized for Making "Sexist" Comment about Jennifer Lopez's Dress.

Now, come on! Renner is criticized for Lopez wearing a dress that reveals and props up her boobs and draws more attention to her two golden globes than attention was drawn to any of the awards handed out that night. Come on, really?

This is what kills me about women who wear clothing that reveals their boobs and/or their ass and THEN they complain when or if someone makes a comment about what they are revealing. Come on! If men wore pants that were cut with a v-cut in the back showing their crack, you don't think someone would look or say something? If you answer, "I would discretely look away," you are a liar. You would notice, and you would want to say something THEN you might look away. Women wearing v-necklines that show part of their bare boobs are asking, "Please stare at what I believe are beautiful boobs." Women wearing bikinis or short shorts or short skirts or tight pants are saying, "Please stare at what I believe is a beautiful ass." To say otherwise is a lie. It is easy enough for women to wear tops and bottoms that do not reveal boobs and ass, but then, "who would look?"

Women have to start admitting the truth that the reason they wear revealing clothing is because they believe people will want to look at them, and they believe they have something they want to show off. So the next time you see a woman wearing a low-cut top that shows off her boobs, stare right at them and say, "Nice boobs!" I think everyone should. Or try wearing pants with a v-cut in the back that shows your crack, and count the number of women that cop a peek. Trust me. Most women will not be able to look away. But do not confuse their stares for interest. And every one of them who sometime later complain about you staring or remarking about their low-cut top or short shorts, you can reveal as a hypocrite.

Just a thought.

Assimilate?

Listening to news reporters and commentators over the last few days following the killings in France, I keep hearing the word *assimilate*. I keep hearing news reporters and commentators declare how many, many French Muslim citizens are living in poverty and being treated as second-class citizens. I hear these same news reporters and commentators saying, or at least implying, the French must do more to assimilate the Muslim population into the greater French population. It almost seems as if these same news reporters and commentators are implying the attacks on the French and the French Jews in the deli are somehow the fault of the greater French population and not the fault of the Muslims, or at least that the greater French population needs to shoulder some of the blame. I wholeheartedly disagree!

The problem with many such groups as of many Muslim groups relocating to neighborhoods in other countries is that they do not want to "assimilate" themselves into the greater population. Many of these Muslims group off—into their own separate neighborhoods— creating a country within a country. Many of these Muslim groups do not want to "assimilate" into the greater population. Assimilation means becoming a part of and very much like the greater population, not separate and different. Many Muslim groups live under such laws as Sharia Law, which is considered a higher law, a higher code, to live by than the law of the governing country they have relocated to live within. Many of these Muslim groups do not want to change or to adopt the customs of the host country. They want the host country to change and adopt the Muslim way of life. The French are the French. Why must the French change their laws and their customs to accommodate those groups of people who ask to live in France? If I move my family to Saudi Arabia and ask for citizenship, can I expect that my daughters be able to walk the streets in bikinis and behave and act and seek and gain employment just like any other Saudi? Can I wear a T-shirt with Muhammad's picture plastered on the front side and "Long live Satan" on the back side? I do not think so. If I wanted to move my family to Saudi Arabia (and I don't), I would expect that I should "assimilate" myself and my family into THE SAUDI way of life and abide by SAUDI LAW. Why, because it is THEIR country, and I am asking to join THEIR culture, THEIR civilization. I am not asking them to join mine. Well, some people are, but should they be?

So why is it that some Western societies feel that OUR countries, OUR cultures, OUR beliefs, OUR freedoms, and OUR philosophies of life and law and freedom should change for some foreign cultures asking to live amongst us? Western societies, Eastern societies, religious societies, countries ruled by laws equal to all, countries ruled by religion—these countries exist for a reason! A country exists because someone has decided its culture, its beliefs, its laws, its freedoms are what it is all about. And when a country has established itself as such, it should not have to change because immigrants move to it with a different philosophy and different ideas. If you agree with how the French live their lives and run their country, then move to France. If you do not agree with the French lifestyle, then stay where you are and do not move to France. To say this is not being inflexible. It is not being racist. It is not being hateful. It is being proud of one's OWN heritage. It is being proud of one's OWN culture. It is being proud of one's OWN outlook on life, freedoms, and rule of law.

So I disagree with the news reporters and commentators use of the word *assimilate* when discussing the French Muslims or any Muslims moving to any country in the world that does not live by Islamic religious law. IT IS THE MUSLIMS WHO MUST ASSIMILATE when moving to France or England/or the United States—or any other non-Islamic run legal and social system—or stay home. We in the West are just as proud—if not more—of our way of life, our freedoms, our culture, our philosophy of life—as others are of their life choices. It is disrespectful to our culture and values of freedom of expression for someone to dictate to us that we cannot show a picture of some guy by the name of Muhammad just because some people believe him to have been a religious prophet. It is disrespectful to our culture and our values for someone to treat our women or anyone's women as less than equal to men and with the same respect. I have daughters, and my culture and my beliefs dictate everyone treats my daughters with the same respect they expect for themselves and that they are expected to treat men. Do not try to force your beliefs upon me or my fellow Americans in OUR land. And if you feel you must and if you do, I will refuse to give you the respect of your cultures when I am upon your soil. RESPECT IS ONLY GIVEN IF GIVEN IN RETURN.

Just a thought.

Prison Is Cruel and Inhumane Punishment

I have been watching the television show *Lockup* over the last several weeks, and I came to the conclusion that prison is cruel and inhumane punishment. To force men and women to be individually locked into a small, six-by-eight-foot room with nothing close to comfort is cruel and inhumane. It is cruel and inhumane enough to lock someone in such a small room for a short period of time, say a week or several months, but imagine how cruel and inhumane it is to lock someone in such a small space year after year, decade after decade. It is unimaginable to me! I understand—I am not naive, nor am I a bleeding heart who refuses to feel for the victims of many of these prisoners—but what does prison actually accomplish? I see no evidence that imprisoning anyone is accomplishing anything.

There is a large percentage of prisoners forced to live in squalor like caged animals with less rights and privileges than most animals who have done nothing to hurt anyone but themselves. Being imprisoned for possession and/or use of drugs is a crime in itself! What is a society saying about itself by imprisoning alleged drug abusers? Is society not saying it does not care about the health and welfare of the alleged drug abuser—which I assume is the given reason for the illegality of the drug use in the first place? What society appears to be saying is that it doesn't like users of "specific" drugs—prescription legally sanctioned and profit-making drugs are acceptable and, hence, legal. And these "illegal" drug users must be locked up and hidden away like animals? If a society really cares about the harm certain drugs may do to users of those drugs, then society should hospitalize and treat and "cure" these individuals of their dependency on said "illegal" drugs, not lock them up like animals to be labeled as outcasts and former prison inmates when and/or if ever released from prison. Drug use is not murder or rape, and yet it seems drug users are treated as badly, if not worse, than many murderers and rapists when sentenced to prison. How does a user of an "illegal" drug merit being locked up like an animal for as long as an individual who has been convicted of killing another human being? He and/or she do not merit punishment by prison!

I fail to see any merit to the prison system. I do not believe prison rehabilitates anyone. I do not believe prison solves any problems for society. I do not believe prison brings back the dead or recoups lost money or does anything beneficial to anyone in or out of prison. Prison is just an archaic and cruel and inhumane way of extracting revenge and torture on someone who has been convicted of doing something against societal law. There must be a better way.

I do not know what that better way may be. I just know prison is not the answer. Maybe society should go back to the preprison days and kill convicted murderers. Maybe death is the answer for murderers, rapists, and pedophiles. But that said, maybe fines and community forced labor is a more justifiable sentence for robbers, burglars, embezzlers, and other such "criminals." There has to be better answers, better ways to treat lawbreakers than forcing said individuals to live in cages. There has to be.

Just a thought.

There Will Never Be Peace in the World

I do not believe there will ever be peace in the world. Why is that, you might ask? My answer is, I believe very few want peace. I believe most people to be self-centered egotists posing for local and national exposure. Most people are self-centered egotists who want to be rich and famous at all costs. Most people are self-centered egotists who care little about anyone else unless that someone else has some influence or effect on their life. Most people are self-centered egotists who want to own guns they allege are for their protection when the reality is they just like killing things and/or people. Most people are self-centered egotists who will kill people if they can get away with it. Most people are self-centered egotists who thrive on power and will do anything to get power and maintain that power. I do not believe there will ever be peace in the world. People do not want peace.

Just a thought.

My Daughter Asked Me, "Daddy, Why Does Everyone Make Such a Fuss over a Policeman Being Killed but Not So Much over Other People?"

My daughter is a very smart young girl. That is a very good question. People die every day for various reasons: old age, disease, crime, accidents. And yet when a cop is fatally shot, all of a sudden the cops come out of the doughnut shops and get serious about their jobs; they then actually care about the dead person. Cops do not serve and protect "us." Cops serve and protect each other and themselves. We just happen to be part of the job description—the part of which they earn their money via our tax dollars. We are a faceless object that is a potential threat in the cops mind to the cop and they treat us like a threat. It is no surprise to me that the people of Ferguson reacted how they reacted to a teen's death by the gun of a cop. It seems so often that cops react to "us" all as if we are all criminals. Cops appear so often to treat us like criminals, to talk to us like criminals, and to react to us as if we are all criminals. Cops so often appear to treat us all as if we are potential killers intent on killing them. It seems to me that many cops have itchy trigger fingers. It seems to me that cops relish the opportunity to shoot us, not protect us. My answer to my daughter's question is that "There is no good reason for everyone to make such a fuss over a policeman being killed more so than other people." WE ARE ALL IMPORTANT; WE ALL HAVE FAMILIES; AND WE ALL DESIRE TO LIVE." The term *brotherhood of police* is insulting to all us civilians! The police should be just as concerned about our deaths as their fellow cops. EVERYONE IS IMPORTANT, NOT JUST COPS! We should ALL be a brotherhood of man.

Just a thought.

I'm So Tired Hearing People Lecture How the Rest of Us Drivers on the Road Should Watch Out for Motorcycles

The inference that drivers of nonmotorcycles are reckless and motorcyclists are innocent careful riders and hence drivers should be careful and watch out for motorcyclists is nonsense. Although I do agree most nonmotorcyclists are terrible drivers, I do not believe motorcyclists are innocent careful riders. The motorcyclists I have seen riding the roadways are reckless, careless, and unconcerned about all other riders on the road, including themselves, and they are anything but innocent rule-of-the-road abiders. I have witnessed motorcyclists riding between vehicles. I have witnessed motorcyclists create their own lanes on the road. I witnessed motorcyclists driving in excess of the speed limit (and they are more vulnerable in crashes than most others). In my opinion, motorcyclists are the worst drivers on the road. Motorcyclists create potential for deadly accidents. The motorcyclists I have witnessed on the road are reckless and unconcerned about the rules of the road or the right of way for all other drivers. They are impatient and lack concern for other drivers. There seems to be a mind-set that implicitly overtakes so many motorcyclists. As soon as a rider of the road mounts a bike, they ink on tattoos. They begin to wear leather with the excuse it is the only clothing that keeps them warm, and overall, they cop an attitude that they are kings and queens of the road. It is kind of funny really. A motorcycle is nothing more than a motor vehicle on two wheels with no roof. Riding a motorcycle does not make one easy rider. Watching motorcyclists and the dress and attitude they adopt upon mounting a motorcycle brings to mind all the other idiots who play role games upon taking up a hobby or whatever. Take bicyclists for example. How often do you see pointed, helmeted, skin-tight European-glasses-wearing bikers on the road riding with an attitude like they are professional racers competing in the Tour de France? Come on now. I have ridden my bicycle nearly two hundred miles on a two-day trip and averaged fifty to seventy miles on one-day trips, and I never dressed pretending to be a professional cyclist. I just wore comfortable clothing. Take runners as another example. I knew a woman who wanted to take up running, so she spent all this money on running outfits and then ran three houses on her first and only run and then called it quits. I just dress comfortable when I run. Too many people are too intent on being performers, actors. Just be yourself. No one cares what you think you are. I'm not impressed. No one really cares except you, so don't bother spending the money dressing for an onstage play.

But I digress. Let's get back to the topic of road safety and motor-cyclists. I watch out for every driver on the road, not just motor-cyclists, because most drivers are terrible. Almost no one can stay within the lines of the road for more than one minute. Watch your fellow drivers, and you will see I am right. Almost no one uses warning signals (now wrongly referred to as turn signals) when switching lanes or turning corners, and if they do use them, they use them AFTER they switched lanes or AFTER they turned the corner. So what is the point I am trying make midst all this rambling verbiage? My point is that ALL drivers should be careful and mindful of each other and the rules of the road. It doesn't matter whether you ride a motorcycle or a van or a sedan or a truck. Most drivers are terrible and need to improve on their driving skills; they to focus on the road and not their cell phones. AND motorcyclists need to be especially careful and mindful of other drivers and the rules of the road as they are more exposed to harm if they collide with other vehicles. We must look to ourselves for protection first and not merely depend on others.

Just a thought.

Most People Will Hate Me for Saying So, but I Think Tattoos Are Childish

It is a fad these days for children of all ages to mark up their bodies with one ugly ink picture or word on their body . . . then another . . . then another . . . then another. Obsessed with covering their body with "art," they fail to stop. To me it appears to be an obsession that the tattooed cannot control.

Now, I know many of you—if not most of you—reading this commentary have at least one tattoo, but that does not change my opinion. Many people like me have been ostracized from the crowd or even imprisoned for having a "different" belief, but then that is human nature. People follow beliefs, ideas, and fads like sheep and persecute all others who see things differently. In fact, you can argue the same of my dislike of tattoos and my reasoning therefore. I am sorry if I offend any inked individuals reading this commentary, but I find tattoos similar to a fad as in other cultures where the piercing of one's nose with bones or one's lips with plates is considered cool. I do not find tattoos attractive; I think tattoos detract from the beauty of one's body and draw attention to unattractive features. To me, tattoos are like Mohawk haircuts; tattoos are tacky. I do not think tattoos are attractive. I do not think tattoos are art. This is my opinion, yes; and I am in the minority on this matter, most likely yes. But I am merely being honest as to my true feelings about tattoos. I think tattoos make men look less professional, less civilized, and more like they believe they are tough guys. I think tattoos make women look less attractive. Of the two sexes, I find women's bodies extremely attractive in their hairless appearance (yes, I know you shave your legs and underarms), and I think tattoos detract from a woman's beauty. This is just me—again, I'm sure I am in the minority.

I believe the human body to be a beautiful thing to look at. I believe women's bodies are like a beautiful deer whereas a man's body is like an unshapely hippopotamus. Tattoos do not add but detract from beauty. Tattoos turn a deer into a mule and the unattractive hippo into a warthog. Tattoos make me think you are insecure with your physical appearance and you need to dress your body with things to draw favorable attention to you. Tattoos also make me think you are not an individual thinker but a follower who needs acceptance by others to feel included. I dare you to be different. I dare you to be an independent thinker. I dare you to be unique. I challenge you to be the beautiful naked human being you—naked of ink, naked of jewelry, naked of makeup. I think you are beautiful.

Just a thought.

Guns Don't Kill, People Do?

Guns don't kill, people do? Sorry, but I don't buy into that slogan. **GUNS DO KILL!** If a person comes at me with a piece of paper, I get a paper cut. If a person comes at me with an eraser, I get little pieces of eraser all over me. If a person comes at me with a scream, I get irritated. If a person flings a paper airplane at me from his or her car, I usually reply "what the . . ." and that is only if the paper plane hits me. If a person throws his uneaten McDonald's Happy Meal at me from his car, I get a messed up shirt, and again I reply "what the . . ." **But if a person fires a gun at me from his or her car—and the bullet(s) hit me—I say nothing, because I am dead.** So I have to disagree and proclaim, **"YES, GUNS DO KILL!"**

Just a thought.

Why Are There So Many Crazy People?

Why are there so many crazy people? Maybe that is not the nicest way to ask the question, but it is a good lead-in to the point I want to make. It seems every day the media reports to us another story about someone with a gun—remember guns don't kill, people kill—right. Someone with a gun who shoots at complete strangers and some innocent(s) die and others lay wounded and the story culminates in the death of the shooter. One such tragic story reported of a gun that doesn't kill ended recently with the death of seven people. Six of those innocent people killed by a gun that doesn't kill allegedly shot by a crazed young man who believed beautiful young women should fall in love with him and because they did not fall in love with him, he believed they deserved to die, and this crazed young man apparently believed the young men whom the beautiful women paid attention to also deserved to die. Is this crazy? Yes, I believe so.

I believe a great many people of this world of ours believe they must play out a story the way they have this story pictured in their head. I believe many people live their lives as if acting out a scripted play, and so many people cannot handle things when life does not play out the way they believe it should play out; people hate to go off script. Many people might think this to be ludicrous, but then a lot of people keep their crazy side hidden. Most people play out their lives according to scripted behavior as taught by their particular social, national, religious, or cultural group. Most people behave as instructed to do so, and when the script is interrupted or lost or someone fails to follow along, they reveal their crazy side.

So is there a solution that can resolve this crazy behavior that pops up so often? I don't know, but I suggest we try not to live a scripted life. We cannot all be the leading man or the leading lady in the movie of life. We cannot all be celebrities, so give Facebook and all those other social media outlets a rest. Stop trying to be the center of attention. We are not all going to be the eye-catcher of the opposite sex. We are not all going to be the popular one at the party. We are not all going to be the quarterback, the musician, the CEO, or the famous artist. We are not all going to marry. We are not all going to have children. We are the same, and yet we are all different. We are all looking for positive attention, yet we are not all going to get positive attention. And don't mistake negative attention for positive attention. Don't hurt others to draw attention to you. It is not the fault of others that we do not measure up to be what we believe we should be. Remember, if you want to be the apple of everyone's eye, that means someone has to not be the apple of everyone's eye. How many apples can one stare at, let alone eat? I hate apples; give me chocolate. Why should you or I be the center of attention rather than someone else anyway? I cannot think of any other reason than that you are you and I am me.

Life is short. Live the best life you can. Look for happiness with what life gave you. Play the cards you were dealt with. There is always something and/or someone that can make your life worthwhile. Don't hurt others to punish them for shortcomings in your life. Remember, they are no different than you; everyone is looking for acceptance and attention. Some people will be blessed with lives that we dreamed we could have, but if we fail to achieve that dream, should we punish someone else for achieving that dream? I don't think so. Be happy for others. Don't be jealous. Live your life, and live it well. There is so much to this world that there must be something within it that can make you happy. Don't stop looking if you have not found it yet. If it means anything at all, I do not know you, and yet I care for you. That is why I am writing this. And if I care for you, there has to be someone close to you that cares for you that much more. Love and do not hate. Love yourself, and others will love you as well. Don't release your crazy side.

Just a thought.

When Will Peace and Equality
Truly Exist in This World?

When will peace and equality truly exist in this world? Only when people stop identifying themselves as separate groups and only when people stop striving for fame and fortune and only when people stop glorifying violence. It is common practice in America today to identifying oneself as African American or Spanish American or Asian American or European American or female or male or gay or lesbian or Catholic or Protestant or Jewish or Muslim or Atheist. Me, I'm a realist. But is not identifying oneself as a good and caring person truly better? It is common in America today for people to strive to be rich and famous, to amass more money than they can ever spend on things they do not need, to be known and worshiped by everyone else. Isn't it better to have just what you need to care for you and your family and enough to help friends, neighbors, and others you find may not have what they need? I believe it better to be known to your family and friends as a caring and loving person, someone who is always there when they need you. It is common in America today to worship guns and violence, to quickly cry for war, to pay to watch people shoot each other in movies and on cable, to learn to fight and to fight, to hit each other with fists and hurl hurtful words at each other. Isn't it better if we talk to one another and even better if we listen to one another, if we take the time to understand our differences, if we strive to prevent fights and wars rather than to initiate wars? Peace starts at home, and we can extend its reach by our willingness to understand others and by our striving to be understood, in nonviolent ways. We need to realize we do not have all the answers and that the world may be moving in the wrong direction but at the same time not give in to misdirection and know we cannot make change for the better without effort and without the realization that positive change is necessary.

Just a thought.

Freedom of Speech Is Not Allowed in the USA

It is a myth that Americans are allowed freedom of speech. The freedom of speech so many Americans believe in and fight for is the freedom of the mob to dictate what others can and cannot say. Some may say freedom of speech is only applicable when the government is involved. It is true that the US Constitution requires freedom of speech in matters concerning citizens and their government—although even that is limited by legislation and the Supreme Court. A Supreme Court politically motivated in all its decisions and controlled by godlike men and women who hold their position of power for life. Ever since I was a child, I was led to believe—as many other Americans like myself—that freedom of speech is an American right whether the government is involved or not. That may not be true, but it is what I believed growing up in America. Think a moment. If we can only speak what is on our minds when voicing opinions in situations where the government and nothing or no one else is involved, do we really have the right to free speech? I think not. Every day Americans are punished for attempting to exercise free speech, not punished by imprisonment but punished by their ostracism from society, a group or a potential job, punished financially by being refused work or having their ability to work taken away, punished by their loss of ownership rights, punished by the slinging of nasty and vulgar language at them and/or harassment. There are worse punishments than imprisonment, and Americans with power, prestige, and employment possibilities know them well. You may exercise free speech only to then be judged by other Americans at the risk of financial and social punishment—yes, the mob rules our speech. No one in America can say anything the mob disagrees with without risking punishment. America can be cruel to whoever challenges the mob. Democracy may not fear a dictator, but it still must fear the mob. Freedom of speech is a myth. And just so you understand, freedom of speech is not just saying what the mob thinks is nice and pleasing to the mob. Freedom of speech includes stupid and nasty comments. Stupid and nasty comments made by European Americans and stupid and nasty comments made by African Americans and Arab Americans and Hispanic Americans and Asian Americans and Native Americans as well as every other race, national background, sex, age, size, intelligence, athletic ability, etc. As Americans, we should support freedom of speech no matter the content, no matter how stupid we personally believe the words to be. No matter if government is involved in the use of our speech or not. You can disagree with what is said. You can argue about what is said. But support everyone's right to say it. Support freedom of speech. Don't punish freedom of speech. The wrong message is sent, and the wrong message is received when any of us punish freedom of speech.

Just a thought.

Feed the Homeless

PLEASE FEED THE HOMELESS. During a family vacation to California, I came up with an idea that I think is great (he has no trademark on the word), and my family and I executed while in California and other places since that vacation. We spent four nights in San Francisco, three nights in Los Angeles, and three nights in San Diego. My family and I ate only half of every meal, and we boxed the other untouched half of every meal and handed it out to the homeless in all three cities. It is a little thing to do, but it felt good to help even if only in a small way. What felt as good as giving food to the homeless were the reactions of the homeless receiving the food. At every handout of no less than several boxes (at one handout ten boxes), at least one person in every group of homeless made sure that the most needy of their group got the most and that everyone in their group shared the food. I was nearly brought to tears witnessing such kindness and concern, such selflessness, from men and women in obvious personal distress. Those people—especially the rich—who hoard possession after possession, more than needed, and waste food like it is available in abundance for all should take note of the selflessness, kindness, and concern for others that I witnessed by a shunned group of people living their daily lives in perpetual need of help. Anyone reading this writing, right now, at this moment, I beg you to help the needy. Help the homeless; help anyone you come across who appears in greater need than yourself. And if at all possible, and if it can be done safely (do not put yourself at risk), help the needy directly, not by charitable contributions. In my opinion, charitable organizations are not the nonprofit groups they claim to be but profit-making businesses that give only a percentage of your donation to those in need while keeping a good percentage to cover their "expenses" and provide many a living wage. I do not deem most charities as "charitable." I believe a true charity to be one where no one involved in the charitable organization receives any financial remuneration whatsoever, where every last penny goes to the intended recipient and no tax deduction is given to the donator. Charity should not be about reward or repayment; charity should be about helping others in need. So give directly to the needy if you can and if you can do so safely. Be smart and know not everyone on the street—like everyone else in the world—is to be trusted, but many are in great need of our help. So please give to the homeless and others in need, but be safe and smart when doing so.

Just a thought.

I'm Apologizing before You Read as I'm Sure I Will Offend Someone with This Thought

Despite my probably offending you, I have to get this off my chest as this has been driving me nuts for years. I am so tired of hearing people say "We must support the troops. Our soldiers are heroes." Many are not heroes. Some may more correctly be labeled "mercenaries." We have not been in a declared war since World War II. The men and women that participated in World War II are/were (live and dead) heroes. Those men and women fought for what so many claim our current day soldiers fight for—but many do not—our freedom and the defense of our nation and our allies. I also honor the men and women who fought in World War I and the Revolutionary War that birthed our country. I only have feelings of sadness for the men and women participating in and who died in our Civil War. The Civil War is a war that never should have been fought. Our government should have negotiated and reasoned out their differences without war. No man, woman, or child should EVER have been a slave to any other man, woman, or child—for that I fault the South for putting economics ahead of what this country claims to stand for—individual freedoms of all men, women, and children. But I digress. The soldiers I'm referring to are the soldiers participating in the many conflicts this country seems to be finding itself embroiled. Most of these "conflicts" being fought by our country today to me appear more like corporate battles for assets and commerce—not Congress-declared wars, not battles to defend our homes or our families or our way of life. They are battles to control oil, land, and the flow of money around the world. Unfortunately, not too many Americans agree this as reality. Many Americans buy into the media and political rhetoric orchestrated by the behind-the-scenes command of the corporate masters. And all these "conflicts" that thrive on our hard-earned TAXED money goes toward making the rich richer, while our infrastructure, our Medicare, our Medicaid, our Social Security morph into the color red. We have a multitrillion-dollar deficit, and yet our millionaire congressmen and congresswomen continue to tax us to death and start "conflicts" all over the world. I don't feel any safer. I don't feel any richer. It does seem to me, however, that the rich are getting richer. Our government, which is comprised of rich millionaires, gets richer; corporations get richer; and all the while somehow we get poorer. And all the while Americans proclaim how proud we are of our soldiers. Well, I am not proud of mercenaries.

If our nation falls under attack by a foreign power, if our homes and our lives are threatened by a foreign power, if a foreign power attacks our nation and/or declares war on our nation, THEN I will say "support our troops." Then I will be grateful and proud of the men and women who stand before the enemy and risk and give their lives to save our lives. Because then and only then will we have brave American men and women fighting for our freedom and our way of life and our lives, not merely men and women fighting "conflicts" for political reasons and corporate agendas . Then and only then will I support the troops and give them what I believe then to be their just due.

Just a thought.

Should Government Pay Defendant(s)' Court Expenses?

In criminal actions, government brings charges against a civilian and government prosecutes the defendant, all at the taxpayers' expense. The prosecutors and the judges are paid by the taxpayers to try defendants charged with breaking the law. Whether a defendant is found guilty and no matter the cost of trying the defendant, the prosecutors and the judges are paid. The defendant, however, must pay for his or her defense out-of-pocket; the defendant must hire an attorney and incur all legal costs entailed to defend her or himself and clear her or his name. Is this fair? I think not!

The American legal system favors the rich. The system taxes the middle class and the poor who by way of their taxes pay for the very prosecutors and judges working to put them in prison, while also having to mortgage away their savings to pay for their own defense. Where is the fairness in this our legal system?

If the prosecuting side of the law—which includes the courts and judges, who lean heavily toward assisting the prosecution of defendants rather than assisting the defense of defendants—is to be financed by the tax dollars of the poor and the middle class, then so too should a defendant's defense be financed by those same tax dollars. It is only fair. If we are a nation where every man, woman, and child is innocent until proven guilty, why do we have to pay to prove our innocence? Should not it be incumbent upon the state to prove the innocent guilty? But that is not the case in America. In America, if you are charged of a crime, you are guilty until proven innocent. The courts can even hold you in prison or force you to place bail until the conclusion of a trial. I thought you were innocent until proven guilty?

Think about what it cost a defendant to defend a serious criminal charge—a charge of murder, for example. A defendant potentially can spend thousands defending him or herself. And what if the defendant proves his or her innocence? The defendant is in no better a financial situation, win or lose. A defendant must pay the cost of his or her successful defense in the way of attorneys' fees and more, regardless of the outcome of his or her case. This can potentially cost a defendant his of her life savings. Yet the prosecutors walk away unscathed financially. In fact, they walk away richer. Why? Because it is their job to prosecute, and they get paid no matter the outcome. Just as it is the judge's job to judge, and the judge gets paid no matter the outcome. So after a trial is done and over, the defendant is poorer than before the trial, and the prosecutor and the judge are richer. Is this fair? If a defendant must pay to prove his or her innocence in a legal system that claims he or she is innocent until proven guilty, should not the state pay the defendant's cost of defense at least if the defendant proves his or her innocence?

You have probably been in court yourself at least in defense of a small traffic infraction. While in court, did you wonder about the system and whether it could be conducted in a more efficient and cost-effective manner? Had you mused about how the court conducted itself? A judge sits behind a large bench on a raised platform surrounded by armed guards. You, on the other hand, are made to sit and wait for as long as the court deems necessary. maybe for hours. Eventually, a pompous judge, who expects you to believe it is HIS or HER courtroom (not everyone's courtroom), and that you owe him or her nonreciprocated respect, condescendingly speaks to you from his or her throne. Do you get paid to quietly sit there for hours on end? How much time and possibly money did you lose sitting there? Were you missing time at work? If you are a parent responsible for young children at home, did you have to pay someone to babysit your children? Did the judge or assistant DA lose any time or money all the time you quietly waited your turn to be heard (or merely talked at) by the court? No, the court made money! Why, because it is their job. Is that fair? No! This is just the outcome of a legal system where we are all "guilty until proven innocent."

So what do you think? Should government pay defendants for their time in court, their lost time from work, their cost of preparation and attorney fees for their defense? I think the answer is a resounding "yes!" At the very least, if the state is unsuccessful in its attempt to prove a defendant guilty of an alleged crime, the state should put the defendant back in the same financial position the defendant was in prior to charges brought and a trial conducted against her or him.

I would add that defendants should be allowed to pursue lawsuits against state officials when the defendants prove their innocence, but then the state would tax you and me to pay their defense expense; that is what they do now. State officials are insulated from such lawsuits in most situations. Is that fair? I think not. But then we do live in a country where we are all guilty until proven innocent.

Just a thought.

Separation of Church and State

Our Constitution calls for separation of church and state, but does this country enforce that? Not in the least! Churches, temples, mosques—however they label themselves—find themselves exempt from taxes. All a church must do is claim a belief in invisible gods and that their objective is doing some invisible god's work and refrain from government affairs, and they are exempt from the payment of taxes that you—and the people who don't claim to see invisible gods—have to pay. How is this separation of church and state? The fact that these pagan religious groups are tax exempt means the rest of us rational citizens must pay more taxes than we would otherwise; we must foot the bill for the existence of churches. In effect, the churches live off of us. Churches are not separated in a "good" way for the rest of us; churches are separated from us by laws that elevate them to a higher class than us.

So what is a true separation of church and state? True separation of church and state means everyone pays taxes or no one pays taxes. We are all equal in the eyes of the law, and the church is owed no favoritism in tax relief or otherwise. This is not the case in America, however. You do not have to look very far or very hard to find examples of churches being favored by the state.

If you live in a community that has even a little money to spend on luxuries, look at all the land some of your community churches own. I own barely a half acre and pay thousands in taxes every year while trying to pay my bills and feed my children, and all the while local, state, and federal governments continue to raise my taxes. None of the taxing authorities care about us working men and women who struggle to get by, who live in communities suffering from increasing unemployment and lack of jobs, yet the taxing authorities care enough for the community churches to give them tax relief. Many of these churches own large amounts of land, acres and acres of land, and they fail to pay their fair share back to the communities that pay for their existence. The government is helping them thrive, but where is my government tax relief? If I lose my job, will government stop collecting taxes from me? If I claim to see invisible gods, will they give me tax relief? In my community alone, I know of at least two churches that both own large buildings and what appears to be hundreds of acres of land—buildings that could be used to house the poor; land that could be used to build parks, senior homes, housing for the poor, and many other uses; at the very least, buildings and land that could be taxed to lessen the tax burden on the rest of us who actually work for a living. I know of one church building big enough to house my entire street. Imagine if that building was taxed like your house is taxed. My guess is the church leaders would quickly look for real jobs.

Take a look around your community. How much land do the churches in your community own? How large are their buildings? And ask yourself and your neighbors who do not go to that church, temple, or mosque, why you or they should have to support someone else's belief in invisible winged creatures by way of tax breaks you are not also entitled to claim. Ask why you or they should have to pay taxes and said church should not have to pay their fair share of the community's taxes. Maybe we should all become ordained ministers and declare our homes churches, temples, or mosques and forget paying taxes altogether? What makes them higher-class citizens than us? Certainly not the US Constitution.

In this country, we are all supposed to be equal. There should be no "first lady, no first family." There should be no class of people held out by government as better than any other. We should all be equal. We should all pay taxes, or no one pay taxes. The state should honor the meaning of separation of church and state—and separate the state's favoritism thereof.

Just a thought.

A Thought on How to End Corruption in American Politics

The question as to why there is so much corruption in American politics as well as a possible answer to redress the problem of corruption in American politics might just be found in legislation. Congress, the executive branch of government, the judicial branch of government—they all answer corruption with more law. But more legislation has not solved the problem. Corruption is running rampant in America. In fact, corruption has become acceptable in America. Americans assume all their politicians are corrupt and accept this belief as a fact of political life. I believe Americans even encourage corruption. Comedians make fun of corrupt politicians and make a very comfortable living off of joking about politicians. Ask comedian Bill Maher what discussions about politicians and political corruption has done for his wallet. I like Bill Maher by the way. I even admire Bill Maher. Our political comedians are our most vocal and avid fighters against political corruption. So unlike our political comedians, should we continue to accept the status quo regarding our belief in corrupt politicians? Or should we do something about it? Can we do anything about it? I think we can.

One thing we could do is to redress requirements to hold a public office. Control and manipulation of legislation is an incentive for politicians to become corrupt and that incentive is something that must be eliminated. Temptation for corruption should be removed from politics. So how do we do that? Our government is supposed to be, or should be, small and efficient and run to help most of us, not merely a few of us. Our government is not supposed to be running our daily lives and making personal decisions for us.

Our government has a legitimate purpose for its existence, but it is not to be our nanny. Government is to protect us from outside forces that may harm us. It is necessary in a violent world with many world governments of varying philosophies and allegiances to have a standing military force that can protect us—defend us—from outside interference and/or harm. That does not mean a military force to be used by corporate America to conquer and control world assets. It means a military force to defend us and our chosen way of life—just that. Another purpose of our government is to protect our economic system. It is not government's job to control the running of said system. It is government's job to make sure no one and no entity interferes with the people's right to run, join, or implement the system. Another purpose of the government is to ensure the country's laws are implemented, followed, and honored. But this latter purpose should be construed tightly, not loosely. Laws should be enacted that are desired by the people, which are beneficial to the people such that the laws allow Americans to live, work, and play as intended by the people.

But what is the most effective way to run government for the people and by the people where government aids people in running their lives but does not run their lives and does not favor the few over the many? I believe changes in regulation of public offices would make a positive difference. I believe all publicly held offices should have restrictions placed upon said offices with the intent purpose of avoiding the possibility of corruption and malfeasance. Easily said, but what restrictions on the job description could possibly eliminate or lessen the possibility of corruption? I believe no one holding public office should be allowed to hold a financial or political interest in any business or charity or political group, organization of investment other than the interest of the office they hold. The salary paid by the public office they hold should be sufficient in of itself as compensation for the job therein done, and said salary should be the only payment they receive while in office and for a specified time thereafter their leaving office. Maybe a severance package could be offered after service, but commensurate with the salary, time served, and only for a limited time period thereafter. This is not perfect. There will always be "wiggle room" for corruption, but it is a start. We have so many rich congressmen and congresswomen, senators, and judiciaries, who are making money off of investments that have nothing to do with carrying out the duties of their public office but do conflict with the carrying out of their public office. We need politicians who truly care about government and the people. We need to weed out the money-seekers and the elite who thrive in corrupt systems such as ours by moving from corporations to politics and back to corporations after enacting favorable laws or commencing military action intended merely for corporate asset gain. We do not need to give said individuals a system they can thrive within. We need to restrict who can hold political office, and we need to restrict the business interests they may have that will assuredly affect their governmental decision-making.

Charitable organizations are another form of corruption in America, which needs reform. Creative definitions of what is defined as "profit" and what is defined as "expenses" allow corruption to run rampant in so-called charitable organizations. How much of your hard-earned dollars that you donate to charitable organizations are actually going to the purpose the charity claims it exists to fulfill? And how much of your hard-earned dollars donated to charities end up buying some charity executive or employee a car, jewelry, and a house? If those running a charitable organization are making a living off of the charity or even one dollar off of our charitable donations, if those working for the charitable organization are earning a living from the charity or earning even one dollar off of the charity dona-tions—it is not a charity. I cannot understand how a charity cannot receive ALL needed to run the charity as charitable contributions. A "true charity" should seek donations to ship, pack, and deliver their gifts. A true charity should seek philanthropist to donate their time at their expense. A true charity should not make a profit by any defi-nition of the word. Charities need reform or at the least redefinition. And I am as guilty as the next, but none of us should deduct our charitable donations from our tax debt.

Religious organizations are not supposed to be supported by government. Our Constitution calls for separation of church and state. Yet most religious organizations escape, paying their fair share of taxes. How is that separation of church and state? There is a church in my hometown that is the size of a palace and situated on what looks like one hundred acres of land tax-free. This kind of thing should not be allowed. A religious organization by definition is spiritual and its beliefs carried forth by word of mouth, helping and charity. So why do so many of these organizations need buildings larger than life and land used for nothing—all tax-free. Atheists and other philosophies abound in America, yet they pay taxes and follow their philosophical beliefs. Why do religious organizations such as Christianity, Judaism, Islam, and others receive special treatment under the law? All peaceful philosophies should be allowed to practice their beliefs according to our Constitution, but no one should receive special treatment under the law. The special treatment of religious organizations in this country needs to be reformed.

Corruption in America is rampant, but we should not just accept corruption as a given. None of us are naive enough to believe corruption will ever disappear in any form of government. It is human nature to want to rule the world. It is human nature to want to be rich. Many will do what they can to obtain fame, riches, and/or power—many, but not all of us. So to those of you who consider yourself in the minority, to those of you who believe the best interests of all over the few is most important, to those of you who also have the ability to effect change, I challenge you to tackle the problem of political corruption and all other forms of corruption in America. Use whatever power you have to redefine who your elected officials are and what they can do on your behalf. Hold your charitable organization accountable for the donations they accept on your behalf of the needy. Hold our religious communities to modest means as they preach from the pulpit. Don't accept the status quo.

Just a thought.

Hypocrisy

I am proud to be African American. Don't call me black. I am proud of my African heritage, and to celebrate my pride, I have African American churches and African American clubs and African American organizations and my sports heroes are all African American and my celebrity idols are all African American. I am African American and proud of it. Not racist, just proud.

Now read this:

I am proud to be European American. Don't call me white. I am proud of my European heritage, and to celebrate my pride, I have European American churches and European American clubs and European American organizations, and my sports heroes are all European American, and my celebrity idols are all European American. I am European American and proud of it. Racist!

I am proud to be homosexual. Don't call me a homo. I am proud of my sexual orientation, and to celebrate my pride, I have gay parades and gay clubs and gay organizations, and my sports heroes are all gay, and my celebrity idols are all gay. I am gay and proud of it.

Now read this:

I am proud to be heterosexual. Don't call me homophobic. I am proud of my sexual orientation, and to celebrate my pride, I have heterosexual parades and heterosexual clubs and heterosexual organizations, and my sports heroes are all heterosexual, and my celebrity idols are all heterosexual. I am heterosexual and proud of it. HOMOPHOBIC!

I am proud to be a woman. I am proud of my sex, and I demand to be treated equality—no more, no less. I vote only for women politicians because they are female like me. Proud of women!

Now read this:

I am proud to be a man. I am proud of my sex, and I demand to be treated equally—no more, no less. I vote only for male politicians because they are male like me. Sexist!

There is hypocrisy in America. Equality means just that . . . equality. Equality does not mean those as perceived to be treated unjustly are to be favored in every event, conflict, and happening of the day. Equality means equality. But that is not the reality in America today. Today to be a European heterosexual male in America means to be automatically labeled racist, sexist, homophobic, and white. The most unfairly treated group in America today is arguably the European heterosexual male. We are grouped together and labeled as "white." We can be insulted by African American comedians while the slightest joke made of African Americans by a European American comedian is met with a public whipping and a career-ending result. To show any pride in one's sexual orientation is only acceptable if one is homosexual. To be a heterosexual with pride is equated with "homophobia." To be a European American male is to be open to constant insults and being portrayed on television and in movies as the bumbling idiotic father, the cowardly male, and evil villain while the African American men and women and European American women are portrayed as good, kind, intelligent, and saviors of the day.

Just because an individual is considered a member of a group considered the largest group in America does not make that individual racist, sexist, and/or homophobic. And it does not obligate that individual to be representative of said group. Equality is about individuality and the rights of all individuals to be treated as individuals, not as members of a group. Racism, sexism, and sexual phobia run across ALL GROUPS and can be ANY INDIVIDUAL in America. And it usually is! Racism knows no color; there are many racist African Americans even though they are regularly ignored and/or considered acceptable by America. Sexual phobia knows no boundaries. Sexism favors neither one sex nor the other. So if you are going to celebrate who and what you are, if you are going to proclaim pride in who and what you are, WE ALL DESERVE TO DO THE SAME! I am no more racist, sexual phobic, or sexist than an African American, a homosexual, and/or a woman just because I am male, heterosexual, and of European descent. I have just as much right to be proud of who and what I am as anyone else. I have just as much right to proclaim my pride. If others have exclusive clubs aimed toward their perceived identity, then I should be able to have an exclusive club aimed toward my perceived identify as well. And I have as much right not to be grouped and labeled as anyone else wishing not to be grouped and labeled. Equality is equality is equality.

Just a thought.

A Man's Thoughts on Women and Beauty

Which one of the two TV actresses, Mayim Bialik and Jennifer Connelly, is a scientist in her "real" life? If you know anything about these two wonderful actresses, you know the answer. Mayim Bialik is not only an actress but a neuroscientist. Quite a lifetime accomplishment for Mayim—to excel not only in the field of acting. But to show she is so much more, so much more versatile, by obtaining a degree in the sciences. Know I am not demeaning Jennifer Connelly in any way. Jennifer is an attractive woman and a fine actress. But I am trying to make a point here.

A woman be so much more than the persona projected onto her by society. A woman does not have to become the outer shell that society attempts to box her into. Just because a woman is considered physically attractive does not mean she can never be a scientist or corporate leader or engineer or doctor or lawyer or whatever else she chooses to be. Just because a woman is considered physically unattractive does not mean she cannot be a newscaster, a model, or whatever else she chooses to be. Many women only compete for the jobs society's image-making machine has cast them as their perceived role. I can only give the male perspective on this topic. This topic should really be written by a woman. But I feel somewhat compelled to say something. I dated a lot of women when I was younger, and it was the outer shell that attracted me. I have grown a little wiser with age. But I certainly was not alone in this my shallow attraction to women, and this shallow attraction is still prevalent today. And not just amongst men. I have met numerous women who have told me that "you have to be physically attracted to the person first before you can date and learn to love them." Really? I don't agree. I believe this kind of thinking is why 50 percent of marriages end in divorce. What I have learned, and what I would like to pass on to others—what has resulted in my blessed fortune to have met and married my wife— what you should know as the success to any long lasting relationship is that one must look deep within a person and ignore the outer shell. Listen. Listen. Listen. Hear what (s)he says. A person should be defined by their inner self, not their outer shape, their hair, their lips, their eyes, their butt, their chest, their smell, or their walk. It is what is inside that defines us all with more power and love than any outer shell. If you fall in love with what is inside a person, it doesn't matter if the outside is fat, skinny, short, tall, shapely, or not. You will remain in love, for the inside grows stronger while the outside weakens with age.

There are a lot of outwardly attractive and beautiful women, but there are also a lot of outwardly unattractive woman that are amazingly beautiful. My point is, do not allow society to dictate what you must be based on its arbitrary decisions as to what you should be based on your physical appearance. One does not look like a scientist or a lawyer or a doctor or a model. You are anyone of these professions because you choose to be anyone of these professions. I'm not naive. I realize as you do that society will continue to dictate. A short, heavyset, outwardly unattractive woman will most likely not be hired to be a model. Even though I believe BEAUTY is a light that shines from within such that it overtakes the outer self, and I believe many others do as well; many do not. But even so, do not allow society to force you to be what it chooses. Do not let society dictate how you must act based upon your outer shell. You are what is inside you. Be you!

Just a thought.

Truth, Logic, Reason, Empathy, Sympathy, Love, Concern for Others

What do these words mean? I know. And so do others. But do we all agree to the same meanings? I doubt it. *TRUTH*—to more of us than not, it means something someone else does not tell us rather than one is not a lie. It is a word more often than not used to denigrate the integrity of others by claiming and/or proving others lack thereof. All the while, those using the word *truth* against the claim of others are many times far from exhibiting the truth themselves. But if they have not been caught telling a lie, truth is theirs to control and manipulate. *REASON*—to more of us than not, it means rationalizing something to one's advantage. The word is rarely used in the context of its original intended meaning. It describes disconnected links in a mismatching chain of facts explained in a cloudy context with the title of anything but reason. *EMPATHY*—very few people really understand/or care about the feelings of others. What they understand and care about is how feigning empathy will reward them with recognition, fame, power, acceptance, and anything else favorable to them rather than its true understanding and concern for others. The self is most important to most. *SYMPATHY*—this is something that most people want for themselves, not to give to others. But of all the aforementioned terms, it is the one that most people come closest to truly giving. Why? Because sympathy cost them nothing, and it makes them feel better to know others are worse off than them and to some sympathy is an attention drawer where one can say, "Hey, that's how I feel too. Feel sorry for me." *LOVE*—what exactly does *love* mean? The word means a thousand different things to a thousand different people. Mostly, it is a self-love thing. That is why so many people marry and divorce. Self-satisfaction of sexual desires tends to be labeled as love when it is really a label for a future divorce. Despite all the negative descriptions I have put forth, there are true and noble meanings to the aforementioned words. Sadly, very few of us actually live them, however. This is very sad, indeed.

There is one more word I would like to mention, and that is *smiling*. The first thing many of us learn about smiling is, "don't." Smiling is not allowed. If a man smiles at a stranger who happens to be a woman, she tends to think you want to shag her. If a man smiles at a child, many people think he's a pedophile. If a man smiles at another man, another man may believe he's gay. If a man smiles at strangers in general, a lot of people believe something is wrong with him. Why is that? This should not be. We should all smile at each other, and we should all welcome being smiled upon. But we live in a cold, self-centered society that thinks little of anyone else unless that someone else has something that benefits them in some manner. I'm sorry to disappoint women, attractive and unattractive, but you need to know there are nice men who smile at you merely because they are nice men being friendly. I'm disappointed in you, paranoid mothers, who believe only women can smile at children and not be a pedophile. Many men are fathers and smile at children because they like children in a fatherly way no different than women claim to like children in a motherly way. And I am sorry to awaken some of you, delusional women, but there are some men who are better parents than some women. There are men who raise their children as the primary caretaker and do a better job at doing so than women raising their children. I was the stay-at-home parent who raised my three children. I even took my first child to work with me the first three years of his life, and I worked out of my home with the other two children. All my children have been at the top of their classes in school, well adjusted, and have many friends. And I'm sorry, guys, just because a man smiles at another man, it does not mean he wants sex with that man. Some men are just friendly and sociable by nature. Man, there are so many paranoid and self-focused people. Smiling in general should not be a terrible thing. Smiling should not be a sign of "weird." What is really "weird" and sad is the multitude of people who frown and scowl at strangers. What is really sad is the multitude of people who cannot look a stranger in the eye. People walk by one another like they are passing by an inanimate object. It is so very sad. Smiling is a good thing, and there is nothing wrong with smiling, so all of you, SMILE.

Just a thought.

War Is Hell on Earth

Why do so many people trumpet a desire to do battle? Why are so many people quick to demand a war? Why is the word *negotiation* used more often as a disguise masking the intent to do battle, the desire to conquer, the desire to rule, the desire to destroy, maim, and end the life of others? Oh, there is always a good reason put forth. They will kill us if we do not kill them first. They live an evil, whorish lifestyle. They are not followers of the true god. They are enemies of god. They are a decadent society. Their government is cruel and evil. Their people want us to liberate them from the dictatorship that rules them. We are good. We know what is best. We are only helping them to become a democracy—to be free, like us; to have morals and a belief in the true religion, like us; to have a government like ours that rules with love and justice for all.

It is easy to fool yourself. It is easy to be fooled by others. Others who care nothing for you except how you can be used to get them what they want. Others who need you to shape the world into their personal vision of what they believe it should be. Others who need you to obtain their desires and a comfort that few of us will ever realize. Yes, we are easily fooled, manipulated. But we hardly ever see it that way. No, we see ourselves as patriots. We see ourselves as freedom fighters. We see ourselves as spreading the true faith to the nonbelievers who will burn in hell but for us. We have no desire to rule the world like them. We are trying to save the world. We know what is best for all. Only we can save the world. And . . . our leaders . . . know what is best for us all. We must trust our leaders to know, when they wage war on others, it is in our best interests. We must trust our leaders see the evil that we sometimes do not see. Must we? I think not. Do not believe rumors or tales of evil without proof. Believe in corporate greed and its control of government; that is a fact that few of us can dispute. Leaders may shout we are a free and proud people and proclaim they share our ideals and that they would never steer us wrong. They will convince you that you must trust every word and every prepared speech and every command they issue forth. Follow blindly. Believe us when we tell you we must wage war on others. We must believe everything they tell us, mustn't we?

It seems war is waged too easily. Living in a powerful nation as we do, war can be waged and carried on for decades without our noticing its effects whatsoever—oh, except for maybe the financial cost thereof and how it affects our taxed incomes. But besides our pocketbooks, war can be waged very indiscreetly. Except for 911, wars have been waged away from our homeland; it has been many years since a war was fought here at home.

But how easy it is to wage a war aside, have you given much thought to what really goes on in a war? Is a war merely a verbal argument between one country's leaders and another country's leaders? Like a game of chess or the game of battleship? Ha, we all know better than to believe something like that, but do we ever think about what really goes on during a war? Do we ever think about the effects of war? The result of the battles during the war and after the conflict has ceased? Do we?

The following are only estimates, estimates of the numbers of deaths and causalities resulting from a few wars fought, so please do not hold me to the exactness of the figures. I am only trying to paint a picture, not quote statistics. The Afghan Civil War resulted in near 2 million deaths. The Iran-Iraq War resulted in near 2 million deaths. The Rwandan Genocide resulted in about 1 million deaths. The Vietnam War resulted in near 3 million deaths. The Korean War resulted in near 4.5 million deaths. World War II resulted in the deaths of somewhere near 72 million people. The Holocaust of World War II accounted for about 17 million of those deaths. World War I resulted in near 65 million deaths. The American Civil War resulted in near 800,000 deaths. The Taiping Rebellion in China resulted in near 100 million deaths. The Napoleonic Wars resulted in near 7 million deaths. The French Wars of Religion resulted in near 4 million deaths. The Mongol Conquests of Eurasia resulted in near 70 million deaths. The religious Crusades resulted in near 3 million deaths. The aforementioned are only a few of the conflicts that history has suffered resulting in casualties and death. They are only a few of so many more that history has suffered. I could fill pages and pages with historical wars and conflicts amongst peoples and never reach an end. How do we merely accept all these deaths? How do we just view all the pain and suffering that occurred therein and therefrom as a mere passage of history. War is truly hell on Earth. War is not a TV movie. War is blood and pain and loss of limbs and death of children and death and more death.

So why do we rush to war? Why are we so quick to attack and kill others? Is it because we feel isolated from the deaths and destruction and pain resulting therefrom? We certainly are not isolated from injury, being disabled, or from death if we are a soldier fighting that war, or if we are a civilian—men, women, and babies, caught up in the battles. But if we are not there but here at home, we are safe in our houses while our sons and daughters and husbands and wives fight the wars for us and for our leaders and for our corporations. And innocent women and children and babies are maimed, bloodied, and killed. But we rarely see the deaths of the innocents, unless their deaths make good press to convince us to join a battle.

So who suffers the most because of these endless wars? Those people in the thick of the battle suffer: soldiers and innocents. They cannot hide. They cannot take lightly the horrors of war, which the survivors thereof bring home with them. In World War I, there were approximately 21 million military personnel wounded. Near 1 million civilians died as a result of military action. Near 6 million civilians died as a result of famine and disease and accidents. Nearly 1.2 million died as a result of the use of chemical weapons. In World War II, nearly 55 million deaths were those of civilians due to military action and crimes against humanity; the Holocaust accounted for near 17 million of those deaths. About 135,000 casualties resulted from one atomic bomb dropped on Hiroshima and another 64,000 casualties from a second atomic bomb dropped on Nagasaki. We have become so good at killing we can now kill thousands with just one bomb and leave thousands more who survive its blast to suffer debilitating disease and injury. So many innocents die.

War is not a video game. We don't play, die, and live to play again. War is not a movie. We don't get to sit in our armchairs eating popcorn when bombs are dropped on our home. Well, maybe we can, but that might be our last meal. War is final. War is destructive. War destroys families, lives. It kills children, mothers, daughters, sisters and brothers, fathers, sons, friends and neighbors. War destroys homes, schools, hospitals, churches, bridges, roads, supermarkets, and historical monuments. War destroys dreams, hopes, and love. War is hell on earth. Please think before yelling "yes" to our leaders who sit comfortably in their mansions while waging war with your sons and daughters on men, women, and children. Think about the destruction that war causes. Think about the innocents who lose their lives, their loved ones. Please remember, war is not something to be proud of. War may sometimes be a necessary evil, but not something to rush into. Remember war is hell on earth.

Just a thought.

Chapter 6

ENTERTAINMENT

In the Ali Versus Liston II Fight, Did Liston Take a Dive?

I've been a big Muhammad Ali fan since I was ten years old. I'm sixty years old as I write this commentary. Muhammad Ali was my first and probably only celebrity hero that I ever looked up to as a role model while growing up. And no, I'm not black. And no, I'm not a Muslim. I come from a white lower-class family with no money (not all white people are rich, just like not all black people are poor). There was just something about Ali's character. There was something about Ali's willingness to stand up for his beliefs. There was just something about Muhammad Ali that brought out an admiration for him within me. Ali got me—a pacifist—to like and follow the sport of boxing. Go figure.

The first time I heard the name Muhammad Ali and the first boxing match I ever watched on television was the first Fraser versus Ali fight. And I was hooked on Ali' fights thereafter. I would sweat and smoke (I used to smoke—not until I was fifteen years old, however), watching Ali fights and praying to I don't know who that Ali would never lose. When Ali did lose, I was depressed (get a life, Greg). In my defense, I was just a stupid kid. But unlike many in white America at that time, I liked and I admired Muhammad Ali. And like most of America this year, I liked and I admired Muhammad Ali. BUT . . .

But just recently, I watched for the first time the first Ali versus Liston fight. Actually, I watched the old black-and-white films of both of Ali's fights versus Charles Sonny Liston. I had an attack of nostalgia hearing of Ali's recent death, and I decided late the one night to watch Ali's two fights with Sonny Liston, which I discovered were both available to watch on cable TV.

The first Ali versus Liston fight was more of a one sided win for Ali than all the stories I remember being told or that I read or heard about. But the second Ali versus Liston fight . . . the rematch . . . This time . . . appeared to me to be a joke. I was obviously not in attendance at the second Ali versus Liston fight. I was just a kid under ten years of age at the time of the fight. The fight took place in another state from where I lived, and even if the fight had taken place in my state, I couldn't have afforded to attend nor would I have ever had the opportunity to attend. My point being that I was not present to witness firsthand the battle between these two great heavyweight fighters. But now, as an adult making use of film and its replay feature, specifically slow-motion replay, and with the added plus of an older mind with greater experience and understanding of the fight game resulting from my having watched thousands of boxing matches over the years and my arguably greater capability for reasoning and objectivity I amassed over these nearly fifty years—I saw this fight in a different light. I saw in this fight what I believe to be Sonny Liston taking a dive.

History tells the story of the phantom punch Ali threw at and which took out Liston, sending Liston to the canvas and solidifying Ali's claim to the heavyweight championship. However, I believe history needs a rewrite. I believe Ali's "knockout" punch was truly a "phantom" punch. I believe it a phantom punch because I don't believe Ali's fist came anywhere close to touching Sonny Liston. I believe, like a phantom, the punch in question would not have knocked out a fly. What I saw when Ali threw the "phantom" punch was not a punch at all, but Ali pulling his punch. I saw Ali's elbow bent throughout the punch—never straightening out—never coming even close to touching Liston's body anywhere thereon. I don't believe Ali's "knockout punch" knocked out Liston. I believe Liston took a dive. And I have to suggest that if Liston had been a little smarter than he appeared not to be, he would have at least waited for Ali to throw a punch that hit him before he threw himself to the canvas. It appeared to me as if Liston thought Ali's "phantom" punch was going to hit him, and so Liston took that as a cue to drop to the canvas, thinking it the time to take a dive. I believe it was only after he hit the canvas that Liston realized Ali's punch was not going to connect, and then it was too late. At least this is what I believe I saw and what I believe really happened. I could be wrong, but you will have to convince me why I should believe otherwise.

In my mind, what made the so-called "knockout" more laughable than credible was what I perceived as a pitiful acting job by Liston: Liston's falling down, getting up, and falling down again looked to me like a night out at the WWE. Liston appeared as if he was acting—and acting terribly. I've seen better acting at professional wrestling matches. When Liston stood up after "falling" to the canvas and then "fell" down again, it looked soooooooooo comical, so contrived, so fake. I cannot believe anyone could believe the second fall was anything but faked and a poor job of acting. And if the "phantom" punch wasn't bad enough, the supposed trying to beat the 10-count was ridiculous as well. I think Liston intentionally beat the 10-count, but it looked as if he miscalculated the clock. And upon realizing his mistake of getting to his feet too soon, Sonny rather poorly pretended to fall back to the canvas, and the referee (a seasoned fighter himself), apparently too absorbed with Ali's celebratory dance around the ring, lost track of Liston and the 10 count and decided to count Liston out despite Liston's getting to his feet, beating the 10 count, before the referee's attention got back to Liston.

Now, these observations of mine and my opinion that Sonny Liston took a dive are merely my personal opinion(s) based on my personal observations. I could be wrong, so don't quote my opinion and/or my observations as gospel. I'm not making these statements as truth. I wasn't at the fight. But these are my observations, and this is my opinion based on my observations as a near fifty-year veteran boxing fan. I THINK LISTON TOOK A DIVE, and the results of that fight were not a testimony to Ali's greatness but a testimony to corruption in boxing and a soiling of the memory of Ali for me. That said, I still believe Ali could have won the fight if there had been no "phantom" punch or early stoppage. I still believe Ali was a great boxer and a charismatic individual. Sonny Liston, however, is another story. I have heard stories that Sonny Liston had ties to the mob. I can conjecture that maybe the mob demanded Liston take a dive in the fight—that maybe some people stood to make a lot of money as a result of Liston's stumbling to the canvas. I can also conjecture that maybe a brash, loudmouthed young fighter who reminds me of many professional wrestlers was what boxing needed to draw more fans and bring in more money to the sport. Maybe, but whatever the reason or whatever the truth of the events of that night, in my mind, Ali did not win that fight. Liston threw that fight.

Whatever the truth behind Sony Liston's being knocked out in Ali versus Liston II, I will forever more—in my mind—believe Liston took a dive. I will forever more believe Ali did not win that fight but that Liston threw that fight. No matter the truth, in my mind the legend of Muhammad Ali will be forever more tarnished. That said, I still will remember Muhammad Ali as the greatest ever.

Just a thought.

Boxing and the Weigh-In

I have to preface this commentary with the statement that I'm a pacifist who likes to watch boxing matches. This does not make sense. It is not logical, I know, That said, I want to comment on the topic of weight classifications that decide championship titles in boxing matches, and I want to comment on the required weigh-in procedure.

I just watched an NBC telecast of a boxing match between Adrien Broner and Shawn Porter. An interesting fight and an interesting matchup between two very different fighters with two very different ring styles. I am not surprised that Sean Porter won in a decision. What I am surprised about and I remain continually surprised about, however, is the weigh-in procedure that takes place before these fights. I do not like it! And I will tell you why by example.

The Broner-versus-Porter fight was a welterweight match; welterweight is 147 lbs. maximum, although the fight terms for the Broner/Porter fight called for a maximum weight for each fighter of no more than 144 lbs. At the official weigh-in, which was the day before the fight, Shawn Porter weighed in at 144 lbs. exactly and Adrien Broner weighed in at 143.5 lbs. The day of the fight, both fighters were some 10 lbs. over the 144 lb. limit. I think there was a contractual clause in the Broner/Porter fight allowing a maximum rehydration weight limit of an additional 10 lbs. But this leads into my issue with boxing's weight classifications and their weigh-in procedure. If the maximum weigh-in for the welterweight classification is 147 lbs., why is either boxer allowed to enter the ring at a weight exceeding 147 lbs. the day of the fight? To my knowledge, both Broner and Porter exceeded the 147 lb. welterweight limit at fight time. It does not appear a welterweight contest to me if the boxers fight in the required weight range of the super welterweight classification of 154 lbs. or the middleweight classification, which is a maximum of 160 lbs., rather than in the required weight range of welterweights. I believe boxers should be weighed on the day of the intended fight, not the day before. Why are boxers weighed a day or so before the fight instead of minutes before the fight? I believe this to be one of the many problems with the sport of boxing today—this and the fact that there are several so-called world champions in every weight classification in boxing. Heck, either a boxer is the world champion, or he is not the world champion. How can two or three fighters all be THE world champion in their weight classification? If the boxing world recognizes more than one fighter as the world champion in a boxer's weight classification, then I have to believe there is no world champion in that weight classification. Come on, boxing, straighten out the sport. Make fighters fight at the required weight limits, and let's have just one champion in each weight classification. Bring back credibility to the sport. It's not professional wrestling . . . yet.

Just a thought.

Not Much in the Way of Role Models

It's Sunday. I worked in the morning and read most of the afternoon. I found some time to watch a little football. I watched the Buffalo Bills play the Denver Broncos. I rooted for Buffalo despite my belief Denver would win big. Denver has a talented team. Watching the game, I was surprised, but not really surprised by this one play—but plays like this one play never fail to disappointment me whenever I see occur what I saw occur. The Bills' quarterback, Kyle Orton, throws an incomplete pass into the Denver end zone. It was obvious to anyone watching on TV the ball bounced off the ground before landing in the hands of a Denver Bronco defender. The Bronco player picked himself up with the ball and ran unmolested all the way to the other end of the field, and the referees signaled a touchdown for the Denver Broncos. If any of the referees had eyes or took the time to look at the same play I saw and probably most of America saw, Bills' coach Doug Marrone would not have had to throw the red flag to challenge the call. After review of the "touchdown" by the referees, the signal of a touchdown was overturned, and Buffalo was awarded the ball, and eventually, Buffalo moved the ball downfield and into the Denver end zone for its own touchdown.

What bothered me about the play, more than the incorrect signal of a touchdown, was that in my opinion, the Bronco defender had to have known he picked up an incomplete pass, and yet he and his team would have accepted a touchdown as originally signaled by the referees. The only thing preventing the Denver Broncos from celebrating an unearned and in my opinion an "unethical" touchdown was a red flag thrown by the Buffalo Bills coach. I was told once, many years ago, that football taught kids to play together as a team and the game itself is the living embodiment of fair play and competition. I don't see it that way, especially after watching this game. To me football is less a sport than a business all about money, and being a business where money is the bottom line, this means your team must win. This means your team must win at all costs apparently—even if winning means cheating when the opportunity to do so arises. Maybe the NFL doesn't consider a referee's signaling a touchdown off an incomplete pass cheating if the referees make the call and the call goes undisputed, but that's not the way I see it. I cannot help but wonder what happened to a player "doing the right thing"? What happened to the ideal of "fair play"? As another example, let me make an observation about the Broncos quarterback Payton Manning. I admire Peyton Manning's ability as a quarterback. I believe as do many others that Payton Manny is a talented football player. But what I don't like about Payton Manning is his "hard counts." I don't understand why tricking the defense to jump offside so as to be awarded a five-yard penalty as a talent of a talented quarterback. I see it as a cheap way to gain free yards. As another example, I don't buy into those "domestic violence" commercials by the NFL featuring players like Eli Manning. It looks like $$money$$ talking bullshit in an attempt to fix the NFL's image damaged by incidents involving players like Ray Rice and others. Tell me you're not buying their publicity crap. Bottom line, I just don't see football players as role models.

Just a thought.

Why Do People Think They Are
Their Favorite Sports Team?

Time and again, I watch and I listen to sports fans screaming and yelling and jumping up and down with excitement when their favorite sports team wins. Time and again, I watch and I listen to sports fans screaming and yelling and crying when their favorite sports team loses. What did you win? What did you lose? NOTHING! When your favorite sports team wins the championship, you don't win. When your favorite team loses the championship, you don't lose. When your favorite team athletes win contracts or championship prizes of millions upon millions of dollars, you don't earn a dime. Your favorite athletes earn millions of dollars because of all the money you spend to watch their games and buy their shirts and shoes, but they don't share any of it with you. They spend all the money you throw at them on mansions, expensive cars, yachts, expensive clothes, expensive jewelry, vacations, and wild, wild, beautiful female models who become their trophy wives. You get none of that. NONE OF THAT! Oh, your favorite athlete might throw you a bone pronouncing to a crowd of fans, "I couldn't have won this without you—the fans." But does he really mean it? Don't you think he's just throwing you a bone? Don't you feel like a dog? And when your favorite athlete is throwing that bone, he's not even throwing at you specifically! He's just throwing the bone into the air for whatever dog thinks it is his or hers to catch. Do you really believe your favorite athlete has any idea you're even alive. Do you really think he cares as long as the money keeps flowing into his pockets? Maybe he does. Personally, I don't think so.

So wake up! Stop spending hundreds or thousands of dollars on tickets to watch your favorite athlete play your game or on clothes with his name or shoes he endorses. YOU SHOULD BE PLAYING THE GAME YOURSELF! Stop spending hundreds or thousands of dollars on shirts and shoes and jackets that have your favorite team name or logo on them. BUY A BETTER PAIR OF SHOES for less money! I doubt your favorite athlete made that shirt or those shoes or that jacket. Most likely, they sold their name to be put on that shirt or as an endorsement for those shoes so as to make a big buck, and I hope you realize wearing a shirt or shoes or a jacket with your team's logo or the name of your favorite athlete on them does not make you part of the team nor does it make you the athlete. You just look like someone who is an obvious fan and probably spent too much money on the shirt, the jacket, or the shoes. But be happy knowing your purchases made some athlete (not you) that much richer.

I love sports, but athletes are overpaid! I do not intend on helping them get rich, and I don't think you should either. If you want to waste your hard-earned money on cheap shirts and shoes and jackets with logos on them, spend your money on shirts and shoes and jackets that benefit people in need, not the rich; most professional athletes are already rich. THINK! The more dollars you continue to throw away at rich, overpaid athletes, the more they will demand of you, knowing you are easily duped into wasting your money. We all make the rich richer and ourselves poorer when we throw our hard-earned money at people who do not need it to get by. GET SMART! Be your favorite athlete. Play the game. Save your money, and buy yourself a better car or at least cheaper shoes, a cheaper jacket and a cheaper shirt. Save your money and buy yourself your own sports equipment with your name on the shirt, and PLAY the sport yourself with some friends. Spend the money on YOU! Stop wasting your hard-earned money on nondeserving overpaid jocks.

Just a thought.

Why Do People Pay Athletes and Celebrities So Much Money?

We are a nation of watchers. Dreamers. Why not be a nation of doers? Why pay hundreds and sometimes thousands of dollars to watch two guys beat each other up? Why pay hundreds of dollars to watch other guys play basketball, football, soccer, tennis, baseball, or hockey? PLAY basketball, football, soccer, tennis, baseball, and/or hockey YOURSELF. Why pay hundreds of dollars to buy shirts, jackets, and/or shoes with some athlete's name on them? They didn't make the shirt, the jacket, or the shoes. My wife wanted to buy me tickets to the US Open Tennis tournament. I love tennis, but I said no thank you. Why? The US Open wanted near $300 just for tickets to the third round matches for nosebleed seats up in the clouds where you cannot tell who the tennis players are on the court. What a waste of money. I'm already paying too much money to watch sporting events on cable. At least I can see the athletes close up from a comfortable seat in my living room near my kitchen.

Why pay hundreds of dollars to listen to somebody tell a bad joke or two or three? Listen to your friends tell the bad jokes for free. Not only will your friends tell the jokes for free, but they will share food with you, drink with you, and drive home with you. Your friends will talk to you without asking to be paid. There is too much money spent—no wasted—on spectator sports and actors and no-name celebrities like the Garbashians. Live your own life. Play your own games. Make up and tell your own jokes. KEEP YOUR HARD-EARNED MONEY, and spend it on a vacation for you and the family or just for you. Spend your money on your husband/or wife, your kids, or your parents. Buy a new tennis racket and go outside or inside and play tennis. Spend your money on a basket-ball, and hit the town park courts. Stop giving your money to these undeserving athletes and celebrities. These strangers get rich from the money you waste on them, and you are that much poorer as a result of your spending your money on them. Just know when your favorite basketball team wins that big game; the team is not com-ing to your house to thank you for supporting them. More likely, they are rushing to the bank to withdraw some of that money you helped provide so they can buy a bigger mansion, a showcase wife, an expensive car, and then fly to some exotic resort to vacation with bodyguards also paid with your fan money in order to make sure people like you stay clear of them. Be smart, and keep your money. Save and invest, and/or enjoy your money spending it on you. Make yourself rich, not others. Let the jock, the comedian, the actor, and the celebrity get a real job.

Just a thought.

Bathroom Etiquette in the Twenty-First Century

What is the correct bathroom etiquette in the twenty-first century? Bathroom etiquette has always been around in this the old US of A. It started out simple, one room for the men and one room for the women. Easy enough, right? If you have a penis, you use the men's room. If you have a vagina, you use the women's room. Of course, this was complicated when the Jim Crow Laws were in effect. Then if you had a white penis, you went into one room; and if you had a black penis, you went into another room. And if you had a vagina with black labia, you went into another room; and if you had a vagina with white labia, you went into another room. Simple, enough, right? Well, maybe not. Jim Crow Laws did complicate things a bit, but fortunately, the Jim Crow laws are no longer in effect, and it doesn't matter what color your penis or what color your labia. Bathrooms were simplified again so that the men's' room accepted all penises of any color and the women's' room accepted all vaginas no matter the color of a woman's labia. Whew! This is just a room to piss and poop, right? I mean, we aren't living there, right?

But wait. Now here we are in the twenty-first century. Fast-thinking computers in our phones that fit in the palm of your hand, cars that talk to us, men and women equal in job opportunities and bread winning (or so the men tell the women); men marrying men and women marrying women; women born with a vagina now sporting a penis; men born with a penis now showing breasts with ample cleavage . . . wait . . . what? Oh, boy, is this going to complicate bathroom etiquette again? How can surgically altered sexual equipment affect bathroom etiquette anyway? Well, apparently, it is having an effect on bathroom etiquette. Oh my, here we go again.

Well, let's examine this a little bit. Why have bathrooms for men and bathrooms for women been separated all these years? My guess is etiquette? What does that mean actually? Most women are uncomfortable with strange men having visual access to their sexual parts, especially when they are peeing and pooping; this is not the position most women feel comfortable in. I really cannot speak for women. I can only assume most women prefer to do their bathroom business in private or at the very least outside the presence of people with equipment unlike their own. They want their privacy. On the other side of the building, most men that I know could really care less who sees their junk whether they are doing their business or not; that's just men (we are slobs, you know). I think women are a little more particular about who can see and hear what goes on while they are in the bathroom doing their business than men. So how do all the sexual lifestyle changes in the twenty-first century affect bathroom etiquette? Before gay became acceptable, women were only concerned about strange men trying to sneak a peek at their vaginas, and I believe they have always been particular about who they showed them off to. Now it's no longer just men they worry are trying to sneak a peek. They are now worried there are some women who want to sneak a peek at their vagina; this makes them a little bit uncomfortable. On the other side of the building, some men who really did not care if a woman snuck a peek at their penis do not like the idea of another man trying to sneak a peek at the old Johnson. The bathroom etiquette for men has always been go in the bathroom look straight ahead at the urinal—never look around; do your business and leave. Now some men are paranoid the guy at the urinal next door is checking out his clutch. Whether these new fears of both men and women are valid, I do not know, but I do believe they are concerns of both men and women.

Well, what to do? Here are my suggestions. We create more bathrooms. Besides a men's room and a ladies' room, we have a gay room and a lesbian room. That way, anyone not wanting someone checking them out can comfortably pee and poop without a worry. Sounds good, right? But wait, wouldn't the gays in the gay room be checking each other out and the lesbians in the lesbian room being checking each other out? Hmm, that might not work. How about the gay men use the ladies' room and the lesbian women use the men's' room? The gay men aren't interested in vaginas, so they'll do their business and stare straight ahead while doing so, and the lesbian women aren't interested in penises, so they'll do their business and stare straight ahead—well, they will be sitting while the gay men are standing, so they will miss each anyhow, right? Of course, lesbians in the men's' room mean it may be difficult for a man to ever find a seat. And gay men in the ladies room doesn't affect time for seating as men are quick, but men do pee on the seat, which adds time for the ladies cleaning the seat before they sit. Hmm, I almost forgot there might be an issue concerning bisexuals. How do we work bisexuals into bathroom etiquette? If biwomen use either the ladies' room or the men's' room, they might be sneaking a peak, and that could make straight women and straight men uncomfortable doing their business. And if bimen use either the men's room or the ladies' room, they might be sneaking a peek at or at least making the straight men and straight women nervous about the possibility of sneaking a peak at their junk. Hmm, what to do?

I'm really confused. What to do? Do we need a men's' room, ladies room, lesbian room, gay room, a bisexual men's room and a bisexual ladies' room? Oh, shit, this is getting complicated. I really don't know what to do. Maybe we should all just stop going to the bathroom anywhere but at home. Maybe we should have one bathroom and only let one person go in at a time. Maybe we should all use the same bathroom but wear a blindfold before we go in and do our business. That might lead to injuries and a messy bathroom, but it might ease the tension during our time in the bathroom.

Well, I guess this issue requires some more thought. What do you think? How do you think we should resolve this issue, making everyone happy in the end (pun intended)? Should we even care? Someone is going to see our junk if we use a public bathroom, so either use and know it, or don't use it at all. I'll tell you this: this is one topic that really deserves less time than I gave it. Let's focus on world peace and leave the shit for someone else to clean up.

Just a thought.

White People Started an Earthquake That Only Affected Black People

A California quake caused injuries and property damage to a local community this morning. You've seen and heard the media reports on the devastation the surprise quake caused in the local county region in the great State of California, but what the media has not told you is that white people started the earthquake and targeted solely black people and their neighborhoods for destruction. Yes, once again, the evil white people are on the move, attacking innocent good-hearted black people. I know it is hard to believe. How could a group of evil white people start an earthquake and cause the earthquake to only target black people? I'm white, and I'm at a loss. But I have it on good authority from the media that that is exactly what happened. I spoke to a couple of newscasters while they were encouraging the looting of a local Target store. These newscasters claim they have definitive proof that the evil white people were behind the earthquake. I asked what that proof was, and they said . . . well, their white people and the neighborhood affected were predominately black. How can you argue that? Well, I for one feel ashamed to be white, and I have decided to give the looters free pizza while they loot and protest no matter how long they plan to loot and protest. I imagine the looting and the protesting will go on for some weeks or months as the looters and the protestors are being encouraged by the media to not go back to work. So yeah, pizza! And I have to applaud the looters and the protestors who are keeping their baby children out until all hours of the night and early hours of the morning. Children can never learn soon enough to hate white people and to blame white people for every bad in their lives. Oh, hold on.

I'm being told by the media that all white people are being offered free tacos and $100 if we leave the vicinity shouting, "They deserved this!" I wanted to help, but it is $100, and I love tacos, and I'm sure the police and emergency crews will help the neighborhood.

I am hearing some people in the neighborhood are questioning whether white people are behind the earthquake. The media is responding to their doubts with what they say is proof positive—a photograph they happened upon, which clearly has printed on the back in bold print, "This photo has not been Photoshopped." They claim this photo is proof positive that white people started this earthquake and targeted black people. The perpetrator's face is fuzzy, but he is obviously white, on a cell phone in the middle of the quake. And as can be seen in the photo, he's a white man on his cell phone obviously coordinating the earthquake effort—what else could he be doing on his cell phone in a black neighborhood? If the photo could talk, I have no doubt what this obviously evil white man was saying on his cell phone. I'm sure he was saying, "Start the earthquake now, and make sure it only affects black people." Isn't it obvious from the look on his face and the posture of his body? I don't know how anyone can dispute this evidence. There is no need for a trial. Let's just hang this guy. Well, good thing the media found this evidence. "You won't get away with this one, whitey," shouts a voice from the crowd! Wait, that man looks familiar. Haven't I seen him on the news before?

This thought is purely entertainment, and none of the events written are true except there are a lot of earthquakes in California. My heart goes out to all the victims of any earthquake—no matter your color, race, creed, sex, age, or national origin, etc. Best wishes and quick recovery to you all! And remember that the media is about making money. A lot of us of all colors are pretty nice people who don't want to start earthquakes.

Just a thought.

Oh, Why Didn't a Shark Eat Ann Coulter?

Some time ago, I was extremely bored. I could not find the will to pick up the television remote control and turn the channel. You know those kinds of days when you are so bored you just want to sit on the couch and eat and fall asleep to a bad movie. Well, I go my wish. On TV comes *Sharknado 3: Oh Hell No!* Yeah? Not really, yeah. More like, are you for real, America? You liked the first one so much you raised interest in someone making a sequel, and you actually watched it? And the sequel was obviously so good someone make us a third *Sharknado*? I have to agree with the *Oh Hell No!* part in the title because those words came to my mind within the first few minutes of the movie—actually, as soon as I saw the title in the movie description. Well, I struggled with my laziness, and I reached for the remote control, and then to my astonishment, I saw Ann Coulter. I shouldn't be surprised. A movie as crappy as *Sharknado* can only star actors who can't make it in a good movie—washed-up actors who can't find work anywhere else and celebrities who will do anything for money and to get themselves exposure in a movie no matter how dumb the movie. Of course, this is my personal opinion only. So here is Ann Coulter, the Constitutional expert attorney? Whenever I see or hear that woman, I think of words like *stupid, idiotic, moronic, bleached so blond the dye must have dripped inside her skull and done something terrible to whatever reasonable thought and logic might have existed in that tiny, pea-brain skull*; but then, this is my opinion and my opinion only. So I put the remote control down. And I waited for the *Sharknado* attack.

But as always with any experience, I've had watching and listening to Ann Coulter on TV or reading a book of hers (I admit I did read one of her books, and I liked it), I was disappointed. She continually escaped the jaws of shark after shark. I so wanted to see her eaten and torn to pieces by a shark. Not really eaten. I mean, I wouldn't really want to see Ann Coulter eaten by a shark in real life. But through the imagination and special effects of TV, I hoped to see Ann Coulter eaten by a shark. I hoped to see Ann Coulter sucked up into *Sharknado* and torn to pieces by shark after shark. Instead what I saw was Ann Coulter surviving shark attack after attack and sliding down the White House stairs on a painting. I guess I knew it would never really happen, even in a cheap movie. So *Sharknado 3*, all I can say is, "Oh, hell, no! A shark didn't eat Ann Coulter." The world would be so much better if one had.

Just a thought.

Chapter 7

POETRY

Life, What It Is

What it is, what we are,
We are near, we cannot go far.
Tethered to the Earth like a kite on a string,
We attempt to soar high, but the Earth doth
    call and we must answer its ring.
We cannot leave, we cannot go.
We are here. On Earth forevermore.

We manipulate the elements. We reshape
    the planet with gaiety and mirth,
But still we remain grounded, tethered to this old Earth.
It is a prison. It is heaven. It is our home.
Here we live. We breathe. We are born.
But we cannot help but look beyond the walls
    of our home. We try to escape our cage.
Yet we cannot see outside. We cannot escape beyond.
    We are trapped in our own mediocrity.
So we invent gods. We invent angels.
    We invent heavens above.
But they are always out of reach, out of sight,
    above and beyond our heads like doves.
We cannot bear not knowing why. We
    cannot stand being alone.
So we dream. We imagine. We try to
    bring forth water from stone.
And all the while, we remain. We
    are never allowed leave.

We dream and we dream, and some-
    times we even scream.
But the answers do not come. Not even some.
For here we must remain, teth-
    ered, tethered to the ground.
And again and again, those born of us
    will ask the same things.
What it is. What it is. Why and where.
What it is. What we are. As we gaze at the stars.

A Little Rhyme about Time

Today I moved forward and thus forward in time.
I then moved backward and thus again forward in time.
I moved up. I moved down. I moved right. I moved left.
It mattered not where I moved, only that I moved.
This way I traversed forward in time.

To move backward in time is a dream of rhyme.
Truth hath no moment transgressing backward in time.
For backward in time is always a forward thought of thine.
And standing still is no movement at all. It is silence. It is no
    time at all.

I cannot think backward. To do so would imply I am a tape
    recording, static and dry.
It would imply I existed before I was born, that I am but a
    video in someone's archive of before.
Though, I admit, if I could reverse time, I would not know,
    for my thoughts would be unraveling in the direction of
    the after to the before.
I have to believe that time is forward, you see.
But for no other reason than logic says cause before effect is
    reality.

A Really Bad Poem about Sex and Marriage

One day I pondered, while walking my baby in carriage. What is it that makes love and marriage?

Is it the joining of male and female? Is it the pleasuring of each other's genitalia?

Can love and marriage be two separate things? Can love and marriage be two people loving to swing?

I know I love my partner, my wife. I am a man. She is a woman. Together we created a little person, a new life.

I have a good friend, a man is he. I love him and share with him, but no sex between we.

Sex feels good. I love it, I know. But marriage and friendship are two different ships on the go.

My wife too is my friend, but what we share is different than what with my male friend.

My wife and I share what my male friend, and I cannot. We share our DNA, half from me, half from my wife, and one plus one makes one brand-new little child, a child who grows up to know both his parents all the while.

I guess one can borrow from someone else. But it is not the same as owning your own. So I say love and marriage is better original than communal grown.

Same-sex marriage be all the rage. But it will never be a real marriage. It is merely a mirage of the day.

A Poem about Religion

Religion they say is about peace and love; it flutters above like a pretty white dove.

Yet despite all the rhetoric about peace and love, it spews hatred when questioned, its followers must always be treated with kid gloves.

Religion claims only it brings ethics, morality, love, and peace, yet it sanctions war, its priests molest little boys, and it threatens damnation on all who question its flock.

Even now the religious who read this poem think "Blaspheme," "Damnation," "I hope he goes to hell, how dare he question, how dare he suggest I am wrong." I will turn my back on his words, and I will walk.

The religious claim they need not prove they are right; they shout, "Faith is all I need." All that is needed is to blindly follow and do what is told, no different than every little tyrant who listens to voices in his head and shouts, "Do what I say, or suffer damnation and hell."

But there is another voice in the world the religious strive to hide, a voice of reason and thought. A voice of peace and love, ethics and morality, honesty and truth, it is the voice of reality. Religion is but one of many a philosophy. There is another philosophy, a belief of what is real and the most real in life is not invisible winged men or bearded, sandaled supernatural men living on clouds. Real is simply reality, which is itself a philosophy of truth, love, and one that spews no hatred when questioned. Reality begs for the search. It begs for the truth. And it loves those who do too. It relies not on faith but fact. It is sane. It is rational. It is international.

So lose those shackles of hatred and ignorance, and seek the philosophy of love and truth. Be real, be logical. Stop listening to voices in your head, and become a sleuth. Search—search for reality, and peace will be yours.

Chapter 8

QUESTIONS AND ANSWERS AND RIDDLES

Question 1:   What is the difference in freedoms between Communism, Socialism and a Republic?

Question 2:   What is the same about the financial situations between a Communistic, Socialistic and Republic Nation?

Question 3:   How many continents are there?

See Appendix for the answer.

Albert Einstein's Riddle:

Question: ARE YOU IN THE TOP 2% OF INTELLIGENT PEOPLE IN THE WORLD?
SOLVE THE RIDDLE AND FIND OUT.

There are no tricks, just pure logic, so good luck and don't give up.

1. On a street there are five houses, painted five different colors.
2. In each house lives a person of different nationality
3. These five homeowners each drink a different kind of beverage, smoke different brand of cigar and keep a different pet.

THE QUESTION: WHO OWNS THE FISH?

HINTS:

1. The Brit lives in a red house.
2. The Swede keeps dogs as pets.
3. The Dane drinks tea.
4. The Green house is next to, and on the left of the White house.
5. The owner of the Green house drinks coffee.
6. The person who smokes Pall Mall rears birds.
7. The owner of the Yellow house smokes Dunhill.
8. The man living in the center house drinks milk.
9. The Norwegian lives in the first house.
10. The man who smokes Blends lives next to the one who keeps cats.
11. The man who keeps horses lives next to the man who smokes Dunhill.
12. The man who smokes Blue Master drinks beer.
13. The German smokes Prince.
14. The Norwegian lives next to the blue house.
15. The man who smokes Blends has a neighbor who drinks water.

See Appendix for the answer.

CONCLUSION

If you read the entire book from cover to cover, you may now agree with me as to reality's objectivity, or you may not. All I hope is that at the very least, I got you thinking about reality from a different perspective and a little deeper than before. As I wrote at the beginning of this book, and as I tried to convey in my thoughts throughout this book, I believe reality is closer to absolute objectivity than time and most other things in life that we have time to think about. I hope you will now look at life in as objective a manner as possible and see how so many others skewing reality into a subjective perspective hurts us all in how we live, how we treat each other, and how we think and solve problems. Know that reality is reality is reality—nothing more, nothing less.

APPENDIX

Answer to Question #1:

What is the difference in freedoms between Communism, Socialism and a Republic?

In a Communistic Nation, its people know they are not free.

In a Socialistic Nation, its people think they are free.

In a Republic Nation, its people delude themselves into believing they are free.

Answer to Question #2:

What is the same about the financial situations between a Communistic, Socialistic and Republic Nation?

Just a few elite are rich and powerful, while most of the populous are relatively poor and subject to laws made by the rich and the powerful.

Answer to Question #3:

How many continents are there?

In North America, they teach you there are seven continents: North America, South America, Antarctica, Europe, Asia, Africa and Australia.

In Europe (except France), they teach there are six continents: The Americas (considered one continent), Antarctica, Europe, Asia, Africa and Australia.

In France, they teach there are five continents: The Americas (considered one continent), Europe, Asia, Africa and Australia. They don't see Antarctica as a continent.

Many geologists see Europe and Asia as one continent, so they believe there are six continents: North America, South America, Antarctica, Euro-Asia, Africa and Australia.

But I agree there are seven continents: North America, South America, Antarctica, Euro-Asia, Africa, Australia and Greenland. I agree with the geologists that Europe and Asia being one land mass is one continent, not two. I see North and South America as two separate continents. I agree that Antarctica is a continent as it is a land mass with ice on top. But where I disagree with everyone else is that Greenland is also a continent. Greenland is larger than Australia and both are islands surrounded by water. I do not see a cogent argument for Greenland's exclusion as a continent. Greenland may not have its own tectonic plate like Australia, but Europe and Asia share one; and, India has its own, but is not considered a continent. Greenland is also larger than Australia. It all seems pretty arbitrary. But then this is my opinion only.

Answer to Einstein's riddle.

My answer to Einstein's' riddle: The GERMAN owns the fish. Is your answer the same?

1	Yellow	Norwegian	water	Dunhill	cats
2	Blue	Dane	tea	Blend	horse
3	Red	Brit	milk	Pall Mall	birds
4	Green	German	coffee	Prince	**FISH**
5	White	Swede	beer	Blue Master	dogs

ABOUT THE AUTHOR

Gregory P. Lomb, Esq., is a USA-born son, brother, husband, father, lawyer, a computer programmer/graphics/website designer, tennis hacker, avid nonfiction reader (physics, science, history, biographies, politics, etc.), recreational soccer coach, bike rider, and avowed realist—chronologically in that order, not necessarily prioritized in that order.

CPSIA information can be obtained
at www.ICGtesting.com
Printed in the USA
BVHW031812070419
544845BV00001BA/48/P

9 781640 828438